STRATEGIC INFORMATION PLANNING METHODOLOGIES

Second Edition

JAMES MARTIN

with

Joe Leben

PRENTICE HALL, Englewood Cliffs, New Jersey 07632

Library of Congress Cataloging-in-Publication Data

Martin, James.
   Strategic information planning methodologies / James Martin with
Joe Leben.—2nd ed.
   p. cm.
  Rev. ed. of: Strategic data-planning methodologies. c1982.
  Bibliography: p.
  Includes index.
  ISBN 0-13-850538-1
  1. Business—Data processing. 2. Data base management.
I. Leben, Joe. II. Martin, James, 1933-   Strategic data-planning
methodologies. III. Title.
HF5548.2.M343 1989
658'.054—dc19

88-35468
CIP

Editorial/production supervision: *Karen Skrable Fortgang*
Cover design: *Ben Santora*
Manufacturing buyer: *Mary Ann Gloriande*

The publisher offers discounts on this book when ordered
in bulk quantities. For more information, write or call:

  Special Sales
  Prentice-Hall, Inc.
  College Technical and Reference Division
  Englewood Cliffs, NJ 07632
  (201) 592-2498

Printed in the United States of America

10 9 8 7 6 5 4 3 2

ISBN 0-13-850538-1

PRENTICE-HALL INTERNATIONAL (UK) LIMITED, *London*
PRENTICE-HALL OF AUSTRALIA PTY. LIMITED, *Sydney*
PRENTICE-HALL CANADA INC., *Toronto*
PRENTICE-HALL HISPANOAMERICANA, S.A., *Mexico*
PRENTICE-HALL OF INDIA PRIVATE LIMITED, *New Delhi*
PRENTICE-HALL OF JAPAN, INC., *Tokyo*
SIMON & SCHUSTER ASIA PTE. LTD, *Singapore*
EDITORA PRENTICE-HALL DO BRASIL, LTDA, *Rio de Janeiro*

TO CORINTHIA

THE INFORMATION SYSTEMS PYRAMID

It is useful to draw a pyramid to represent an organization's information systems function. The three sides of the pyramid represent an organization's data, the activities the organization carries out using that data, and the technology that is employed in implementing information systems activities.

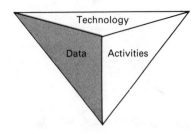

Each of the three general books for managers and users discusses all four levels of the pyramid, but with different orientations. The three detailed books on database emphasize different levels of the data side of the information systems pyramid. This book is concerned primarily with the data side of the strategy level of the pyramid.

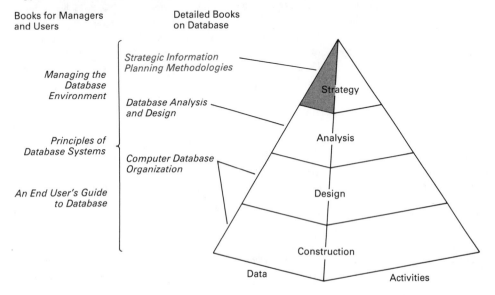

JAMES MARTIN BOOKS

BOOKS FOR TECHNICAL STAFF

Strategic Information Planning Methodologies

Strategic Information Planning Methodologies, Second Edition, was first published in 1982 under the title *Strategic Data-Planning Methodologies*. This book is for executives, managers, and business-oriented database administrators who will be involved with the high-level strategic planning of information systems and for the technical staff members that will assist management in performing these functions. This book concentrates on the strategic planning functions that involve creating an overall model of the enterprise and indentifying individual business areas for detailed analysis (the first level of the pyramid). This book has no prerequisites and can be read by those having no previous information systems knowledge or experience. *Strategic Information Planning Methodologies* could be used as the text in a course on strategic business planning.

Database Analysis and Design

Database Analysis and Design, published in 1989, is for information systems technical staff members who require an in-depth understanding of the tasks that are performed in all aspects of database analysis and design. It emphasizes the analysis and logical design of the subject databases used by individual business areas (the second level of the pyramid). This book has a how-to-do-it orientation and uses numerous examples and case studies to show how the job of database analysis and design is done in the real world. This book assumes the reader has a thorough background in business information system fundamentals, but no programming background is required. *Database Analysis and Design* could be used as a text in a course on the logical design of databases.

Computer Database Organization

Computer Database Organization was orignally published in 1975, and the second edition was published in 1977. This book is for information systems technical staff members who require a knowledge of the technical and theoretical aspects of database technology. This book emphasizes database theory and examines the workings of modern database management systems (levels 3 and 4 of the pyramid). It includes detailed discussions of IBM's IMS, Cullinet Software's IDMS/R, and IBM's DB2 and assumes the reader is has an in-depth understanding of information systems fundamentals. A programming background is helpful in reading some of the more detailed chapters. A general knowledge of database fundamentals is also assumed; this prerequisite can be satisfied by reading either *Principles of Database Systems* or *Database Analysis and Design*. *Computer Database Organization* could be used in an in-depth course on database techniques.

ON DATABASE

BOOKS FOR MANAGERS AND USERS

Managing the Database Environment

Managing the Database Environment was initially published in 1983. This book is for executives, managers, and senior information systems technical staff members who will be involved in ensuring that database techniques are successfully inplemented throughout the organization. This book concentrates on the management and organizational implications of database technology. It uses technical terms, but all new terms are clearly defined when they are first used. This book has no prerequisites other than a general knowledge of information systems fundamentals. *Managing the Database Environment* could be used as the text in a management-oriented course on database techniques. Some of the same technical content is covered in this book as in the more technical books described on the facing page, but it has a management rather than a technical staff orientation.

Principles of Database Systems

Principles of Database Systems was first published in 1976 under the title *Principles of Data-Base Management*. This book is for programmers, analysts, and managers who require an introduction to the database environment and the technology that surrounds it. This book provides a thorough introduction to all aspects of database technology without overburdening the reader with detail. Technical terms are used, but all are clearly defined when first used. The book has no prerequisite other than a general understanding of information systems fundamentals, and no programming background is required. *Principles of Database Systems* could be used as a text in an introductory course of database fundamentals. The content of this book is adapted from the more technical James Martin books on database described on the facing page and forms a shorter introduction to the subject matter.

An End-User's Guide to Database

An End-User's Guide to Database uses nontechnical terms to present the basics of database management to people who will use information systems that employ database techniques. After reading this book, the end user will be in a better position to assist information systems technical staff members in ensuring that application systems meet user needs. No technical terms are used and no previous database or information systems background is assumed. *An End-User's Guide to Database* could be used as the text in a course on database techniques that is given to end users who will provide direction to technical staff members carrying out the tasks of information strategy planning, business area analysis, and database analysis and design. The content for this book has been adapted from the more technical books described on the facing page and forms a completely nontechnical introduction to the subject.

The only liberty I mean is a liberty connected with order.

Edmund Burke

Those who expect to reap the blessings of freedom must, like men, undergo the fatigues of supporting it.

Thomas Paine

We are in bondage to the law in order that we may be free.

Cicero

Individualism is a fruit of organized society.

Ralph Barton Perry

The building of a computerized organization requires the combined efforts of each individual in the organization working toward common objectives. These objectives should reflect an overall strategy for the new methodologies and should be clearly understood by everyone in the organization.

CONTENTS

15   The Follow-on Plan   *247*

Choice of Business Areas to Analyze 248;
Analysis of Current Systems 249;
Strategic Technology Planning 253;
Keeping the Planning Study Up-to-Date 255

16   Business Area Analysis   *257*

Keep It Simple 258; Short Project 258;
Independent of Technology and Organizational Structure 260;
Organizational Changes 260;
Identification of the Business Area 261;
Solving the Communication Problem 263;
Four Types of Diagrams 265; The Initial Diagrams 265;
Links with Other Business Area Analyses 265;
Staffing a Business Area Analysis Project 267; References 269

PART **III**   EPILOGUE

17   The Future of Information Systems   *273*

Where Should Decisions Be Made 274;
Flattening the Bureaucratic Tree 274;
The Orchestra-Like Structure 276;
Computer-Integrated Manufacturing 278;
Automated Links Between Corporations 279;
Rigorous Engineering 280; Integration of Systems 281;
Knowledge Bases 281; Networks and Standards 282;
Building Human Potential 282;
Three Waves of Entry in Technology 283; Government 285;
Summary 285; References 286

PART **IV**   APPENDICES **287**

Appendix I   Entities and Normalization   *289*

Normalization 291; First Normal Form 292;
Second Normal Form 293; Third Normal Form 297;
Fourth Normal Form 299; Fifth Normal Form 301

PREFACE

During the 1970s it became clear that computerized information is a resource of high value to corporations and other organizations. It also became clear that this resource needs planning from the top. The planning needs a formal and preferably computerized methodology that links to database design.

Although many organizations perceived the importance of information resource planning, few knew how to set about the task. Some consulting firms stressed the importance of the subject but did not have a hard methodology that led to the design of the resources needed. This book describes methodologies that *have* been used to achieve this and discusses the practice and experience of using them.

In the 1980s, isolated information planning methodologies were integrated into the broader disciplines of information engineering, which carries the planning and modeling through into implementation and maintenance. Information engineering has become very powerful as tool kits have evolved that automate its activities and as the tool kits provided design and code generation capabilities. This is not a book on information engineering, but it mentions this subject throughout. There is now much experience with the implementation of information planning methodologies in an information engineering framework.

This book was written in conjunction with my book on *Managing the Database Environment* and a trilogy of books on information engineering. It would help to read those books together with this one, although any of these could be read by itself.

Throughout the text, quotations are printed, in boxes, from persons with different implementation experiences. Some of the quotations are from ALI James Martin video interviews. Some are from other interviews with management and database implementers. A few are from corporate memos. The quotations have been selected to make the voice of experience speak from the pages. In some cases it is bitter experience; so to protect the guilty, the individuals and organizations have not been named.

Chapter 1 in the Prologue of this book is addressed to both information systems staff members and to business executives. It stresses the cooperation that must take place between top management and the information systems department if the strategic planning of databases and information systems is to be effective. The chapters in Part I are addressed to more technically oriented readers and describe a collection of techniques that are used in carrying out the methodologies of strategic information planning. The chapters in Part I can be skipped by more business-oriented readers, especially on a first reading. The chapters in Part II are addressed to both information systems technical staff members and to nontechnical business executives. It describes, in detail, the methodologies that are used in carrying out the strategic information planning process.

Acknowledgments

We wish to thank the staff of *KnowledgeWare,* Atlanta, Georgia (a corporation which specializes in this area), for reviewing the manuscript and making many helpful suggestions. Brilliantly creative in this were Ken Winter and John Hope. We would also like to thank Adrian Tidswell for sharing with us various experiences in applying strategic information planning. Particularly, we must thank the staff of James Martin Associates for their help and for the evolution of the disciplines of information engineering. Thanks also to Ken Primozic and Ed Primozic, both of IBM, who generously supplied information on their innovative methodology of linkage analysis planning, discussed in Chapter 7.

James Martin
Joe Leben

STRATEGIC INFORMATION PLANNING
METHODOLOGIES

PROLOGUE

1 THE ROLE OF TOP MANAGEMENT

It would be unthinkable to build a battleship without an overall plan. Once an overall plan exists, separate teams can go to work on specifying the details for individual components. The design of databases and the corporate information systems that access them is often as complex as building a battleship, yet in most enterprises it is done without an overall plan of sufficient detail to make the components fit together. The overall architect of a battleship cannot conceivably specify the detailed design of the guns, electronics, and other subsystems. These have to be developed by different teams working autonomously. But imagine what would happen if these teams enthusiastically created their own subsystems without any coordination from the top.

The information systems world is filled with inspired subsystem designers who want to be left alone. Their numbers are rapidly increasing as personal computers proliferate, end users learn to acquire their own facilities, and easy-to-use software spreads. In many cases they are doing an excellent job. However, the types of data they use overlap substantially, and this is often not recognized. The subsystems need to be connected, but often this cannot be done without conversion. Conversion, when the need for it becomes apparent, is often too expensive to accomplish, so incompatible systems live on, making it difficult or impossible to integrate the information that management needs.

In the late 1960s the dream emerged of a totally integrated corporate database. This has turned out to be completely unworkable. The task of building a single database to support all the information needs of an enterprise is unthinkably complex. It is far beyond the capability of any one team to design, and even if it could be designed, machine performance considerations would make it unworkable (except in small organizations).

Good system design avoids excessive complexity. Corporate information systems ought to be composed of discrete modules, each of which is simple enough to be efficiently designed; completely understood by its design team;

low in maintenance costs; susceptible to high-productivity development methods, including the use of fourth-generation languages (4GLs); and possibly capable of employing inexpensive small computers where possible. The modules must fit together, and they must employ shared databases that have been carefully designed. The main emphasis of this book is on the high-level planning of the data resources that the enterprise requires, now and in the future.

BUSINESS PLANNING AND INFORMATION SYSTEMS PLANNING

At least a third of the largest corporations in the United States (more than $1 billion in revenues) do long-range information systems planning; however, McLean and Soden [1] reported that in many of these corporations the planning is done with little involvement from end users and even less from top management. They comment about a conference attended by a group of long-range data processing planners:

> Interestingly, only a very few of the participants reported any involvement whatsoever in their longer range MIS planning effort by members of the business planning staff of the corporation. One might conclude from this that the MIS planning activities were not closely tied to the strategy of the overall corporation—a hypothesis that is further supported by the observation that only one-third of the participants linked their MIS planning process to the overall business planning effort of the enterprise.

Today, most corporate presidents are well aware of the importance of information technology. They know that they are building a computerized corporation and need help. They need a vice-president of information systems who talks the same language as themselves. The methodologies of information strategy planning that are presented in this book provide an excellent means for establishing rapport between top management and the top information systems executives and planners.

To do strategic planning of databases and information systems in isolation from strategic business planning is to ask for trouble. It is likely to lead to expensive systems that do not fully serve the needs of the enterprise. Unless the long-range information systems plan reflects the long-range business plan, future organizational changes may not be factored into the information systems plan. Conversely, if information systems executives and technology professionals are not involved in the *business* planning, the business plans may overlook major technological opportunities and competitive threats. The information strategy planning methodologies discussed in this book should be used by the *business planners*—not merely the *computer system planners*.

The business plans need control mechanisms to monitor progress and make adjustments so the plans can be implemented as successfully as possible. As in all control mechanisms, feedback is essential. When the business plans are created, the information systems organization should be involved to ensure that the desirable databases and information systems come into existence. Sometimes these systems are complex because they involve information from multiple functions in the enterprise and from outside the enterprise as well. An overall information architecture is needed to ensure that the different types of data are compatible and are available.

OVERALL ARCHITECTURE

Strategic planning of information resources involves more than merely project development plans. It requires an architectural framework into which separate systems fit. Many separate systems are built in an enterprise by separate teams of people. It is desirable that these separate building blocks of a computerized enterprise should fit together. This will not happen without an overall corporate information architecture. The methodologies discussed in this book create the framework of this architecture. Strategic information planning, then, has three overall purposes:

1. To link information technology and systems planning to the strategic business planning.
2. To help in the building of control mechanisms to implement the plans.
3. To create an architectural framework into which further analysis and design will fit so that separately developed databases and information systems will work together.

THE COMBINATION OF TOP-DOWN PLANNING AND LOCALIZED DESIGN

So we can see that corporatewide *planning* of information is vital, but corporatewide *design* of a totally integrated database is impractical. What is needed is bottom-up design of individual subsystems with maximum encouragement for local initiative in creating such subsystems and a methodology for top-level planning of the information resources these systems use—like the building of a battleship.

To build a computerized enterprise, it is essential to have a linkage between the *top-down* planning of databases and information systems and the *localized design* of systems in many different user areas. It is necessary to ensure that localized designs evolve according to an information architecture that describes the databases and information systems that will be required to implement the business plan. This architecture needs to be developed with sufficient detail.

THE INFORMATION STRATEGY PLANNING STUDY

The methodologies for doing the bottom-up design of individual databases and the information systems that use them are now well understood, and many aspects of this are discussed in other books in the James Martin series. (See listings in the front matter.) The methodologies that are used to perform the required top-down planning, however, are newer. This book describes organized methodologies that can be used to perform an *information strategy planning (ISP)* study. The results of the ISP study form the basis of the information architecture needed by the enterprise to implement its business plan.

INFORMATION RESOURCES PLANNER

The information strategy planning study needs to be coordinated by a single individual. Some organizations have a committee for information strategy planning. A committee can be desirable for review and feedback, but the overall design *must* be the responsibility of one strong, competent individual, equipped with the right tools and techniques. In some cases the information strategy planner is responsible for planning file and database resources alone; in other cases this individual has the broader responsibility of overall planning of information systems. The information strategy planner must have the ear of top management, and top management must sign off on the plans that are developed by this individual. Where this has not been the case, the plan has often caused bitter political controversy and has never been fully implemented.

The information strategy planner must have a corporatewide perspective in order to be able to determine what databases and other data resources the organization needs. After the information strategy planning process has been completed, other members of the technical staff can then do the detailed data analysis for each database that needs to be created. The information strategy planner and the technical staff members that do detailed database design all need help from end users, but in different ways. The information strategy planner needs help from every functional area, but not at a fine level of detail. The detailed designers need user committees looking at individual database in fine detail, attempting to make them as stable as possible.

CONSISTENCY OF INFORMATION

A major objective of an information strategy planning study is to achieve *consistency of information.* *Inconsistency* results from the historical evolution of computer usage that usually occurs without overall planning. Data can be inconsistent in five ways:

1. **Field definition.** Different parts of the organization do not agree about the definitions and meanings of a field.

2. **Field structure.** The same field is structured differently in different places (different lengths, binary versus decimal, different code structures, etc.)

3. **Record structure.** Records having the same key are differently structured in different places.

4. **Time of update.** Data can be processed monthly, weekly, daily, or interactively in different subsystems, making different copies of the data have different values. Managers often perceive inconsistent data.

5. **Inconsistency of update rules.** Processing and update logic may be different for different copies of the data.

The dangers of inconsistency are much greater now that computing systems are becoming inexpensive and widespread, with many end-user departments and many individual users having their own computers. Distributed processing and the widespread use of personal workstations greatly increase the need for corporatewide strategic planning of information resources. Incompatible architectures and data used by different systems can prevent, or make difficult, the integration of data that is required to generate the information required by management in a world where information systems will reach out beyond the boundaries of the enterprise itself.

DECOUPLED PROJECTS   Subsystem designers, and sometimes end users, are often concerned that if they have the design of data imposed on them from elsewhere, they will lose their freedom to be creative. In practice, installations that have been well managed have demonstrated that the opposite is true. Procedure designers are given *stable* data structures and tools with which they can extract data quickly in many forms. The ease and speed of creating new procedures with fourth-generation languages and tools for *computer-aided systems engineering (CASE)* lead to much more creativity in changing and inventing procedures. *Without* good management, the ability to change systems increasingly bogs down in maintenance problems and problems with incompatible data.

The data models that result from good data administration are a foundation on which new procedures can be created quickly by small teams—often by one person. Strategic planning of the information needs of an enterprise permits separate design projects to proceed by themselves. Each project can be reasonably coherent and decoupled from other projects. The separate projects can be small and easy to implement. Yet they are integrated by using data that is centrally defined.

TOWER OF BABEL   The languages and software for creating commercial data processing applications are improving rapidly and will continue to do so. *Nonprocedural* languages and facilities now permit many applications to be created without conventional programming and in some cases permit them to be created by end users. The image of a computerized corporation of the near future, which the reader should keep in mind, is one in which *many* people are creating and adjusting the electronic procedures. They have easy-to-use software that enables them to do this *rapidly*. Inexpensive computers are spreading, and there is today a workstation of some type on most desks. The challenge for both information systems and corporate management is: How do we control this environment? The most important aspect of control is coordinating the data used. If this is not done, there will be a Tower of Babel effect. To build databases and information systems throughout an enterprise without coordinated planning of data would be like running a telephone system without the use of a common directory. In many cases, an additional investment of as little as 10 percent, for careful planning of the data that will be required by future information systems, can produce a large return.

SENIOR MANAGEMENT INVOLVEMENT

In many cases, the attempt to implement corporate-wide planning of data has come from the information systems department itself. This is often not too successful, for two reasons. First, the information systems executives do not have enough authority to make everyone conform to the data definitions and representations they create. Second (although they sometimes think the contrary), information systems professionals do not fully understand the business. It is a requirement to involve senior management *themselves* in the information strategy planning process.

Interviewer:

You've seen data evolve over about eight years in your organization. What do you think is the single most important ingredient for success?

Information Systems Executive:

Top management. Top management has got to understand what's going on and how it affects the future of the organization. If you don't have somebody at the top pulling the pieces together, everybody's going to charge off in their own direction. You might as well have an orchestra with everyone playing a different symphony.

There are many reasons that top management involvement is needed in the top-down planning of the information resources required by the enterprise. Some of these reasons are listed in Box 1.1.

BOX 1.1   Top management involvement

- Information is an extremely vital corporate resource. It affects productivity, profitability, and strategic decisions. Any resource that is important needs planning from the top.

- Where a *technical* group has planned corporate information resources, it has generally been unable to have the perspective of business managers or to understand the overall corporate information needs.

- The best laid plans of information systems designers have crashed on the rocks of corporate politics. Information systems, especially those that employ shared databases, tend to create political problems, often severe ones, and various factions will oppose them. Often, these problems can be solved only when top management has made it clear that it believes that advanced information systems are the way of the future and has signed off on a corporate information systems plan.

- Some of the methodologies for information strategy planning reveal anomalies, waste, and inefficiencies in the *corporate* organization and methods. In many cases the information strategy planning study has led to the reorganization of procedures and to corporate restructuring.

- Productivity in information systems development is vital. An appalling waste of development resources results from redundant uncoordinated application development and excessive maintenance and conversion activity. A top-down corporatewide information architecture is needed to lessen these.

- A formally structured corporatewide view of information processing is needed to set information systems priorities.

- Budgets need to be set for database development independently of application development.

- Orchestration is needed to make the various efforts fit together. Multiple *incompatible* fragments of databases and information systems cause excessive conversion costs and prevent senior management from obtaining the information it needs.

- An infrastructure needs to be planned for distributed systems. The separate database systems should be linked by a common network.

- The methodologies described in this book need the involvement of senior management and staff from user departments working with an overall directive from the top.

We have examined numerous case histories of strategic planning done *with* top management involvement and sponsorship and *without* it. The difference is far greater than is often generally realized. The planning done *without* senior management involvement consists of information systems staff looking outward. However good as analysts, they usually do not have the business experience needed to understand the subtleties of information requirements. When they create an information strategy plan, although it may be ingeniously conceived, it is often not accepted by senior management and has often become the basis for bitter political arguing.

Database Executive:

When we adopted the plan three years ago, we did not go to top management because we felt that, at that time, they were not quite ready because it was so new in concept and they would be very concerned.

Interviewer:

If you look back on that experience now, do you think it was a mistake not to go to top management in the beginning?

Database Executive:

It was a catastrophe! It seemed intuitively obvious to us that the plan was right, but nobody else saw it that way. The whole thing has been a political nightmare.

The primary payoff from executive involvement is solid management support for the databases and information systems that will eventually be developed. The detailed data modeling is more likely to succeed, represent the enterprise correctly, be used, be supported, and be understood.

The second payoff is more subtle, but in some cases has been very powerful—the effect on the enterprise of having a fresh picture of itself and its relationship to the organizations with which it interacts. We might refer to this picture as an overall *strategic vision* that clearly describes where the enterprise is going within its industry. Having such a self-perception evolve, clearly charted and unaccompanied by preaching about how the enterprise "ought" to do things, is often a more effective force toward organizational restructuring than an army of experts who are explicitly trying to change the organization. Many leading corporations have a clearly defined vision; others do not. Chapter 8 presents techniques that top management and information systems executives can employ to formulate the vision that is necessary to guide strategic planning.

COMMUNICATIONS GAP

In many enterprises there is poor rapport between information systems management and top management. There is a variety of reasons for this: the information systems department's use of jargon, management incomprehension and fear of information systems technology, databases and information systems failing to fulfill the promises of an earlier age (especially integrated databases and decision support systems for top management), and top management failing to understand the need for their involvement. Too often senior management regards the data administrator as a technician who lives down in the bowels of the earth.

Information Systems Consultant:

I can remember when the database administrator, who was a senior analyst before he became a DBA, went to the MIS director and said: "I want to understand the corporate needs so that I can take those into account in my planning." The MIS director said: "It's none of your business." In fact, that company today still uses a database management system in an application-by-application manner, although it paid lip service to the idea of database being corporatewide seven years ago.

Interviewer:

Did you have the capability to really communicate with top management to explain the trade-offs to them?

Information Systems Executive:

No.

Interviewer:

What do you think would make that possible?

Information Systems Executive:

It needs credibility, in terms of what you are talking about, and some real-life examples that they can relate to in hard quantifiable terms. So the experience of installing the product and starting to work on it, even if it is in some degree bottom-up, then gives you the wherewithal to go to the management team and make presentations that say: "OK, now look. Here's where we have been, and here's where we see the direction going. Based on this experience I can make some real predictions. I can give some deliverable items and we can move ahead in that direction." I think if you can do that, they will give you resources.

> *Interviewer:*
>
> But that's going to take much more time because you've got to spend three years getting some experience before you can then go to the top management.
>
> *Information Systems Executive:*
>
> That's been our experience, about two to three years.

It is not a good idea to wait for three years, gaining experience with advanced technology, before approaching top management about strategic planning. Information strategy planning is needed from the start, and as part of this process top management must be given realistic expectations about the time scale.

If there is a communications gap between information systems executives and top management, several actions can help to bridge that:

- Bring in a consulting firm that specializes in information strategy planning.
- Show top management videotapes on the subject. Sometimes this is done in a lunch meeting; sometimes executives can be encouraged to take tapes home. A careful presentation should relate the videotapes shown to the particular circumstances of the enterprise in question.
- Ask top management to read this book.
- Arrange for top management to go to a short seminar on the subject.
- Stress to top management that corporate or organizational changes often result from a top-down examination of corporate data usage.

Top management is likely to be turned off completely by technical talk about data structures. It is likely to be skeptical about vague promises of better management information. There are, however, certain aspects of the subject that are likely to interest them. Senior management takes an active interest in decisions about how the enterprise *should* be run:

- The *linkage analysis planning (LAP)* methodology, discussed in Chapter 8, is particularly effective in helping senior executives to formulate the overall strategic vision that we discussed earlier. This strategic vision can be extremely important in linking the information systems plans to the overall business plan to help guide the enterprise as our economy becomes ever more information-oriented.
- Changes in organizational procedures, structural changes, or corporate reorganization are usually suggested by the techniques discussed in Part IV of this book.

- Most senior executives often perceive some areas where they would like better information or where fundamentally different types of information systems seem to be required. Sometimes they have not had an opportunity to articulate this and be listened to.

- Senior executives are often concerned about administrative expenditures. Many enterprises waste money because of redundant procedures or procedures that could be eliminated. A detailed charting of what activities use similar data can help to clean up these anomalies.

- Most senior managers perceive problems in today's information systems operations or have "hot buttons" about what they would like accomplished. The *critical success factor analysis* procedure, described in Chapter 11, is particularly effective at highlighting these.

- Information systems responsiveness, or speed of new application development, is often perceived as a problem. Management cannot obtain new reports when it wants them. One large bank in New York indicated to the author that it had a seven-year backlog of applications. Thorough strategic planning and the effective use of well-designed, shared databases ought to greatly increase the rate at which new information systems can be deployed.

- To be competitive, top management has to build a highly computerized corporation in the near future. The basis for this is establishing an overall strategic vision and performing corporatewide strategic information planning.

INFORMATION SYSTEMS PRODUCTIVITY

Information systems staff productivity is a concern in many organizations. It is becoming a more important concern as computers drop in cost. The cost of a computer is today often much less than the cost of the programmers and analysts who keep it busy. Computers are plunging in cost while programmers' and analysts' salaries are going up. Senior management often perceive productivity problems in terms of how long it takes to develop the new applications that are needed.

Many authorities advocate that information systems productivity be attacked by using structured programming and structured analysis. These techniques help a little. However, the *major* causes of low information systems productivity are *not obvious* and will not be corrected by *structured versions of conventional techniques*. They include the following:

- A seemingly trivial change sets off a chain reaction of program modifications. As systems evolve, the chain reactions grow longer and the unanticipated effects of change grow worse. Information systems managers become reluctant to make changes and sometimes say requested changes cannot be made. This was one of the main reasons for the development of database management systems. To solve the problem fully needs top-down planning of *subject* databases, skilled logical database design, and the use of very high level fourth-generation languages.

- The same data is represented in incompatible ways in different files. This causes severe conversion problems or prevents data from being associated as it must be to meet many of the needs of management.

- There are many different versions of similar paperwork in different departments. Each requires different application programs and maintenance. If the procedures were replanned, they could be similar enough to use the same programs. To perceive this and plan the solution needs strategic planning.

- Much of the logic in today's programs is redundant, with many programmers writing routines that ought to be the same.

- Time-consuming program data coding could be lessened or eliminated with data dictionary techniques. This results in fewer data-related program errors.

- Most of today's commercial programs are written in languages like COBOL and PL/I. In typical installations the rate of program creation varies from 7 to 40 lines of code per day. High-level fourth-generation languages permit much faster development of many (but not all) applications. One line of code in such languages is often equivalent to between 10 and 40 COBOL statements.

- End-user languages are permitting users to create their own queries and generate their own reports and graphics, provided that appropriate database facilities are accessible.

- Slow and laborious systems analysis procedures can be avoided for certain types of transactions and speeded up for others, if appropriate databases already exist. Relatively fast analysis for database *actions* can generate structured English programming specifications or code skeletons of 4GLs, such as MANTIS, NOMAD, FOCUS, RAMIS, NATURAL, and IDEAL.

Good information strategy planning should aim to attack these areas and maximize future information systems productivity.

CORPORATE POLITICS

As we have already mentioned, the move to an information-based enterprise often worries or antagonizes end users. Users sometimes have to be told that data they have regarded as their own will now have to be shared, or derived from an information system maintained by others. End users may regard this approach as an invasion of their own carefully protected turf. Reorganization of procedures or corporate restructuring should often go hand in hand with the creation of new information systems, and that needs senior management involvement.

Often, management or users receive their information from different sources once new types of information systems are operational. This may upset long-time employees who used to provide this information.

> *Data Administrator:*
>
> We had one accountant who was quite determined not to allow me to dig in and understand what his systems were providing. He felt that he could satisfy all the report requirements of his users. It was his prerogative to supply the data *in his* manner. This gave him some status which I think he was afraid of losing. He's still bent out of shape by the idea of users being able to step up to a terminal and retrieve the data themselves.

In many enterprises, politics have left in ruins the attempt to move to a strategically planned database environment. Throughout the short history of database technology, the main reason for failure has been human problems, not technical problems.

There is a world of difference between a situation in which the information systems department is trying to pioneer new techniques on its own and a situation in which top management understands, endorses, and visibly supports the move to advanced information systems. It makes a gigantic difference if top management is saying: "We have to build a computerized corporation. We want you *all* to understand that and help as fully as possible."

The emphasis on avoidance of disruptive politics needs to be an ongoing one because, left alone, such politics will soon reassert itself.

> *Programmer:*
>
> Once database implementation was under way, management left everything "to run on the rails." As often as not, it ran off them.

BUDGET CONSIDERATIONS   Another reason for top management involvement is the budget needed for the development of databases and advanced information systems. It is expensive to develop the databases and information systems that an enterprise needs. The payoff is a long-term one, and the costs should not all be borne by the first applications, or the first user department.

> *Database Executive:*
>
> When we discussed the plan with the end users, they would feel, "Gee! It's going to cost so much money!" We're faced with the question: "Who's

going to pay for that?'' The end users feel that they already have a system that's working, and they don't want to pay the cost of rewriting it under the database umbrella.

Interviewer:

So this concern about who pays for things is a major inhibiting factor in evolving from a file environment to database environment?

Database Executive:

In the past they paid just as much, and possibly even more, under the file systems. *But they knew what they were paying for.* With database, especially at the beginning—startup time—they think they are paying for a system that's not totally their own.

Interviewer:

So what do you think is the right way to deal with that problem?

Database Executive:

We have to come out with a better chargeback system and also we have to come out with some kind of research and startup budget. We have to go to top management and have a total commitment and show them the total picture. In fact, we have to go to them with an information systems architecture. This is what we are trying to do. We have given them a plan with detailed costs and milestones for all that we want to implement in the next two to three years. We didn't want them to just imagine how much the cost would be. I think that in the past, with MIS, we never identified the total cost. We justify the cost in terms of reduction of maintenance costs, which are big, and speeded up application development.

If a company is oriented to a long-term planning horizon, it may be ready to accept a database approach that requires a three- or four-year involvement. If it has a very short-term approach to its business and is trying to squeeze the maximum profit in sales out of every year, or even every quarter, anybody who presents a multiyear project is not going to be too well received. Maximizing return on information systems investment in the short term requires different actions from maximizing it over a three- or four-year period.

One of the world's fastest-growing computer service corporations generated hundreds of millions of dollars worth of business each year installing customer applications that minimized immediate costs. To achieve this end it strictly avoided database techniques. However, the costs of maintenance on these applications rose until it was consuming 80 percent of the service corporation's staff resources. The objective of minimizing *immediate* information systems costs results in high maintenance costs *in the long term* and prevents the development of databases that should give fast, inexpensive application creation when they are complete.

Information Systems Executive:

The problem is that the corporate executive today has to deliver today's profits. And a major database expenditure is going to pull right out of today's profit line.

Interviewer:

Do you see a solution to that problem?

Information Systems Executive:

First, we have to educate senior management. That they ought to be willing to take a little bit of an expenditure in today's dollars in order to get a maximum return on tomorrow's dollars. But if the government would come around to looking at a database or any kind of a major information systems expenditure as a capital item, we could look at it as any other major capital expenditure in the corporation.

The development of advanced information systems that depend on centralized databases is a type of cost that ought to be capitalized. Like the installation of a major piece of capital equipment, it is designed to last for many years. If the designers succeed in creating stable data structures—the objective of data modeling and automated data modeling tools—the database has a life span of at least ten years and probably more. It will last longer than most major pieces of production machinery. To charge such a cost to this year's users does not make sense, especially as it takes some years to develop the applications to use databases fully.

SELECTION OF FAST-PAYBACK PROJECTS　　　　Having said that, there *are* opportunities to obtain *fast* payback from databases in certain applications. After an information strategy plan has been created, it is then desirable to look for those systems with which results can be quickly demonstrated. Often they are systems using fourth-generation languages that permit very fast and flexible creation of results.

Database Executive:

Our own experience is that management has to get a sense of some immediate payback. So an opportunity to deliver something—and in fact delivering it—is critical. The undertaking should not be so ambitious as to seem mystical.

IMPLEMENTATION PRIORITIES
An important part of information strategy planning is to determine implementation priorities. A corporatewide view of the needed systems should be developed in such a way that priorities can be rationally set. The databases and information systems that are implemented first should be those that solve immediate problems, have fast payoff, or are quick and easy to implement.

Multiple systems with these characteristics can be implemented if they are designed to be building blocks in a corporatewide information strategy plan.

A HOUSE UPON THE SAND
It is enormously tempting to build databases and information systems without the proper foundation blocks that are provided by proper information strategy planning. It will become much more tempting as the tools for building systems become more powerful and easy to use.

Most data in an enterprise needs to pass from one department to another. Some data needs to be gathered from a number of areas to form the information needed for decision making or control. In today's environment, it is becoming apparent that data must also be exchanged with organizations outside of the enterprise itself. There are not many areas of an enterprise with which we can afford uncoordinated random design by local enthusiasts who wish to be left alone.

Information strategy planning, if done efficiently with a proven methodology, does not cost much compared with the hidden costs of chaotic data and confused information systems. It is a one-time expense, not an ongoing expense (although it is important for the plan to be reviewed and updated periodically). When done, it does not restrict the freedom of local developers. Once appropriate information systems exist, they greatly enhance the freedom to change the corporate procedures.

To build modern information systems without the proper foundation blocks is like building one's house upon the sand. Sooner or later it will be in trouble and have to be rebuilt. Absence of the foundation stones of information strategy planning is one of the reasons why so much information systems activity steadily bogs down in maintenance. The maintenance caused by absence of planning is enormously more expensive than the planning would have been.

The chapters in Part I of this book describe a number of techniques of interest to information systems staff members that will work with top management in carrying out the methodologies of information strategy planning. Readers who are not technically oriented can safely skip the chapters in Part I, at least on a first reading of the book, and continue with the more business-oriented chapters in Part II.

REFERENCE

1. E. R. McLean and J. V. Soden, *Strategic Planning for MIS* (New York: John Wiley, 1977).

PART I **TECHNIQUES**

2 INFORMATION ENGINEERING

Many information systems are employed for routine work—payroll, invoices, calculations, and paperwork. Steadily, however, organizations of all types are realizing that computers and telecommunications can do much more than automate what was previously done by hand. They are changing the way corporations do business, changing their relationships with suppliers and customers, changing where decisions are made, changing the organization chart, and creating new strategic alliances among corporations. In some cases entirely new industry patterns are evolving.

The complexity of design that is found in effective computer systems is increasing. It is much more complex to design systems for computer-integrated manufacturing (CIM) than for the isolated manufacturing applications of an earlier era. It is much more complex to provide systems in which customers and suppliers are online via networks than the early systems that handled paperwork orders and purchases. The best decision-support systems of today are much more complex than those of a decade ago. The efficient enterprise today is moving to a high level of automation and is highly dependent on computerized information. It is clear that it will have a much higher integration of its computer systems than in the past.

However in many enterprises there is much wrong with the information systems department. As we mentioned in Chapter 1, many organizations have application development backlogs of several years. It takes too long to build systems, and the cost of creating programs is outrageous. Management cannot obtain information from computers when needed. The tape and disk libraries are a mess of redundant, chaotic data. The programs are spaghetti code. When management needs to change business procedures or introduce new products and services, the information systems organization cannot make the required modifications on a timely basis. Application software cannot be changed to keep pace with the dynamic, constantly changing needs of business. *The Wall Street Journal* lamented: "Oil and software are the two principal obstacles to economic progress."

INFORMATION SYSTEMS METHODOLOGIES
The methodologies for creating information systems are rapidly changing. The term "engineering" is today often used in describing modern methodologies to imply that they use formal disciplines with precise, well-thought-out techniques rather than the invent-it-as-you-go and often sloppy methods of much conventional programming. The term *software engineering* refers to the set of disciplines used for specifying, designing, and programming computer software. The term *information engineering* refers to the set of interrelated disciplines that are needed to build a computerized enterprise *based on information systems*. The primary focus of software engineering is the logic that is used in computerized processes. The focus of information engineering is the data that is stored and maintained by computers and the information that is distilled from this data. Software engineering applies structured techniques to one project; information engineering applies structured, automated techniques to

BOX 2.1   Characteristics of information engineering

- It is driven by the user.
- It anchors data processing expenditure in top management's needs and goals.
- It identifies how computing can best aid the strategic goals of management.
- It is based on easy-to-understand diagrams.
- It employs a steadily evolving central repository of knowledge about the enterprise.
- It uses CASE tools to link diagrams with code generators and fourth-generation languages.
- It uses prototypes.
- It assists information center activities.
- It is integrated throughout the information systems function.
- Its goal is full automation of the database and application development processes.

BOX 2.2   High-level objectives of information engineering

- Support the needs of top management.
- Focus data processing on the goals of the business.
- Increase the value of computer systems.
- Manage information so that it is accessible when needed.
- Increase the speed of application development.
- Facilitate reusable design and reusable code.
- Reduce the maintenance problem.
- Involve the users in information system design and planning.
- Improve communication among the planners.
- Achieve coordination among systems.
- Provide understanding and control of the data processing resource.

the enterprise as a whole. Box 2.1 lists some of the important characteristics of information engineering; Box 2.2 lists its high-level objectives [1].

POWER TOOLS

An important trend in information engineering is that the manual methods of the past are being rapidly replaced with *power tools* for the design of databases and data processing systems. It would not be possible to build today's cities, or microchips, or jet aircraft without power tools. Our civilization depends on power tools, yet the application of computers is still largely done with hand methods. The design of the interlocking computer applications of a modern enterprise are no less complex than the design of a microchip or a jet aircraft. To attempt this design by hand methods is to ask for trouble.

Advanced power tools bring the need for engineering-like discipline to the database and application design processes. They change the methods of construction but also drastically change *what can be constructed*. To stay competitive in the future, corporations will be dependent on power tools for the engineering of information systems.

COMPUTER-AIDED SYSTEMS ENGINEERING (CASE)

Software engineering techniques became formalized in the 1970s. They encompass software development methodologies such as structured programming, structured design, and structured analysis, and tools to support these. Automated tools for software engineering and information engineering now exist and are becoming widely used. These are generally referred to using the term *computer-aided systems engineering (CASE)*. The use of appropriate CASE tools is an important part of information engineering. The techniques presented in this book are valuable even when CASE tools are not available. However, they are even more effective when they are used in conjunction with appropriate CASE tools at each step in the information strategy planning process.

Today some organizations have excellent information systems. Information engineering formalizes the techniques by which they were created. It uses different types of diagrams and methods from those used by older methodologies for creating systems. It is our contention that strategic information planning must be carried out using organized disciplines and that the techniques of information engineering provide these disciplines.

The remainder of this chapter introduces the discipline of information engineering. The remainder of this book then focuses on those aspects of the information engineering discipline that are useful in performing the tasks associated with information strategy planning.

THE INFORMATION SYSTEMS PYRAMID

It is useful to draw a pyramid to represent an organization's information systems function. (See Fig. 2.1.) The pyramid has three sides, as shown in Fig. 2.2. The sides represent the following:

- The organization's *data*
- The *activities* the organization carries out using that data
- The *technology* that is employed in implementing information systems

All three aspects of information systems must be viewed from a high-level, management-oriented perspective at the top to a fully detailed implementation at the bottom, as shown in Fig. 2.3. The pyramid describes the four levels of activities that involve data, activities, and technology.

- **Strategy.** At the top of the pyramid is strategic planning for data, activities, and technology. The strategic planning of data, activities, and technology needs to be anchored firmly in the strategic planning of the business itself. At this level, top management must work together with its information systems executives to formulate an overall strategic vision that relates to future technology and how it could affect the business, its products or services, and its goals and objectives. Formulating a strategic vision and performing strategic planning for the information needs of the enterprise is the subject of this book.

- **Analysis.** At the second level, logical models are built that describe the fundamental data that is needed to operate the enterprise, the activities that use the

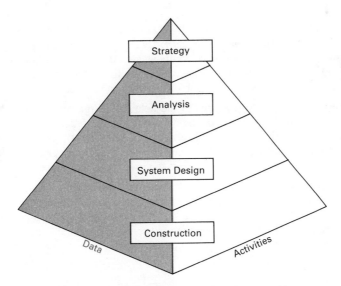

Figure 2.1　The information systems pyramid.

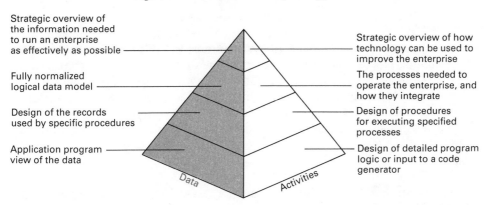

Figure 2.2.　The left side of the pyramid represents data, the right side activities.

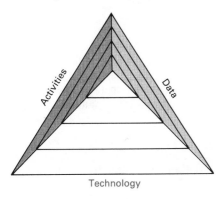

Figure 2.3.　The pyramid has three sides. The third side represents technology.

data, and the technology that will be employed to store, maintain, and manipulate the data. This level is concerned with *what* needs to be done but not, in detail, with *how* it is to be accomplished. At this level, there needs to be a migration plan showing how the enterprise will evolve from earlier unstructured applications to the well-engineered and integrated systems of the future.

- **Design.** The third level relates to the detailed design of data, the data processing systems that interact with the data, and the hardware and software that will be employed. This level is concerned with how the work is accomplished and describes the procedures in user terms. This level, however, is not concerned with implementation details, except for user input and output.

- **Construction.** At the bottom level are all those activities that relate to the construction of physical databases and the application programs that access them using the chosen hardware and software tools. This layer is concerned with the files, database management systems, program structures, technical design, and in general the implementation details.

DIAGRAMMING TECHNIQUES

At each of the four levels in the information systems pyramid, diagramming techniques are important. A major function of most CASE tools is to automate the diagramming process and to produce updatable diagrams using a graphics workstation. Computer-maintainable diagrams are an important part of information engineering. Many different types of diagram are used in documenting different aspects of data and activities at the four levels of the pyramid. The basic building blocks of these diagramming techniques are described in Chapter 3.

DIAGRAMS FOR ACTIVITIES

There are eight types of diagram that are important on the *activities* side of the pyramid. Figures 2.4 through 2.11 show examples of all eight diagramming techniques for activities.

1. **Decomposition Diagrams.** A *decomposition diagram* (Fig. 2.4) is a basic tool for structured analysis and design. With decomposition diagrams, high-level activities are decomposed into lower-level activities showing more detail. This top-down structuring makes complex organizations or processes easier to comprehend. Most decomposition diagrams are simple tree structures.

2. **Dependency Diagrams.** A *dependency diagram* (Fig. 2.5) has blocks showing activities and arrows between blocks showing that one activity is dependent on another. A dependency diagram might be used for analyzing the processes that are needed in a business area.

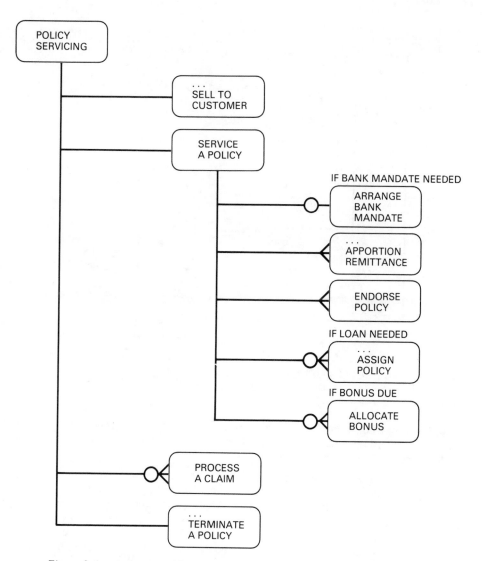

Figure 2.4. A decomposition diagram of the processes performed in *policy servicing*. Three dots in several of the boxes indicate that those boxes can be expanded to show more detail.

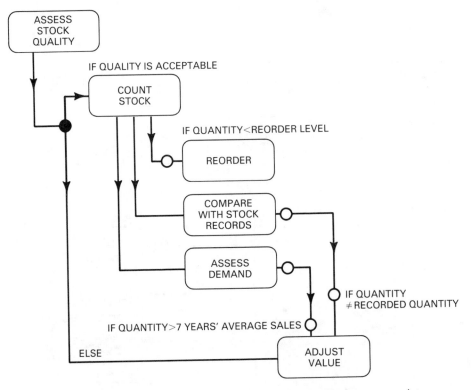

Figure 2.5. A dependency diagram should be drawn with the arrows point-ing down or to the right whenever possible. The root of the diagram (a box with no arrows entering it) should be at the top left.

3. **Data Flow Diagrams.** A *data flow diagram* (Fig. 2.6) shows procedures and flows of data among procedures. It is a high-level design tool for mapping out the proce-dures required to automate a given area.

4. **Action Diagrams.** *Action diagrams* (Fig. 2.7) provide a simple technique for draw-ing high-level decomposition diagrams, overview program structures, and detailed program control structures. Most diagramming techniques cannot draw both the overview structure of programs and the detailed control structures; action diagrams can. Action diagrams can also be used to document management procedures, as we will show in Chapter 3. Throughout this book, we will use action diagrams to illus-trate the steps involved in the information strategy planning methodologies we de-scribe.

5. **Data Navigation Diagrams.** *Data navigation diagrams* (Fig. 2.8) show the access paths through a database structure that are used by a process or procedure. Data navigation diagrams provide a first step in charting procedures that use databases or multiple files. Appropriately drawn data navigation diagrams can be automatically converted to action diagrams using appropriate CASE tools.

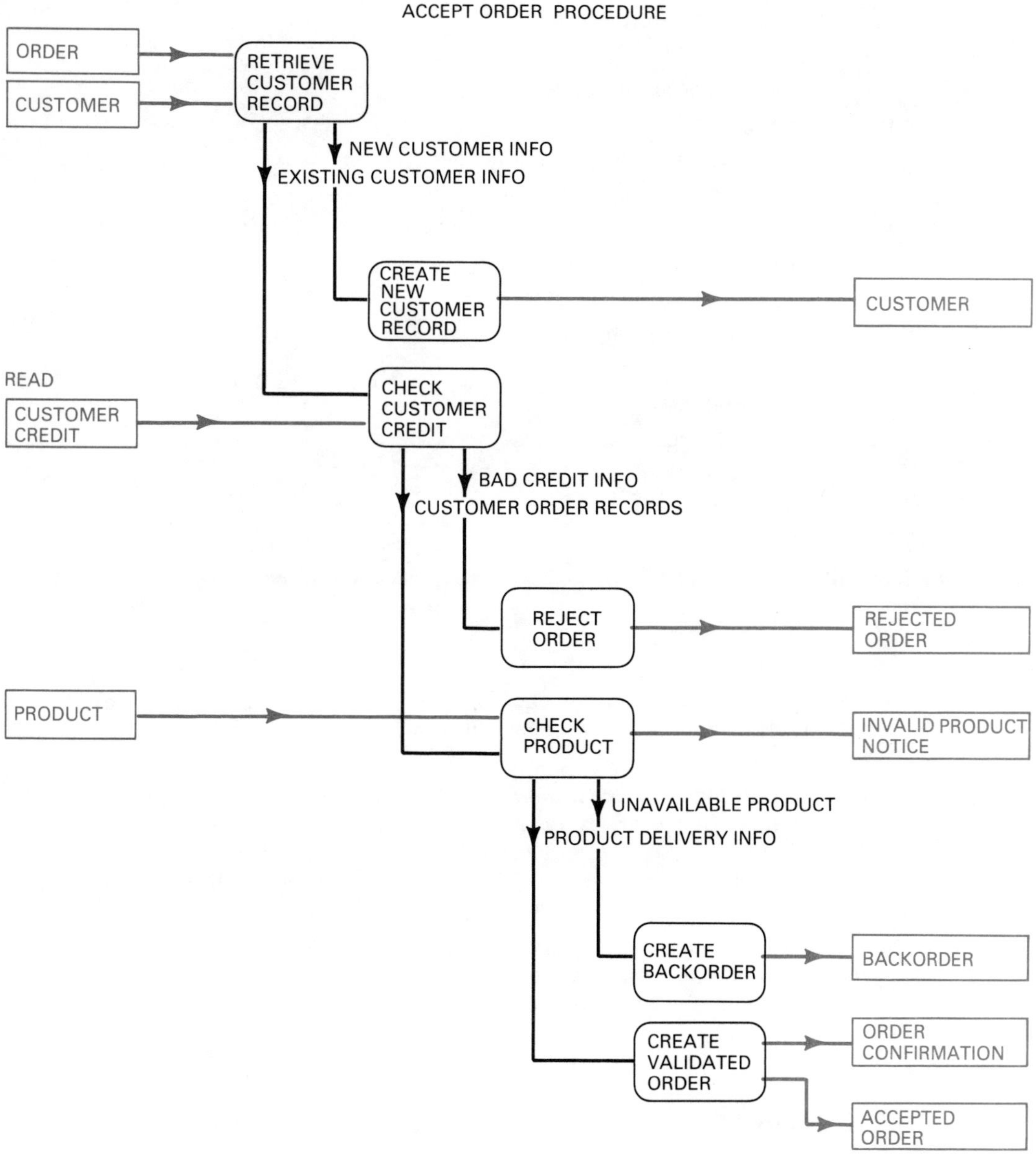

ACCEPT ORDER PROCEDURE

ORDER

CUSTOMER

RETRIEVE
CUSTOMER
RECORD

NEW CUSTOMER INFO
EXISTING CUSTOMER INFO

CREATE
NEW
CUSTOMER
RECORD

CUSTOMER

READ

CUSTOMER
CREDIT

CHECK
CUSTOMER
CREDIT

BAD CREDIT INFO
CUSTOMER ORDER RECORDS

REJECT
ORDER

REJECTED
ORDER

PRODUCT

CHECK
PRODUCT

INVALID PRODUCT
NOTICE

UNAVAILABLE PRODUCT
PRODUCT DELIVERY INFO

CREATE
BACKORDER

BACKORDER

CREATE
VALIDATED
ORDER

ORDER
CONFIRMATION

ACCEPTED
ORDER

Figure 2.6 A data flow diagram shows procedures and flows of data among procedures.

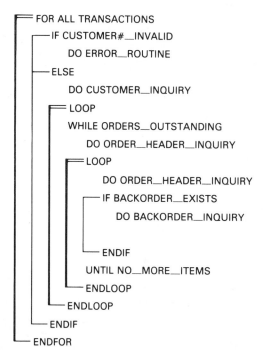

```
┌══ FOR ALL TRANSACTIONS
│   ┌── IF CUSTOMER#__INVALID
│   │       DO ERROR__ROUTINE
│   ├── ELSE
│   │       DO CUSTOMER__INQUIRY
│   │   ┌══ LOOP
│   │   │   WHILE ORDERS__OUTSTANDING
│   │   │       DO ORDER__HEADER__INQUIRY
│   │   │   ┌══ LOOP
│   │   │   │       DO ORDER__HEADER__INQUIRY
│   │   │   │   ┌── IF BACKORDER__EXISTS
│   │   │   │   │       DO BACKORDER__INQUIRY
│   │   │   │   │
│   │   │   │   │
│   │   │   │   └── ENDIF
│   │   │   │   UNTIL NO__MORE__ITEMS
│   │   │   └── ENDLOOP
│   │   └── ENDLOOP
│   └── ENDIF
└── ENDFOR
```

Figure 2.7 An action diagram showing detailed program logic.

6. **Decision Trees and Decision Tables.** *Decision trees* (Fig. 2.9) and *decision tables* provide a technique for drawing logic that involves multiple choices or complex sets of conditions.

7. **State Transition Diagrams.** *State transition diagrams* (Fig. 2.10) provide a technique for drawing complex logic that involves many possible transitions among states. Based on finite-state machine notation, neither decision trees nor state transition diagrams are useful with every type of system or program; both relate to situations with certain types of complex logic.

8. **Dialog Design Diagrams.** A *dialog design diagram* (Fig. 2.11) is similar to a state transition diagram. The states represent the screens or panels of a dialog, and the transitions among states represent various operator actions.

**DIAGRAMS FOR
DATA**

The diagramming techniques that we will use most in this book are those that are used for documenting *data*. There are three types of diagrams that are useful for documenting the data side of the information systems pyramid. Figures 2.12, 2.13, and 2.14 show examples of these.

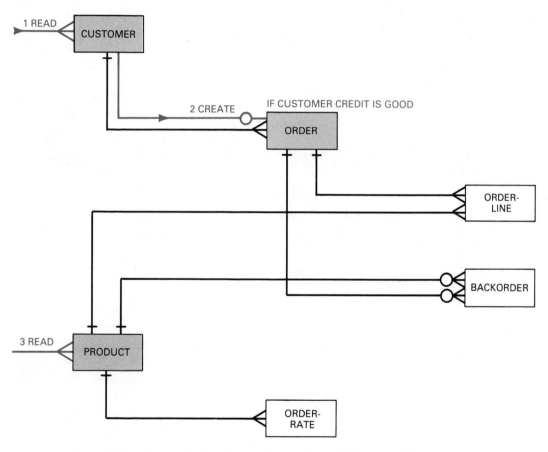

Figure 2.8 A data navigation diagram showing three database accesses.

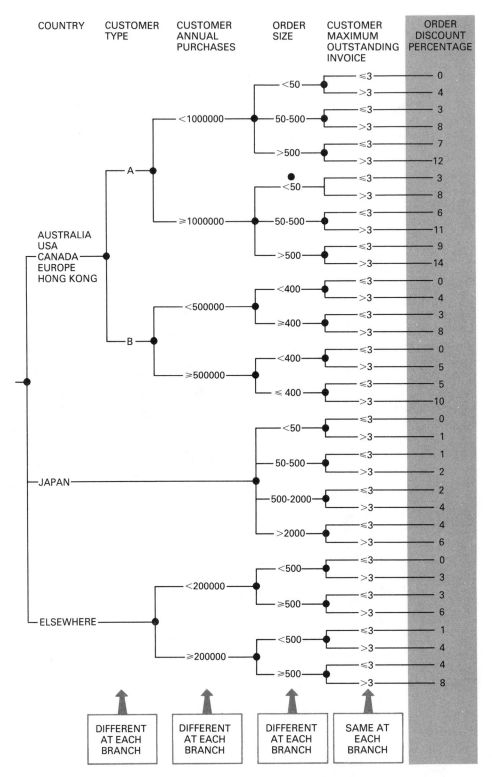

Figure 2.9 A decision tree in which branches are identical for some fields and different for others.

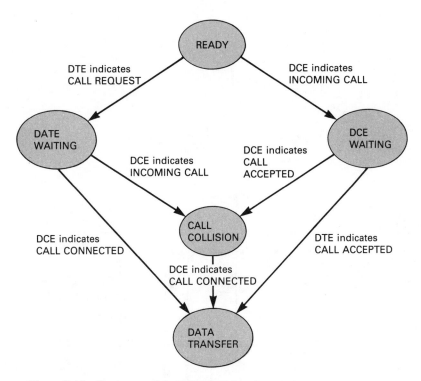

Figure 2.10 The states of the DTE/DCE interface during the setup of a call with CCITT Recommendation X.25.

1. **Entity-Relationship Diagrams.** *Entities* are the people, things, or concepts about which we store data.* An example of an entity is *employee. Entity-relationship diagrams* (Fig. 2.12) are used to document entities and the relationships that exist between them. Entity-relationship diagrams document the high-level data models that are of interest to top management.

2. **Logical Data Model Diagrams.** *Data items* are the individual elements of data that we store for a particular entity, for example *employee name* and *department number. Logical data model diagrams* (Fig. 2.13), also sometimes called *data analysis diagrams,* consist of bubble charts and record diagrams that show individual data items and the dependencies that exist between them. They are used in the logical data modeling process.

3. **Data Structure Diagrams.** *Data structure diagrams* (Fig. 2.14) are similar to the diagrams used in documenting the logical data model, but show the detailed data

---

*To be completely precise, we must make a distinction between an *entity type* and an *entity occurrence.* An example of an entity type is *Employee;* an example of an occurrence of the Employee entity type is *James Smith.* In many cases, we use the term *entity* alone to mean either entity type or entity occurrence. When we do this, it is generally clear from the context which we mean. In this book the term *entity* almost always means *entity type.*

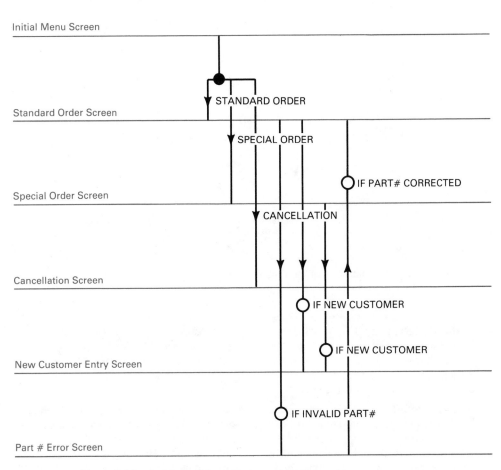

Initial Menu Screen

Standard Order Screen

▼ STANDARD ORDER

▼ SPECIAL ORDER

Special Order Screen

○ IF PART# CORRECTED

▼ CANCELLATION

Cancellation Screen

○ IF NEW CUSTOMER

○ IF NEW CUSTOMER

New Customer Entry Screen

○ IF INVALID PART#

Part # Error Screen

Figure 2.11   A simple dialog structure showing transitions among screens.

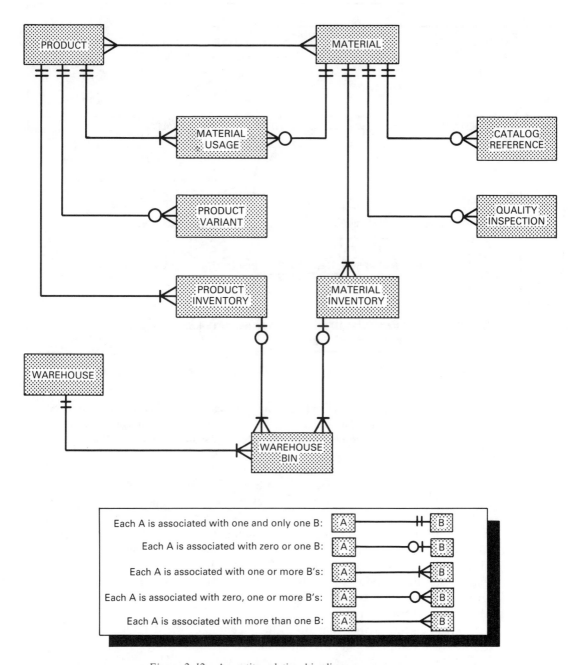

Figure 2.12 An entity-relationship diagram.

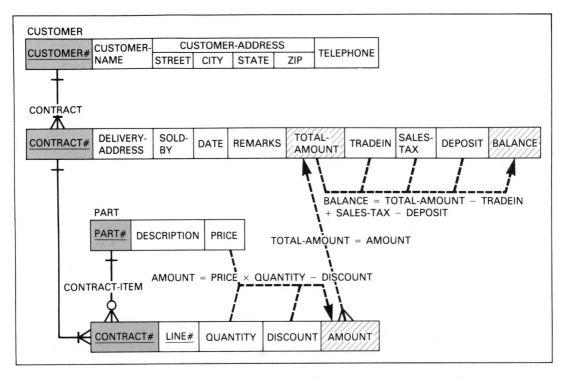

Figure 2.13   A typical record diagram showing derived data items.

structures that are used in implementing a logical data model in a specific database management system. The specific types of diagram used to document this type of structure may be different for different types of database management systems.

THE ENCYCLOPEDIA

As we have been discussing, information engineering is an interlocking set of formal techniques in which enterprise models, logical data models, and process models are documented with various diagrams. Ideally, the various diagrams should be stored in computerized form where they can be interlinked and validated using artificial intelligence techniques. It is the *meaning* of a diagram rather than the graphic image itself that should be stored. If this is done properly, many different types of diagram can often be automatically generated from the stored information.

We call the facility that stores the meaning of the diagrams an *encyclopedia*. An encyclopedia should "understand" the designs that it stores and apply many rules to check their integrity and consistency. The encyclopedia can be large, storing information about an entire business area or the results of enterprisewide strategic planning.

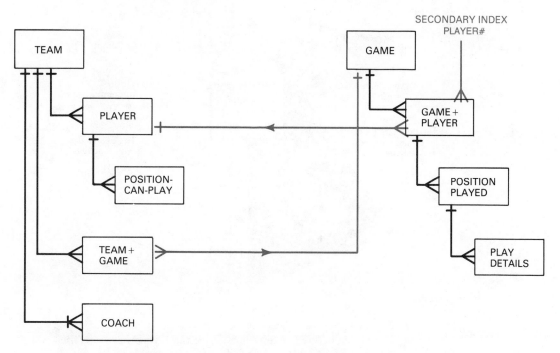

Figure 2.14   A data structure diagram for an IMS database. The red lines are logical linkages that can be followed in the direction of the arrows. A secondary index is shown with PLAYER# as its source field and GAME + PLAYER as its target.

The encyclopedia often stores information that is not shown graphically on diagrams. Some of this information can be collected as the diagram is built. It is desirable that the user of a graphics workstation be able to display the more detailed information. This can be done by pointing to a diagram element and expanding it into a window that contains the details in text or table form or in the form of another diagram.

SEVEN TRENDS   There is a constant ongoing search for better methodologies in data processing. Seven types of approach have been advocated by different authorities, and any one of the seven is valuable in itself. The *integration* of the seven trends to better methodologies makes all of them more valuable. Information engineering creates a synthesis of these seven trends. We will conclude this introduction to information engineering by summarizing these seven trends, illustrated in Fig. 2.15.

1. **Strategic Planning of Information Systems.** This trend seeks to relate the use of computers in an enterprise to top management needs and perspective. It is concerned

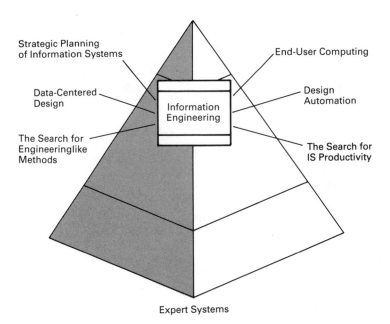

Figure 2.15 Each of these thrusts in the methodology of information engineering is valuable by itself. Information engineering attempts to synthesize them.

with formulating an overall strategic vision that formalizes management goals and objectives, modeling the enterprise, and performing strategic planning of information.

2. **Data-Centered Design.** This set of techniques is concerned with formal data administration and logical data modeling. Systems have proven to be much easier to build and much cheaper to maintain when thorough logical data modeling has been completed.

3. **Engineering-Like Methods.** Conventional structured techniques improved the design of systems but did not go far enough. More rigorous techniques are possible when computers are used to help build specifications and to link these specifications to computerized models of data. Computers can perform comprehensive cross-checks throughout a complex system. As hand methodologies are replaced with computerized methodologies, more rigorous engineering-like techniques are possible that would be too tedious to attempt by hand.

4. **End-User Computing.** The end-user revolution in computing has spread rapidly in some corporations. Many organizations have information centers that help users to employ a wide variety of end-user tools. Creating prototypes that end users can critique has become common in system building. Analysts guide end users through *joint application design (JAD)* sessions to specify what systems are needed. It has become clear that techniques are needed for guiding end-user computing to prevent a Tower of Babel from springing up as a result of randomly designed data and

redundant procedures. Information engineering can provide the necessary guidance mechanism.

5. **Design Automation.** Computer-aided design techniques have spread rapidly in mechanical and electronic engineering. They are even more critical to systems engineering. Diagrams for all aspects of systems engineering can be built at a workstation screen using CASE tools, with the computer aiding the designer and checking the design. With CASE technology, computer-aided design tools can be tightly coupled to the use of fourth-generation languages and code generators.

6. **Improved Data Processing Productivity.** The building of data processing systems currently takes too long. Time and cost overruns are normal. The maintenance problems are intolerable. Major attacks on these problems have been made by means of fourth-generation languages, application generators, prototyping tools, and end-user tools. In some cases, these have dramatically improved data processing productivity. The coupling of CASE tools to fourth-generation languages and code generators is especially important for improving the speed and quality of systems building.

7. **Expert Systems.** Expert systems are a spin-off from artificial intelligence research. They apply inference processing to a knowledge base, which contains data and rules, to make a computer emulate human expertise or to build up a level of expertise more comprehensive than any one human could achieve. Information engineering should use expert systems techniques to help planners, analysts, and designers create better systems.

Experience with information engineering and CASE tools has shown that, once the logical data models are built, the construction of systems proceeds much more quickly. Information engineering makes it more likely that the real needs of end users will be met with the information systems that are built.

REFERENCE

1. James Martin, *Information Engineering,* a report in four volumes from the Savant Institute, 2 New Street, Carnforth, Lancashire, England, 1986, 1987.

3 DIAGRAMMING TECHNIQUES

Modern information systems technology depends heavily on its use of diagramming. Diagrams showing facets of highly complex data structures, and the automated procedures that employ them, need to be as easy to understand as possible. Diagrams need to have precision so that a computer can use them as a basis for design automation and code generation. A complex design is often represented with multiple diagram types in such a way that the computer can interrelate the diagrams.

To gain control of its computing, an enterprise must establish a set of standards for the diagrams that are used to represent data structures and procedures. The standards should be the basis of the training given both to data processing professionals and to end users. Enterprisewide standards are essential for communication among persons involved with computers; for establishing corporate, interdepartmental, and personal data models and procedures; and for managing the move into computer-aided systems engineering (CASE).

Many corporations have adopted diagramming conventions adapted from methodologies of the past, which today are inadequate because they are narrowly focused, ill-structured, inadequate to support database techniques, not suited to fourth-generation languages, too difficult to teach to end users, clumsy and time consuming, inadequate for automation, or, as is usually the case, tackle only part of problems that should be tackled.

This chapter summarizes the constructs that we need to be able to draw. Similar constructs are needed on many different types of diagrams. A consistently drawn set of constructs can be used to draw all the following types of diagrams used to describe various aspects of information systems:

- Decomposition diagrams
- Dependency diagrams

- Data flow diagrams
- Action diagrams showing management procedures
- Action diagrams showing program logic
- Data analysis diagrams
- Entity-relationship diagrams
- Data structure diagrams
- Data navigation diagrams
- Decision trees and tables
- State transition diagrams and tables
- Dialog diagrams

All these types of diagrams should be drawn from the same small set of blocks and symbols. These blocks and symbols are described in this chapter. This subject is examined in more detail in the author's book *Recommended Diagramming Standards for Analysts and Programmers*.

CHANGING METHODS

Diagramming techniques in computing are still evolving. This is necessary because when we examine techniques in common use today, many of them have serious deficiencies. Flowcharts are falling out of use because they do not give a structured view of a program. Some of the early structured diagramming techniques need replacing because they cannot be used to represent some important types of structures. Information systems practitioners are today inventing more rigorous methods for creating better specifications. Vast improvements are needed and are clearly possible in the specification process. These improvements bring new diagramming methods.

Many of the diagramming techniques in common use are old and obsolete. The IBM diagramming template, which many analysts still use, is hopelessly out of date. It contains symbols for "magnetic drum," "punched tape," and "transmittal tape." It was created before database systems, personal computers, or structured techniques were in use. We need an integrated set of diagramming standards with which we can express all the constructs that are necessary for the description of complex data structures and procedures. Box 3.1 lists principles that should apply to diagramming standards.

BOXES

All the diagramming techniques we will discuss here use blocks to represent both activities and data. To

BOX 3.1   Diagramming standards

Principles of Diagramming Standards

- Analysts, programmers, and end users should be provided with a set of diagramming techniques that serve as aids to clear thinking about different aspects of analysis, design, and programming.
- The multiple diagramming tools should use the minimum number of building blocks.
- They should be as easy to learn as possible.
- The diagramming techniques should be a corporatewide standard, firmly adhered to.

Automation of Diagramming

- The diagrams should be the basis of computer-aided systems engineering (CASE).
- Higher-level design diagrams should convert automatically to action diagrams where relevant.
- The family of diagrams should be a basis for code generation.
- The diagrams should be easy to change and file at the computer screen.
- The diagrams should relate to data models.

---

distinguish between these, we will represent *activities* using boxes that have rounded corners, and we will show *data* using boxes with square corners:

ACTIVITY   DATA

ARROWS   Many types of diagrams use lines that connect the various boxes that represent procedures or data. We can use an arrow on a connecting line to mean *flow* or *sequence*.

FLOW   SEQUENCE

High-level decomposition diagrams are usually unconcerned with sequence. They use a tree structure to show how a function is composed of lower-level subfunctions. Lower-level decomposition diagrams, however, may need to show sequence. For example, they might show how an activity is composed of subactivities that are executed in a given order. To show this, we use an arrow pointing in the direction of the sequence. This direction should always be drawn top-to-bottom and left-to-right:

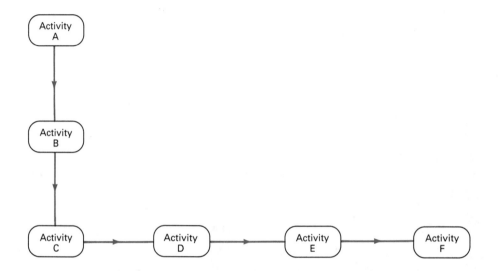

Notice that we draw arrows in the middle of a line that connects two boxes rather than at the end. This is because we use symbols at the ends of the line to represent *cardinality,* which we discuss next.

CARDINALITY

The term *cardinality* refers to how many of one item is associated with how many of another. There can be *one-with-one, one-with-many,* and *many-with-many* cardinality. We sometimes also include numbers to place upper or lower limits on cardinality.

One-with-Many Cardinality

We use a *crow's-foot* symbol to represent a one-with-many cardinality:

This diagram means that each occurrence of A is associated with one or more than one occurrence of B. We refer to this relationship as a *one-with-many association*.

One-with-One Cardinality

To represent a one-with-one cardinality, we use a small bar across the line, like a "1," as follows:

This diagram means that each occurrence of X is associated with one and only one occurrence of Y.

Zero Cardinality

We include a circle, like a zero, as part of the cardinality symbol when there can also be zero occurrences of an item in the association:

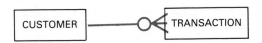

This diagram means that each customer can have zero, one, or many transactions.

We can also combine the circle with the bar:

This diagram states that each employee has zero or one spouse.

Cardinalities at Both Ends

In the foregoing diagrams, we have used a cardinality symbol at only one end of the connecting lines. In some cases, this is sufficient. However, on diagrams that are used to represent data structures, we normally include a cardinality symbol on both ends of the connecting line:

This diagram documents two different relationships:

- Each occurrence of A is associated with one or more than one occurrence of B.
- Each occurrence of B is associated with one or more than one occurrence of A.

In general, a diagram is incomplete if it has lines connecting to data boxes with no cardinality symbols. On diagrams that describe *activities* rather than data structures, the cardinality is usually one with one; because of this we often omit the one-with-one symbol. A line with no cardinality symbol implies a one-with-one cardinality.

Maximum and Minimum

It is sometimes necessary to be very explicit about the minimum and maximum numbers of occurrences that are represented by the cardinality. We can then include two cardinality symbols at each end of a connecting line. The symbol representing the maximum number of occurrences is always placed next to the box to which it refers:

This diagram states that for each occurrence of A there can be one or many occurrences of B. It also states that for each occurrence of B there can be zero, one, or many occurrences of A.

Similarly, the following diagram states that a husband has one and only one wife and a wife has one and only one husband:

In many cases, it is not necessary to state both a minimum and a maximum explicitly. A single crow's-foot implies a minimum of one and a maximum of many; a single bar implies a minimum of one and a maximum of one.

ENTITY-RELATIONSHIP DIAGRAMS

An important type of diagram that is used in database planning and design is the entity-relationship diagram. An entity is any person, thing, or concept about which data is stored. Entity types, drawn using square-cornered boxes, are associated with one another; for example, a PRODUCT entity is purchased by a CUSTOMER entity. Lines linking the entity boxes show these associations. The lines have cardinality indicators. Figure 3.1 shows

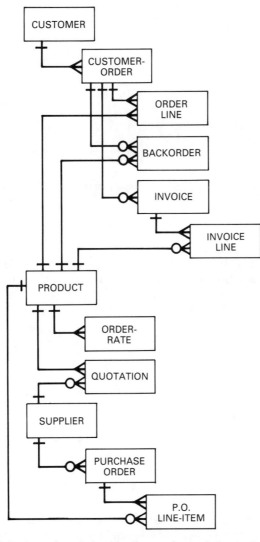

Figure 3.1   An entity-relationship diagram for a wholesale distributor.

an entity-relationship diagram that uses the diagramming techniques we have been describing.

LABELING OF LINES   On some types of diagrams, the lines connecting boxes should be labeled. Lines between activity boxes are undirectional. There may be lines in both directions between activity boxes, but these should be separate lines each with its own particular meaning. Lines between data boxes, on the other hand, are bidirectional. The line could be read in either direction; thus,

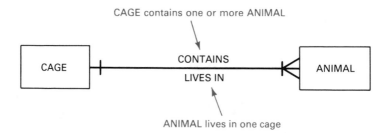

It is usually necessary to label only one direction of such a line.

A label above a horizontal line is the name of the relationship when the line is read from left to right. A label below a horizontal line is the name when the line is read from right to left.

As the line is rotated, the label remains on the same side of the line:

Thus the label to the right of a vertical line is read when going down the line; the label on the left of a vertical line is read when going up the line.

**READING LINES
LIKE SENTENCES**

Lines between boxes give information about the relationship between the boxes. This information ought to read like an English sentence. For example,

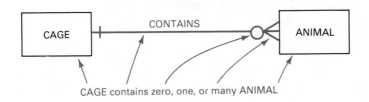

CAGE contains zero, one, or many ANIMAL

LARGE ARROWS

A large arrow on a diagram is used to show that an event occurs:

**DIAGRAM
CONNECTORS**

A pentagon arrow is used as a connector to connect lines to a distant part of a diagram:

The connector symbol may be used to connect to other pages. This is often unnecessary with computerized design tools because the user scrolls across large complete diagrams.

ACTION DIAGRAMS   Thus far we have been discussing diagramming techniques that are well suited for documenting data structures. In the remainder of this chapter we will discuss another important type of diagram called action diagrams. Action diagrams are particularly useful for documenting program logic. We will see at the end of this chapter how they can also be used to describe management procedures.

Of the diagramming techniques that evolved in the 1970s and earlier, some are useful for describing an overview of program structure, and others are useful for describing detailed program logic. *Structure charts, HIPO diagrams, Warnier-Orr diagrams,* and *Michael Jackson charts* show overall program structures, but not detailed tests, conditions, and other program logic. Their advocates usually resort to *structured English* or *pseudocode* to represent details. *Flowcharts* show the logic of a program but tend to encourage a nonstructured representation with GOTO links. *Nassi-Shneiderman charts* show the detailed logic of a program but are not useful for showing a high-level overview.

Unlike other types of diagram, action diagrams are useful for showing both an overview and for showing the details of program logic.

BRACKETS   In an action diagram, we use a simple bracket to draw a program module that is executed a single time each time it is invoked:

Brackets are the basic building blocks of action diagrams. Inside a bracket we can include a sequence of operations. A bracket can be of any length, so there is space in it for as much text or detail as is needed.

A simple control rule applies to the bracket. We always enter the bracket at the top, do the things described in the bracket in a top-to-bottom sequence, and always exit at the bottom. Inside the bracket we can include other brackets, nested to any desired level. The nesting shows the hierarchical structure of a program, as illustrated in Fig. 3.2.

DECOMPOSITION DIAGRAM,
STRUCTURE CHART, HIPO CHART, ETC.

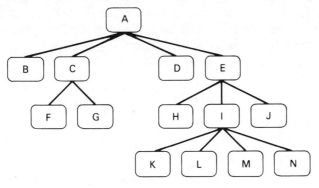

ACTION DIAGRAM

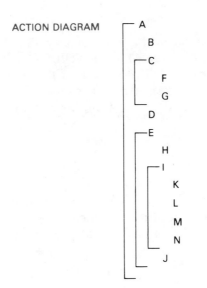

Figure 3.2   A hierarchical block structure and an equivalent action diagram.

REPETITION   Some brackets are used to represent *repetition*. A bracket that represents a module that is executed multiple times each time it is invoked has a double line at its top and bottom:

═ For All Transactions

A repetition structure can be used to document a program loop. Sometimes the test that is performed to determine when to terminate the loop should be made before the actions of the loop are performed and sometimes the test should be made after. This difference can be made clear on brackets by drawing the test either at the top or bottom of the bracket; thus,

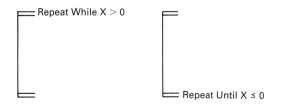

If the test is at the head of the loop as with a WHILE loop, the actions in the loop may never be executed if the WHILE condition is not satisfied the first time the test is performed. If the test is at the bottom of the loop, as with an UNTIL loop, the actions in the loop will always be executed at least once. They will be executed more than once if the condition continues to be met.

SELECTION

Often a program module or subroutine is executed only IF a certain condition applies. To show this, we include a description of the condition at the head of the bracket. Whenever an IF statement is shown, the corresponding ELSE should also be on the bracket:

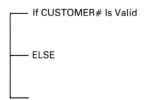

CASE STRUCTURES

When only one of several processes is to be executed (mutually exclusive selection), we draw a bracket that has several divisions:

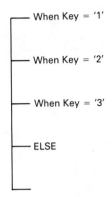

This type of bracket describes the structured programming CASE structure. One, and only one, of the divisions in the bracket is executed.

SETS OF DATA   Sometimes a procedure needs to be executed on all of the items in a set of items. It might be applied to all transactions or all records in a file; for example,

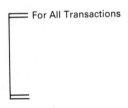

This is a form of repetition bracket.

SUBPROCEDURES   Sometimes a user needs to add an item to an action diagram that is itself a procedure containing actions. We call this a subprocedure, or subroutine, and draw it with a round-cornered box:

In some cases the procedure designer has sections of a procedure that are not yet thought out in detail. This is represented using a box with rounded corners and a right-edge made up of question marks:

Some procedures are invoked from more than one place in an action diagram. These procedures are called common procedures. They are indicated by drawing a vertical line down the left-hand side of the procedure box:

The use of these boxes makes action diagrams a powerful tool for designing procedures at many levels of abstraction. As with other structured techniques, top-down design can be done by first creating an overall structure with procedure boxes, while remaining vague about the contents of each box. The gross structure can then be broken down into successive levels of detail.

ESCAPES

Certain conditions may cause a procedure to be terminated. They may cause the termination of the bracket in which the condition occurs, or they may cause the termination of multiple brackets. This is called an *escape*. Escapes are drawn with an arrow to the left through one or more brackets, as follows:

It is important to note that an escape structure allows only a forward skip to the exitpoint of a bracket. This restriction keeps the structure simple and does not allow action diagrams to degenerate into unstructured "spaghetti" logic. An escape is different from a GO TO instruction. It represents an orderly closedown of the brackets escaped from.

GO TO

When a language has a well-implemented escape mechanism, there is no need for GO TO instructions. However, some languages have GO TO instructions and no escape. Using good structured design, the GO TO can be employed to emulate an escape. However, any attempt to branch to a distant part of the program should be avoided.

It has been suggested (without much justification) that a GO TO should be included in the action diagram vocabulary. This can be done by using a dashed arrow to replace the solid escape arrow; thus,

NEXT ITERATION

In a repetition bracket a next-iteration construct is useful. With this, control skips the remaining instructions in a repetition bracket and goes to the next iteration of the loop. A next-iteration construct is drawn as follows:

The arrow does not break through the bracket as with an escape construct.

SIMPLE DATABASE ACTIONS

Most of the action diagrams drawn for commercial data processing systems relate to databases or files.

A common action of these diagrams is the database or file operation. We will distinguish between simple and compound database actions.

A simple database action is an operation applied to one instance of one record type. There are four types of simple actions:

- CREATE
- READ
- UPDATE
- DELETE

The memorable acronym CRUD is sometimes used to refer to these and to help remember them.

On an action diagram, a simple database action is represented by a rectangular box. The name of the record is written inside the box; the type of action is written on the left side of the box:

COMPOUND DATABASE ACTIONS

A compound database action also takes a single action against a database, but the action may affect multiple records of the same type and sometimes of more than one type. An operation may search or sort a logical file. It may be a relational operation that operates on an entire table or set of tables.

A compound database action is represented as a double rectangular box. The name of the record is written inside the box; the database action is written on the left-hand side of the box:

Often a compound database action needs a qualifying statement associated with it to describe how it is performed. For example,

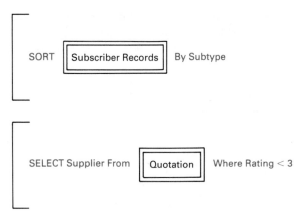

AUTOMATIC NAVIGATION

A compound database action may require automatic navigation by the database management system. Relational databases and a few nonrelational ones have this capability. For a database without automatic navigation, a compiler of a fourth-generation language may generate the required sequence of data accesses.

With a compound database action, search parameters or conditions are often an integral part of the action itself. They are written inside a bracket containing the access box.

SIMPLE VERSUS COMPOUND DATABASE ACCESSES

There are many procedures that can be done with either simple database accesses or compound accesses. If a traditional DBMS is used, the programmer navigates through the database with simple accesses. If the DBMS permits automatic navigation, higher-level statements using compound database accesses may be employed.

Suppose, for example, that we want to give a $1000 bonus to all employees who are sales representatives in the Southeast region. Using the SQL database language, we would write

```
UPDATE EMPLOYEE
    SET SALARY = SALARY + 1000
    WHERE JOB = 'SALES'
    AND REGION = 'SOUTHEAST'
```

We can diagram this with a compound database action as follows:

With simple actions (no automatic navigation), we can diagram the same procedure as follows:

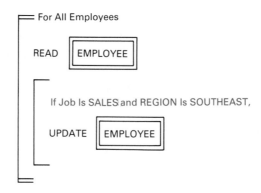

ULTIMATE DECOMPOSITION

At the higher levels of the design process, action diagram brackets represent the names of processes and subprocesses. As the designer descends into program-level detail the brackets become program constructs, IF brackets, CASE brackets, LOOP brackets, and so on. Figure 3.3 shows an action diagram that provides an overview of a program structure.

When action diagrams are manipulated on a computer screen using an interactive editor, developers can edit and adjust the diagram and successively fill in details until they have working code that can be tested interpretively. We

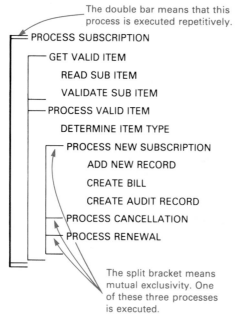

Figure 3.3 A high-level action diagram.

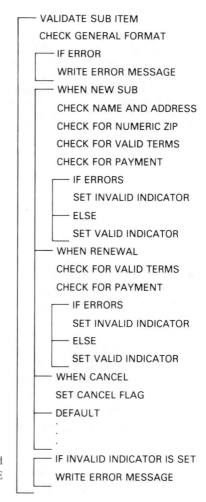

Figure 3.4 An action diagram showing the detailed logic inside the process in Fig. 3.3 named VALIDATE SUB ITEM.

call this process *ultimate decomposition*. Figure 3.4 expands the process in Fig. 3.3 called VALIDATE SUB ITEM. Figures 3.3 and 3.4 could be merged into one chart if desired.

Figure 3.5 shows a diagram describing a simple game program. With action diagrams we can decompose this until we have program code. Figure 3.6 shows an action diagram equivalent to Fig. 3.5. The action diagram gives more room for explanation. Instead of saying "PRINT RANDOM WORDS," it says "PRINT RANDOM WORD FROM EACH OF THE THREE LISTS." Figure 3.7 decomposes the part of the diagram labeled BUZZWORD GENERATOR. The inner bracket is a repetition bracket that executes 22 times. This is inside a bracket that is terminated by the operator pressing the ESC (escape) key. The

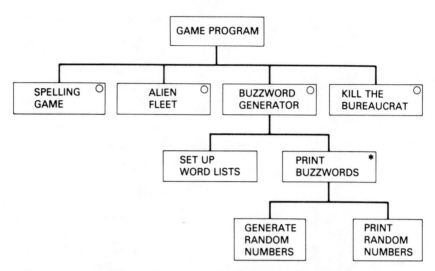

Figure 3.5 The "o" and "*" in the top right-hand corner of the blocks on charts such as this do not have obvious meanings. The form of diagrams should be selected to make the meanings as obvious as possible to uninitiated readers.

last statement in this bracket is WAIT, indicating that the system will wait after executing the remainder of the bracket until the operator presses the ESC key. This gives the operator as much time as needed to read the display. Figure 3.8 decomposes the diagram further into an executable program. This program is written in the fourth-generation language MANTIS, from CINCOM, Inc.

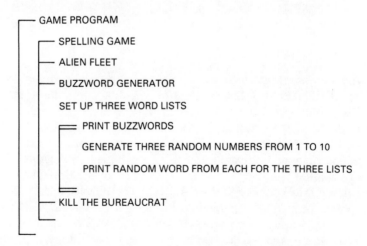

Figure 3.6 An action diagram equivalent to the Jackson diagram of Fig. 3.5.

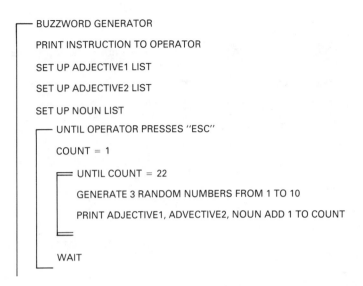

BUZZWORD GENERATOR

PRINT INSTRUCTION TO OPERATOR

SET UP ADJECTIVE1 LIST

SET UP ADJECTIVE2 LIST

SET UP NOUN LIST

UNTIL OPERATOR PRESSES "ESC"

COUNT = 1

UNTIL COUNT = 22

GENERATE 3 RANDOM NUMBERS FROM 1 TO 10

PRINT ADJECTIVE1, ADVECTIVE2, NOUN ADD 1 TO COUNT

WAIT

Figure 3.7   An expansion of the BUZZWORD GENERATOR portion of Fig. 3.6.

INPUT AND OUTPUT DATA

The brackets of action diagrams are quick and easy to draw. If the user wants to show the data that enters and leaves a process, the bracket can be expanded into a rectangle as shown in Fig. 3.9. The square brackets may be thought of as a shorthand way of drawing rectangles like those in Fig. 3.9. The data entering the process is written at the top right corner of the block. The data leaving is written at the bottom right corner. This type of functional decomposition is designed for computerized checking to ensure that all the inputs and outputs balance.

A diagramming technique, today, should be designed for both quick hand drawing and computerized manipulation. Users and analysts will want to draw rough sketches on paper or argue at a blackboard using the technique. They will also want to build complex diagrams using a graphics workstation and use the power of the computer to validate, edit, and maintain the diagrams, possibly linking them to a dictionary, database model, and the like. The workstation acts rather like a word processor for diagramming, making it easy for users to modify their diagrams. Unlike a word processor, it can perform complex validation and cross-checking on the diagram.

In the design of complex specifications, the automated correlation of inputs and outputs among program modules is essential if mistakes are to be avoided. In showing input and output data, Fig. 3.9 contains the same information as would normally be shown on a data flow diagram. Unlike a data flow diagram, it can be directly extended to show the program structure including conditions, case constructs, and loop control.

```
┌── ENTER BUZZWORD GENERATOR
│
│      CLEAR
│      SHOW "I WILL GENERATE A SCREEN FULL OF 'BUZZ PHRASES' EVERY"
│      "TIME YOU HIT 'ENTER'. WHEN YOU WANT TO STOP, HIT 'ESC'.
│
│      TEXT ADJECTIVE1 (10,16), ADJECTIVE2 (10,16), NOUN (10,16)
│
│      ADJECTIVE1 (1) = "INTEGRATED", "TOTAL", "SYSTEMATIZED", "PARALLEL",
│         "FUNCTIONAL", "RESPONSIVE", "OPTIONAL", "SYNCHRONIZED",
│         "COMPATIBLE", "BALANCED"
│
│      ADJECTIVE2 (1) = "MANAGEMENT", "ORGANIZATIONAL", "MONITORED",
│         "RECIPROCAL", "DIGITAL", "LOGISTICAL", "TRANSITIONAL",
│         "INCREMENTAL", "THIRD GENERATION", "POLICY"
│
│      NOUN(1) = "OPTION", "FLEXIBILITY", "CAPABILITY", "MOBILITY",
│         "PROGRAMMING", "CONCEPT", "TIME PHASE", "PROJECTION",
│         "HARDWARE", "CONTINGENCY"
│
│      SEED
│   ┌══ UNTIL KEY = "ESC"
│   │   COUNT = 1
│   │
│   │  ┌══ UNTIL COUNT = 22
│   │  │   A = INT(RND(10) + 1)
│   │  │   B = INT(RND(10) + 1)
│   │  │   C = INT(RND(10) + 1)
│   │  │
│   │  │   SHOW ADJECTIVE1(A) + " " + ADJECTIVE2(B) + " " + NOUN(C)
│   │  │
│   │  │   COUNT = COUNT + 1
│   │  └══ END
│   │
│   │      WAIT
│   └══ END
│
│      CHAIN "GAMES_MENU"
└── EXIT
```

Figure 3.8 An expansion of the action diagram of Fig. 3.7 into program code. This is an executable program in the fourth-generation language MANTIS. Successive decomposition of a diagram until it becomes executable code is called *ultimate decomposition*.

ACTION DIAGRAMS FOR MANAGEMENT PROCEDURES

Throughout this book we use action diagrams to represent procedures for performing the various steps in the methodologies we describe. For example, Fig. 3.10 shows an overall action diagram for performing the information strategy planning process. Notice that many of the lines in the diagram begin with three dots. A line beginning with three dots means that additional detail is available and can be displayed by executing an EXPAND function for that line using the computerized action diagramming tool. Details of individual components are given in the chapters that follow.

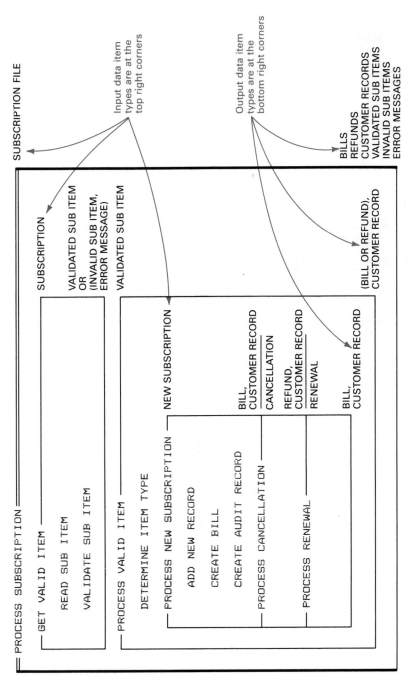

Figure 3.9 The bracket format of Fig. 3.2 is here expanded into rectangular format used to show data item types that are input to and output from each process. This is designed for computerized cross-checking.

ISP procedure

> The procedure given below may be modified with Action
> Diagrammer to meet the needs of the particular situation.

...Initiate
...Obtain top-management commitment.
Prepare

...Establish the ISP team for this project.
...Ensure that the appropriate tools are installed and working
...Ensure that the ISP team is adequately trained
Determine the target date for completing the study.

...Hold kickoff meeting
Create an overview model of the enterprise
Enter the following information into the encyclopedia:
An organization chart showing all organizational units.
The persons who manage the organizational units.
Identify the major business functions.
Decompose into lower-level functions with a function decomposition
diagram.
Identify the data subjects.
Decompose into entity–types.
Add detailed comments to the above diagram where necessary.
Create an initial entity–relationship diagram.
Create a matrix mapping functions against organizational units.
Create a matrix mapping functions against entity–types.
Create a matrix mapping organizational units against entity–types.

Print relevant versions of the above diagrams from the
encyclopedia for the participants to review.

Conduct Technology Impact Analysis

> See TIA action diagram

Conduct Critical Success Factor Analysis

> See CSF action diagram

Conduct Goal-and-Problem analysis
...Obtain any existing documentation which relates to goals
Determine which executives will be interviewed.
Establish the format of the interview.
For each executive
...Conduct goal-and-problem interview
...Record the interview information
Submit the record of the interview to the executive for validation.
Record any changes that are requested.

Refine the enterprise model
Make any improvements to the enterprise model as a result of
the executive interviews.
Complete an entity–relationship diagram.
Create a matrix of entity–types and business–functions.
Obtain approval of the enterprise model.

...Group the enterprise model into natural clusters
...Prepare follow–on from Strategic Information Planning
Make too–management presentation

Figure 3.10 An action diagram showing the steps involved in information
strategy planning.

Action diagrams, especially when a computerized action diagram editor is used, provide a particularly convenient means for showing human procedures. The diagram can be contracted to show an overview or expanded repeatedly to show detailed text or checklists. All the procedures described in this book are likely to be adjusted in practice to meet the needs of the particular situation, or the perspective of a particular team or particular consultant. An action diagram can be quickly tailored to the situation in question, and all participants can be given printouts of the part of the procedure that involves them.

4 DATA MODELING

A basic premise of our approach to information strategy planning is that data lies at the center of modern information systems technology. This is illustrated in Fig. 4.1. The data is stored and maintained with the aid of various types of database management software. The processes on the left in Fig. 4.1 *create* and *modify* the data. The data must be captured and entered with appropriate accuracy controls. The data will be updated periodically. The processes on the right of Fig. 4.1 *use* the data. Routine documents such as invoices, receipts, freight bills, and work tickets are printed. Executives or professionals sometimes search for information. They create summaries or analyses of the data and produce charts and reports. They ask "what-if" questions and use the data to help them make decisions. Auditors check the data and attempt to ensure that it is not misused. The data in Fig. 4.1 may be in multiple data systems. Different databases may be stored in different ways. They will often be distributed. They are often updated and used by means of transmission links and workstations.

A second basic premise of our approach to information strategy planning is that the *types* of data used in an enterprise do not change very much. The entity types do not change, except for the occasional (rare) addition of new entity types. The *values* of data change constantly, like the data in a flight information board at an airport, but the *structure* of the data does not change much if it was well designed to begin with.

The author worked in a large bank when computers were first introduced. There was batch processing, many manual procedures, no terminals, and much form filling. Today the customers use automated teller machines connected to distant computers, there are large numbers of terminals, and the administrative procedures have entirely changed. However, the raw types of data that are stored are the same as 20 years earlier.

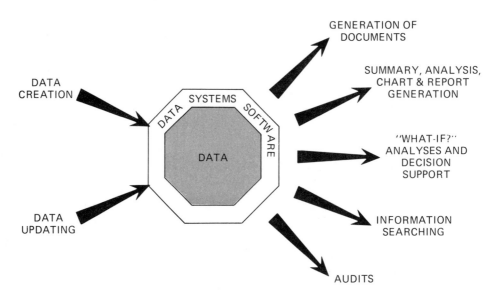

Figure 4.1 Most modern data processing is composed of actions that create and modify data, with appropriate accuracy controls and processes that use, analyze, summarize, and manipulate data or print documents from data.

DATA ORIENTATION VERSUS PROCEDURE ORIENTATION

Because the basic data types are stable whereas procedures tend to change, *data-oriented* techniques succeed if correctly applied where *procedure-oriented* techniques have failed. Many of the procedure-oriented techniques that have been used in the past have resulted in systems that are slow to implement and difficult to change. Information strategy planning seeks to fulfill management's changing needs for information rapidly. We can obtain results quickly, once the necessary data infrastructure is established, by using high-level database languages and application generators.

Traditionally, each functional area in an organization has developed its own files and procedures. There has been much redundancy in data. A medium-sized firm might have many departments, each doing its own purchasing, for example. Before computers, this redundancy did not matter; it was probably the best way to operate. After computers, however, it did matter. There might be a dozen sets of purchasing programs to be maintained instead of one. There might be a dozen sets of incompatible purchasing files. The incompatibility prevented overall management information from being pulled together. Figure 4.2 shows the environment of this data processing style.

When each functional area has its own files and procedures, there is a

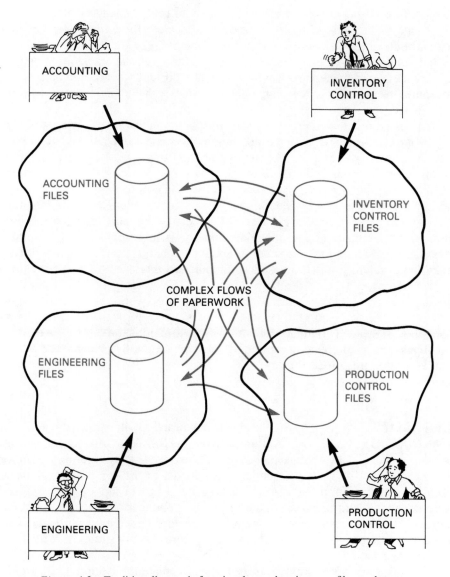

Figure 4.2 Traditionally, each functional area has its own files and procedures. Because of this, there is a complex flow of paperwork between areas to reflect changes in all versions of the data. When this is computerized with separate files, the system is complex and inflexible. Data for different areas is separately designed and not equivalent. Accuracy is lost. Items slip through the cracks in the paperwork processes. Maintenance and change are difficult to accomplish, so the procedures become rigid. Management information spanning the areas cannot be extracted.

complex flow of paperwork between the areas to reflect changes in all versions of the data. When this is computerized with separate files, the system is complex and inflexible. Databases or files for different areas are separately designed and not equivalent. Accuracy is lost. Items slip through the cracks in the paperwork processes. Maintenance and change are difficult to accomplish, so the procedures become rigid. Management information spanning the areas cannot be extracted.

In this nonintegrated environment, most communication of changes is done by paperwork, which is error-prone, time-consuming, and highly labor intensive. Suppose, for example, that the engineering department prepares an engineering change report and makes multiple copies. One for production control concludes that the engineering change requires changes to the product file. This requires a new request for materials to be sent to inventory control. Inventory control must determine the effects of the change on purchasing operations. These affect the costs of raw materials and parts. Inventory control communicates these to accounting. Accounting concludes that a change in sales price is necessary to retain profitability and communicates this need to marketing. And so on.

In one factory, more than $1 million worth of work-in-progress was unaccounted for on the shop floor due to items slipping through the cracks in the paperwork process. This unaccountability was a major motivation for the end-user management to create an online system, which totally changed the administrative procedures of the factory.

CENTRALIZED PLANNING OF DATA

The solution to the problems illustrated by Fig. 4.2 is centralized planning of data. An overall, stable data model of the data needed to run an organization is essential. This model spans the functional areas. When it is modularized for detailed design, it is broken up by *data subjects* rather than by departmental or organization chart boundaries. Each of these data subjects can then be modeled separately to create a collection of *subject databases,* which are discussed in Chapter 5. Figure 4.3 illustrates the use of a common data model.

The steps of information strategy planning create the beginning of a common data model and analyze the fundamental processes of the enterprise, independently from current systems and procedures. The follow-on to the information strategy planning study is *business area analysis,* which we introduce in Chapter 15. During business area analysis, fully normalized data models are specified at the detailed level. Once the data and fundamental processes of an enterprise have been clearly modeled, the systems and procedures can be streamlined to give the most efficient operation.

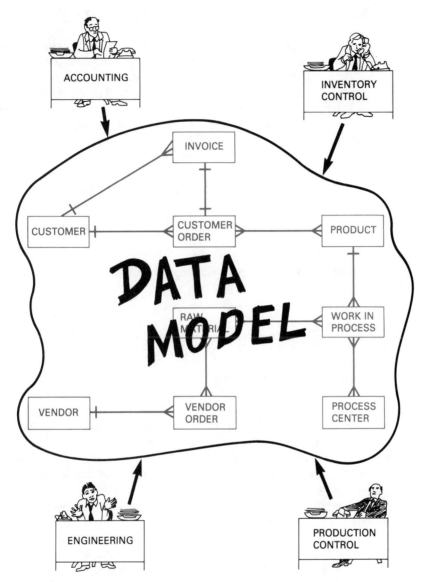

Figure 4.3 When data is consolidated into an integrated database, data modeling is the key to success. The data structures become more complex, but the data flows are greatly simplified. The data is consistent and accurate. New forms of management information can be extracted quickly with fourth-generation languages. Changes in procedures can be made rapidly with these languages. Paperwork is greatly lessened. The administrative procedures of the organization need to be completely rethought. Fundamentally different analysis and design techniques are needed.

STABLE DATA MODELS

Given a collection of data item types, there is generally one correct way to represent them logically. Formal techniques (which are now well-understood and have been automated) can be used to create *models* of data that are *stable*. If well designed, these models change little, and we can usually avoid changes that are disruptive. These models are of great importance to strategic information planning. They become a foundation stone on which most computerized procedures are built. This chapter introduces the techniques that are employed in creating stable data models.

THE DATA ADMINISTRATOR

The person responsible for data modeling is the *data administrator*. The tasks of the data administrator are as follows:

- Determine the information needs of the enterprise.
- Create and maintain the enterprise data models, ensuring that they are as stable as possible.
- Obtain agreement among users about the definitions and format of data items.
- Ensure that system builders conform to the data models as far as possible.
- Resolve conflicts about incompatible representations of data.

It is important to distinguish clearly between a data administrator and a database designer. The *database designer* is a technical staff member who is concerned with the design of a specific database. The database designer designs the physical structure of an individual database to be as effective and machine-efficient as possible. This task may be associated with a given project. The *data administrator,* on the other hand, has a high-level job of planning, modeling, and coordinating the data of the enterprise. This is not a job requiring technical skills but, rather, is a task of understanding the data needed to run the business and making diverse individuals agree about the definition and representation of data items. Many different views of data must be synthesized, ideally with the aid of a CASE modeling tool, into a fully normalized data model.

Many corporations now have years of experience with data administration and have well-established techniques for doing it as effectively as possible. Others have disastrously failed to achieve any overall coordination of data. This failure is extremely expensive in the long run in terms of inflated information systems costs, failure to implement needed procedures, and lost business. Many corporations have not made a serious attempt at data administration and allow systems to be built with ad hoc file design. Some corporations have tried to achieve data administration and have failed. The reasons for the failure are listed in Box 4.1. Many corporations have achieved successful data administration. Box 4.2 lists human and technical requirements needed for success.

BOX 4.1 Reasons for failure of corporate data administration

- Organizational politics prevailed, because of a lack of strong management and direction from the top.
- The human problems of making different accountants or managers agree on the definitions of data items were not dealt with.
- The magnitude of the task was underestimated.
- The data administrator was a low-paid technical staff member.
- Methodologies for the design of stable data structures were not understood.
- The necessary data models were too complex to design and administer by hand, and appropriate computerized tools were not used.
- There was not an overall architect who could use the design methodology.
- Attempts of data modeling took too long and users could not wait.
- Data model design was confused with *implementation* and physical database design.

BOX 4.2 Essentials for the overall control of data in an enterprise

Human

- Top management must understand the need for information engineering.
- Information that is strategic to the running of the enterprise should be identified.
- The data administrator must report at a suitably high level and be given full senior management support.
- The span of control of the data administrator needs to be selected with an understanding of what is politically pragmatic.
- The data administrator must be highly competent at using the design methodology and the methodology must be automated.
- An appropriate budget for data modeling must be set.
- Data modeling should be quite separate from physical database design.
- End-user teams should be established to assist in data modeling and to review and refine the data models thoroughly.

(Continued)

Box 4.2   *(Continued)*

Technical

- Strategic planning should be done of the entities in an enterprise. All entities should be represented in an overview entity-relationship model.

- The overview entity-relationship model should be expanded into detailed data models in stages, as appropriate.

- The detailed data model should represent all functional dependencies among the data items.

- All logical data groups should be fully normalized.

- Stability analysis should be applied to the detailed data model.

- The entity-relationship model and the detailed model should be designed with CASE modeling tools.

- Defined operations can be associated with the data to ensure that integrity, accuracy, and security checks are applied to the data, independent of applications.

- Submodels should be extractable from the overall computerized model when needed for specific projects.

- Ideally, the CASE data modeling tool should provide *automatic* input to the library of the specification language, application generator, or programming language that is used.

REPORTING
HIGH LEVEL

The data administrator needs to report at a suitably high level and to have enough "clout" to ensure that good data models are built and adhered to. Effective data administrators often report to the chief MIS executive, as shown in Fig. 4.4, with a matrix management link to information centers and project managers.

DATA
INDEPENDENCE

Proper use of database techniques allows us to isolate application programs from changes that are made to data structures. We use the term *data independence* to describe this goal. Data independence means that when the data structure changes, the programs keep running because they are isolated from that change. The programs have a "view" of the data that can be preserved even though the actual, physical structure of the data changes.

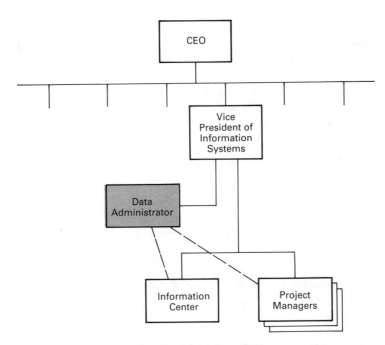

Figure 4.4   The data administrator needs to report at a suitably high level.

Data independence can be achieved through the appropriate use of database management systems. The most important difference between a database management system and a file management system is that database management software translates between an application program's *view* of data and the way in which the data is actually stored. It preserves the program's view of data when the storage structures change in either a logical or physical manner. With database management systems, many application programs can have different views of the same data. However, it is important to point out that the use of a good database management system does not, by itself, give us the protection we need. We also need good logical design of the data structures used.

LOGICAL DESIGN OF DATABASES

Unless controlled, systems analysts tend to design records that group together any collection of data items that they perceive as being useful. All manner of anomalies can arise because of inappropriate grouping of data items. Some of these anomalies are subtle and often not perceived.

A database contains hundreds (and sometimes thousands) of different data item types. If the logical structures are designed badly, a large financial penalty will result. A corporation will not be able to employ the databases as it should, so productivity will suffer. The databases will constantly have to be modified, but they cannot be modified without much application program rewriting. The end users will not be served as they need, and because of this many try to create their own alternatives to employing the database.

In the late 1970s it became clear that many database installations were not living up to the publicized advantages of database techniques. A few rare ones had spectacularly improved the whole data processing function and greatly increased application development speed and productivity. Time and time again the difference lay in the design of the overall logical structure of the data.

STEP-BY-STEP BUILDING OF THE MODEL

The logical model of the data must be created on a step-by-step basis. During information strategy planning, we create only an overview diagram that shows the entity types in an enterprise and the relationships among them. The development of the overview entity-relationship model for the enterprise is discussed in detail in Chapter 8. Ideally, the overview model of the enterprise should be built using CASE modeling tools so that it can be constantly added to and so that a computer can help in organizing the diagram. At this stage there is no attempt to identify attributes, to normalize the data, or even to detect the subtle variations in entities. The initial requirement is an overview of the data across the entire enterprise.

After the overview model of the enterprise has been constructed, details of attributes are added to the data model, and a fully normalized data model is built (Fig. 4.5). This model is usually created for one business area at a time and is part of the work of business area analysis. We introduce this process in Chapter 15. When an entity is examined during business area analysis, the entity may already have been modeled in detail in a different business area. If automated CASE tools are used to perform the data modeling, this fact will be made known. There may be some resolution needed of conflicting representations of attributes. It is the task of the data administrator to resolve such conflicts. There are likely to be certain data for which conflicting definitions remain. A large enterprise rarely achieves perfection in data modeling.

ENTITY-RELATIONSHIP DIAGRAMS

An *entity,* as we have stated, is anything about which data can be stored—a product, a customer, a salesperson, a part. As we described in Chapter 3, we represent entities on a diagram using square-cornered boxes. An *entity-relationship diagram* shows the relationships between entities. The relationships are drawn as lines connecting the boxes. Figure 4.6 shows a simple entity-relationship model. The links are labeled with the names of the relationships. For example, Fig. 4.6 indicates that a *customer* places *customer-orders,* a *customer-order* consists of *order-lines,* a *product* is ordered on an *order-line* or is backordered on a *backorder,* and so on. As we saw in Chapter

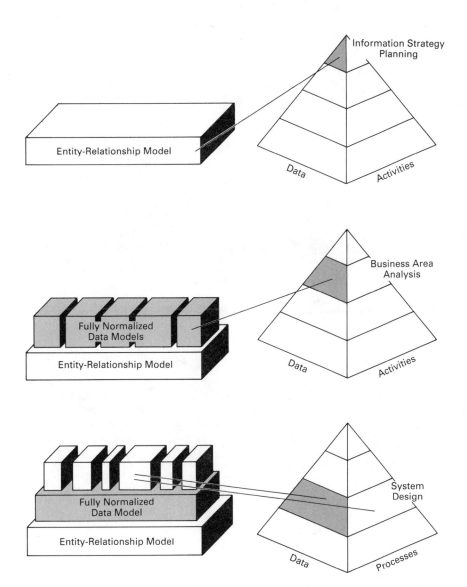

Figure 4.5 After the overview model of the enterprise has been constructed, details of attributes are added to the data model, and a fully normalized data model is built.

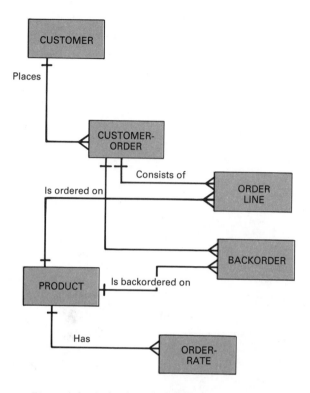

Figure 4.6   A simple entity-relationship data model.

3, other information can be stored about the relationship. For example a crow's-foot end on a line indicates a one-with-many relationship. A bar across a line indicates a one-with-one relationship. A circle means zero. Thus,

means that a CUSTOMER can place zero or multiple CUSTOMER-ORDERS; a CUSTOMER-ORDER relates to one CUSTOMER.

ATTRIBUTES   For each entity, we can store one or more *attributes* that provide information about the entity. For example, a sales representative has a name, an address, a territory, a quota, a salary, a sales as a percentage-of-quota figure, and so on. This level of detail is not appropriate to strategic information planning. However, an entity-relationship data model can be expanded during business area analysis to show the attributes that relate to each entity.

A typical medium-sized corporation has several hundred entities (when redundancies are removed). A large diversified corporation has more, and a separate data model might be created for each of its subsidiaries. There are often 10 to 20 attributes for a typical entity.

**CHANGING
PROCEDURES**

Although the data is relatively stable, the procedures that use the data change fast and frequently. In fact, it is desirable that systems analysts and end users *should* be able to change them frequently. We need maximum flexibility in improving administrative procedures and adapting them to the rapidly changing needs of management. Every business changes dynamically, and the views of management on how to run it change much faster. The procedures, then, change rapidly (or should); the computer programs, processes, networks, and hardware change; but the basic types of data are relatively stable. The foundation of data is viable only if data items are correctly identified and structured so that they can be used with the necessary flexibility.

5 SUBJECT DATABASES

As we look back now on years of database case histories, we can observe two types of approaches: *application databases* and *subject databases*. It is quite clear which has given the best results in the long term: subject databases. Subject databases relate to organizational subjects rather than to conventional computer applications. There should, for example, be a product database rather than separate inventory, order entry, and quality control databases relating to that product. Many applications may then use the same database.

We could regard the whole of data processing as a succession of changes to data. A snapshot of a system or organization at any instant in time will reveal only a data structure. A process is, technically, a series of data changes, including changes to data in working storage and input/output data.

Designing a stable, well-documented, and largely nonredundant structure of data in the long run provides a simpler and cleaner form of data processing than embedding separately designed data into hundreds of processes. Attaching logic, such as integrity checks and decision tables, directly to the data structures so that this is shared by multiple processes can further simplify the overall processing.

One objective of information strategy planning should be to identify the subject databases that are required. Typical subjects for which databases could be built in a corporation are

- Products
- Customers
- Parts
- Vendors
- Orders
- Accounts

- Personnel
- Documents
- Engineering descriptions

Some applications use more than one subject database. The programs make calls to multiple separate databases. For example,

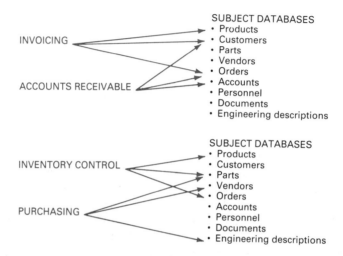

FOUR TYPES OF DATA ENVIRONMENT

There are four types of environment of computer data. It is important to distinguish clearly among them. Box 5.1 summarizes the four types of environment. They have a major effect on management at all levels in an enterprise, including top management. An efficient corporation ought to have a substantial foundation of Class III and Class IV data. These, however, are only likely to be pervasive and successful if there is top management support for them, as we shall see.

Class I: Files

A Class I environment is that of files. A separate file is designed for each, or most, applications. Often as a direct result of structured analysis, the data is embedded in the function. This has caused severe maintenance problems and inflexibility in the use of data. As discussed in Chapter 4, a database environment attempts to solve these problems by separating the data from the applications in order to achieve data independence. Box 5.2 summarizes the problems that are typical of old, established file installations. Good database software combined with knowledgeable design and management (often lacking) can solve these problems.

BOX 5.1   Four types of data environment

Class I Environment: Files.

A database management system is not used. Separate files of data are used for most applications, designed by the analysts and programmers when the application is created.

Characteristics:

—Files are simple and relatively easy to implement.

—A large proliferation of files means a high level of duplication, leading to high maintenance costs.

—Seemingly trivial changes to applications trigger a chain reaction of other changes, and hence change becomes slow and expensive and is resisted.

Class II Environment: Application Databases.

A database management system is used but without the degree of sharing in a Class III environment. Separate databases are designed for separate applications.

Characteristics:

—Application databases are easier to implement than a Class III environment.

—A large proliferation of databases means a high level of duplication, as with a file environment.

—Maintenance costs are high.

—It is sometimes more expensive than a Class I environment.

—It does not achieve the major advantages of database operation.

Class III Environment: Subject Databases.

Databases are created that are largely independent of specific applications. Data is designed and stored independently of the function for which it is used. Data for business subjects such as customers, products, or personnel is associated and represented in shared databases.

(Continued)

BOX 5.1   *(Continued)*

Characteristics:

—Thorough data analysis and modeling are needed, which take time; maintenance costs are much lower.

—Faster application development and direct user interaction with the databases results eventually (but not immediately).

—Traditional systems analysis methods and overall information systems management must change.

—If not managed well, it tends to disintegrate into a Class II (or sometimes Class I) environment.

Class IV Environment: Information Systems.

Databases are organized for searching and fast information retrieval rather than for high-volume production runs. Employs software designed around inverted files, inverted lists, or secondary key search methods. New fields can be added dynamically at any time. Good end-user query and report generation facilities. Most user-driven computing employs Class IV databases.

Characteristics:

—Information systems are often easy to implement.

—They are more flexible and dynamically changeable than traditional database systems.

—Often they coexist with a Class III environment.

Class II: Application Databases

A Class II environment is one of application databases rather than subject databases. The systems analysts tend to create a separate database for each new application, as they do with file systems. Because database management systems are used, there is some degree of data independence, but proliferation of duplicate data grows as with file systems and has many of the problems listed in Box 5.2. It is sometimes said in this environment that a database management system is used like a file access method rather than as a true database system.

BOX 5.2 Problems that are typical of old, established file installations

- High proportion of information systems professionals devoted to maintenance activities.
- High cost and slow speed in developing new systems.
- Inability to respond quickly to necessary changes.
- Inability to provide ad hoc management information.
- Inconsistent definition of similar data items across applications.
- Steadily worsening proliferation of separate files.
- Increasing proliferation of inconsistent values of redundant data.
- The greater the number of programs, the worse the problem of converting them when data changes, so the greater the reluctance to respond to requests for such change by end users.
- Difficulty in maintaining inventory and control of data.
- Cost of duplicate storage.
- Cost of repetitive data entry.
- Lack of overall management of the data resource.

Class III: Subject Databases

A Class III environment is one of subject databases. When a collection of such databases has been built, they represent the data resource we have been discussing—data independent from specific applications. The types of data represented do not change very frequently, whereas the functions that use the data do. Therefore, it makes sense not to embed the data in the functions as in a Class I environment.

By using subject databases rather than application databases, the eventual number of databases is far lower. A corporation builds up a very large number of applications but does not have a large number of operational subjects. If files are designed for specific applications, the number of files grows almost as rapidly as the number of applications and results in the great proliferation of redundant data found in a typical tape and disk library today. Application-oriented databases can also proliferate rapidly. Using subject databases, however, the number of applications grows much faster than the number of databases.

Many database installations have set out to create a Class III environment and have had problems. A new application comes along, and for some reason a new database is created for it rather than using the existing subject databases. It is easier and quicker to create application databases than doing the overall design that is needed for subject databases. However, as the years go by, installations that do this end up with almost as many separate databases as they would have had files had they not used database management. They do not then achieve the long-range advantages of database operation. The use of database management in such installations has not reduced the program maintenance cost as it should.

Too often the attempt to create a Class III environment disintegrates into Class II. This may be due to poor management or to poor subject database design. Sometimes end users or analysts want their own database for reasons of pride or politics, or because it is easier. Management is not strong enough to enforce the principles of the Class III environment, or possibly does not understand them or their significance. Sometimes the analyst needs a new view of data, which cannot be derived from the existing databases. Consequently, a new database is created. This happens over and over again until there is a proliferation of databases. The cause of this is usually inadequate design in the first place.

Class IV: Information Retrieval Systems

This class of data system is designed for spontaneous information retrieval, decision support systems, and office automation rather than for prespecified computing or high-volume production runs. New fields can be added dynamically. The software is designed around inverted lists or other techniques for searching the data. Good end-user languages are provided. Sometimes these languages can flexibly create their own logical data files. Much user-driven computing employs Class IV databases: for example, the Query Management Facility (QMF) product that supports access to a DB2 relational database via Structured Query Language (SQL) and Query by Example (QBE).

Information retrieval systems are often separate from the production database systems that produce the daily paperwork and do the routine data processing. They are often easier to install and are easier to manage. They use different software. The end-user language for interrogating the database is often closely interrelated to the data structures. Some software can handle either a Class III or a Class IV environment, or both at the same time, but one or the other is often handled without the highest efficiency.

It is important in discussing database management to distinguish between Class III and IV environments. They have different problems and are managed differently, and both need to fit into the overall planning of a corporation's data resources.

ADVANTAGES OF SUBJECT DATABASES

As more subject databases come into existence, the rate of application development increases in well-managed installations, as illustrated in Fig. 5.1. Increasingly, *when new applications come along, the data already exists,* although possibly, attribute fields may need to be added to it. New application development can often be carried out very rapidly with high-level database languages, report generators, and application generators.

Database Executive:

As I have looked at the unfolding of the subject database groupings, it has been startling how the same data has been used for many processes. Cash management as we have developed it was a new requirement, but it is using very much the same data that has been available in banking for years. By representing it in database form and enabling access in a number of different ways, we have been able to serve our retail banking group, corporate banking group, and international banking groups.

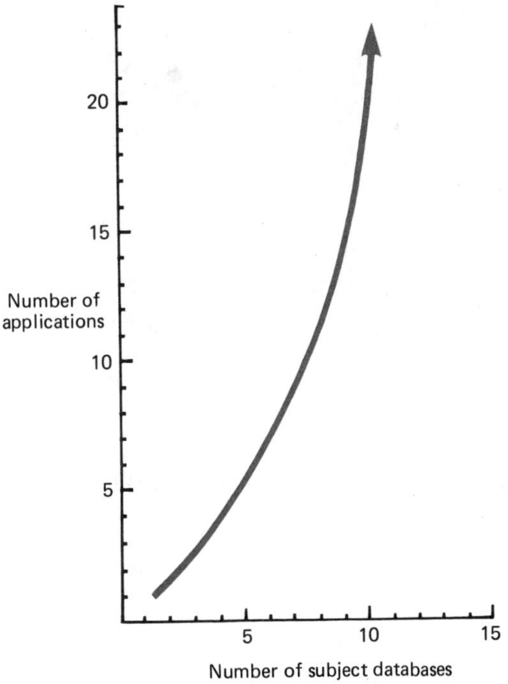

Figure 5.1 As the number of subject databases grows, the number of applications using them grows disproportionately. Eventually, most new applications can be implemented rapidly because the data is available and the software provides tools to manipulate it. This curve was taken from a corporation with five years of experience with subject database development.

Number of applications

Number of subject databases

Information strategy planning should divide the total aggregate of data in an enterprise into manageable units—subject databases. One or more subject databases can be placed under the control of one manager. One subject database at a time can be modeled in detail during business area analysis.

The subject databases should be designed to be as stable as possible. They provide long-term stability for the enterprise's information resources. "Stability" does not imply that they will never change. It implies that most changes will be of such a nature that they can be made without forcing the old applications to be rewritten. The logical structures produced by this process are independent of their physical implementation on current hardware and software. As the technology changes, the logical structures of the subject databases will remain valid.

SELECTION OF SUBJECT DATABASES

Subject databases are sometimes called *data classes*. In most installations their contents have been chosen without a formal methodology. The records relating to customers are in the customer database, the records relating to products are in the product databases, and so on. A relatively simple corporation might have about 20 subject databases; a complex one may have as many as 60. This sounds simple but in fact leaves much scope for argument about what subject databases should exist and what data fits into them. Should purchaser orders be in the vendor database or in the materials database? In Chapter 13 we see how to use simple clustering techniques to identify business areas. Business area clustering often leads to an identification of the subject databases or databases needed by each business area. Chapter 14 presents more rigorous methods that can be used to identify subject databases.

HIGH-LEVEL PERSPECTIVE

It is necessary to have a high-level overall perspective of a corporation in order to plan what subject databases it should have. Such organizationwide planning needs to take into consideration not only the subject databases but also existing or new files and stand-alone databases for certain applications. This is part of information strategy planning. The detailed design and modeling of data items and records that constitute a subject database (or for that matter an application database) is the bottom-up design, which is carried out during business area analysis.

In many corporations it has been discovered that a database implemented for one process happens to serve another process, or a different area in the organization. These happy discoveries ought not to happen by chance. They ought to be planned. If they are not planned, they will often not happen because different areas tend to keep to themselves, be jealous of their own data, and avoid anything "not invented here."

Database Executive:

The customer profile database was implemented initially for use internally in the operations division. Suddenly it became of value in providing information to the commercial side of the organization as well as to the retail side. Again, when we had implemented the demand deposit database for cash management in the head office, we found that its structure also served the branch network.

If subject databases are created quickly, the curve in Fig. 5.1 can be climbed quickly, especially with today's high-level database languages. As the curve is climbed, application development tends to become database driven rather than driven by demands for conventional systems analysis.

A BANK'S DATABASE PLAN

In a large bank a plan was put together incorporating the databases in Fig. 5.2. With these 21 databases it was theoretically possible to run almost all the processing in the organization. The chart in Fig. 5.3 (see pp. 94-95) was drawn up mapping the databases against the main banking processes. This was intended to be a master plan for database development. On the left of the processes listed were production runs, transaction processing, and simple inquiries. They represent fairly straightforward database usage. On the right were information systems rather than production systems. These need complex database usage. Spontaneous new types of inquiry and report generation will occur once the databases are in place and appropriate query languages are available. Some of these uses are very important in the overall management of the bank. This represents a top-down view of the data needed to run the organization efficiently. The crosses on the chart show what banking processes and decision-making support activities use what databases.

Before doing the planning represented by Fig. 5.3, the bank had implemented one database—that with customer information, names, addresses, and customer profiles. It found that that database was usable by applications in many areas of the organization, and so it set out to plan what other subject databases could be used organizationwide.

Interviewer:

The creation of this chart must have needed very thorough knowledge of how the entire bank worked. Did you have a team that understood every operation in the bank?

Bank Database Executive:

One person generated the chart. She does have a great deal of banking knowledge. She used the banker's handbook and talked to many people. The chart had to be verified. All the banking processes were included in the chart. So this person identified the business processes in which the bank was involved and how those processes do deal with essentially the same kinds of data and then looked from the operational level to the next dimension, which was the one of decision support.

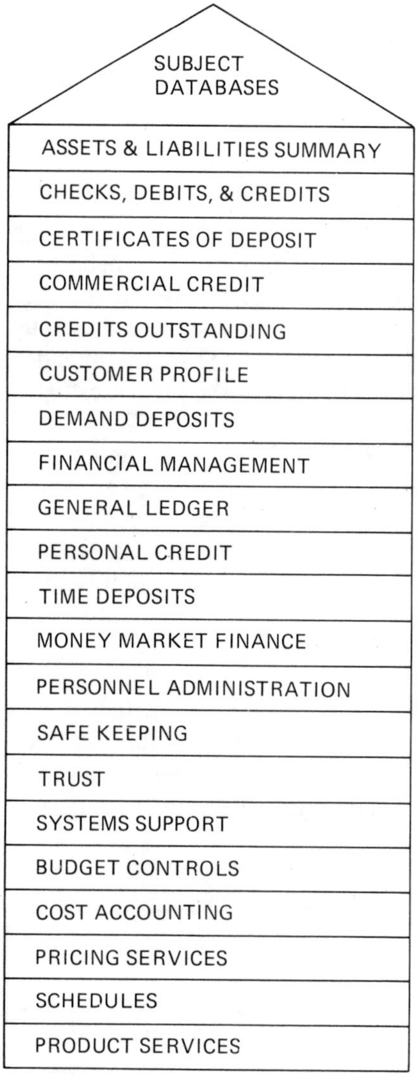

SUBJECT
DATABASES

ASSETS & LIABILITIES SUMMARY

CHECKS, DEBITS, & CREDITS

CERTIFICATES OF DEPOSIT

COMMERCIAL CREDIT

CREDITS OUTSTANDING

CUSTOMER PROFILE

DEMAND DEPOSITS

FINANCIAL MANAGEMENT

GENERAL LEDGER

PERSONAL CREDIT

TIME DEPOSITS

MONEY MARKET FINANCE

PERSONNEL ADMINISTRATION

SAFE KEEPING

TRUST

SYSTEMS SUPPORT

BUDGET CONTROLS

COST ACCOUNTING

PRICING SERVICES

SCHEDULES

PRODUCT SERVICES

Figure 5.2 With these 21 subject databases it would be possible to perform most of the information processing in a large bank. Figure 5.3 shows a strategic plan that maps databases against their prospective uses.

In many corporations, subject databases have eventually been used in application areas beyond those for which they were originally intended. The U.S. banking industry, for example, perceived the need for a cash management service during the 1970s. The need for this service arose because large corporate customers have many accounts: current accounts, interest accounts, time deposit accounts, and investment accounts. The customer has different addresses and accounts in different branches of the bank. It is a valuable service to give the customer reports summarizing these accounts, saying how much cash is available in total and will be available in the future. The bank also needs this information about its customers.

Bank Database Executive:

Cash management is a means to pull together online a very complete picture of a customer's position. We use this to make certain credit decisions about the customer and recognize when funds should be cleared under certain circumstances. At the same time it is a critical part of our customer service. We can transmit information to the customers which enables them to manage their cash portfolios. For some corporations this has become a very critical issue.

The databases in Fig. 5.2 that are used for cash management are checks, debits and credits, commercial credit, customer profile, and demand deposits.

Bank Database Executive:

The cash management process has been one that has steadily unfolded. We have found that more and more parts of the bank are interested in it, and they have new twists on what they want from an application point of view. The initial implementation was a matter of months. We were able to implement demand deposit shortly after and commercial credit within six months. As the cash management capability unfolded, we were able to demonstrate the relationships to global credit and demand accounts. These were implemented in a much shorter time frame than could have been done in a conventional file way.

In some banks the data needed for cash management existed in several previously implemented databases. In other banks, cash management was an impetus toward database technology, and the databases created for cash management were found to also serve the branch bank network. In one bank an online system for branch checking accounts was implemented using the cash

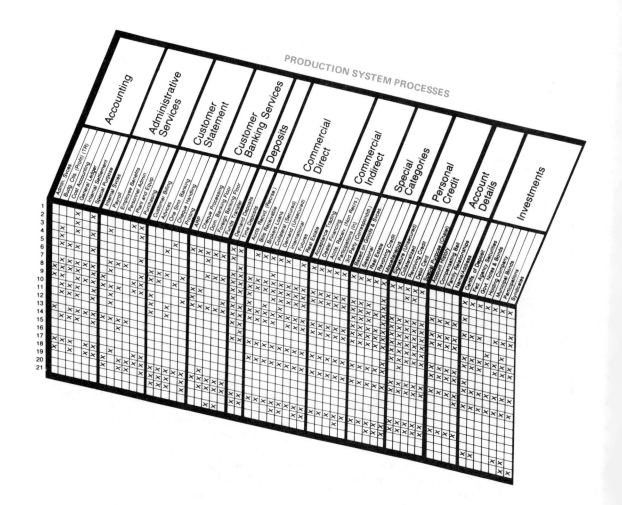

PRODUCTION SYSTEM PROCESSES

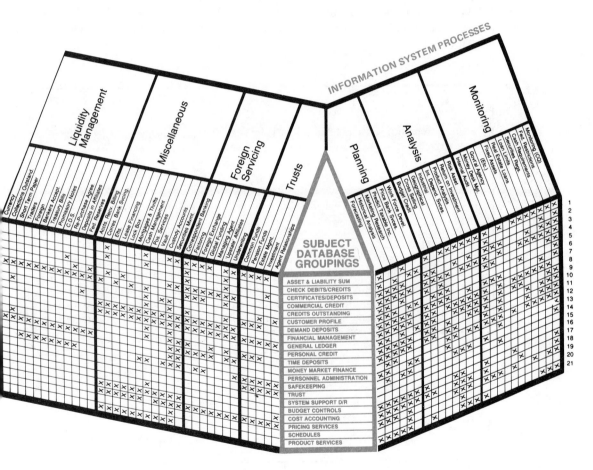

Figure 5.3 A large bank's subject database plan.

management database. Similarly, a customer profile database designed to serve the internal operations division became of unanticipated value later in providing information to both the commercial and retail sides of the organization and in identifying account relationships for cash management.

When such unanticipated evolution occurs, there are often database conversion problems and other growing pains. The intent of a chart like that in Fig. 5.3 is to anticipate in what areas subject databases will or should be used, and then the automated data modeling process can take the needs of these areas into consideration. It is generally essential that senior management be involved in the creation and verification of a plan such as that in Fig. 5.3. As it becomes implemented, it will have a major effect on how the organization is managed.

Database Executive:

In the creation of a plan like this it is vital that the business managers be involved.

Interviewer:

What sort of business managers?

Database Executive:

Without a doubt the people who are involved in the line operational processes. In addition, there is an important need for the people involved in corporate planning and in the process of managing the assets and liabilities of the company. In the long run the greatest use of information services will be the one that deals with planning, analysis, product identification, market identification, and true decision support.

In many cases the business evolves and moves into new areas. It is important that the senior management who can anticipate this be involved in planning the evolution of the information strategy plan.

Interviewer Referring to the Chart in Fig. 5.3:

Do you think you have really identified those subject databases you need for running a big bank?

Database Executive Involved with the
Chart in Fig. 5.3:

As this bank holding company concerns itself with what it is to be, there will probably be more subject data groupings. Some may be distributed.

Interviewer:

That really means that you want a top-level committee reviewing this chart, upgrading it, and making decisions about distribution.

Database Executive:

That's important. Yes. And it's vital that the business managers participate in that process.

RESISTANCE TO THE PLAN

There is almost bound to be resistance to a plan such as that shown in Fig. 5.3 unless it is seen to have senior management backing. If this backing does not exist from the start, a plan such as that of Fig. 5.3 is doomed to cause political fighting, and probably not enough of the plan will be implemented to make the planning worthwhile.

Interviewer:

Looking back at the three years' experience in using this plan, what advice would you have for people starting to create a top-down plan for databases?

Database Executive:

To get this implemented you do need a corporate top management commitment. In the past, when we started, we were faced with a great deal of resistance both inside the DP department and outside it. Inside the DP department we had resistance because previously, especially with tape-oriented systems, they had total control of whatever application they developed. Outside, in the user departments, they felt that they wanted to have exclusive rights over their own data. Databases, they thought, would take away those exclusive rights.

Interviewer:

So you're saying, take the broad plan to top management and get their commitment?

Database Executive:

More than that. Get their commitment before the plan is created. Get them involved in the creation of the plan itself. Make sure that they understand it, believe in it, and say so loud and clear so that the low-level political types don't oppose it.

6 PLANNING TOOLS

Different corporations use different variations on the theme of information strategy planning. The process generates many data items that need to be recorded and analyzed. The results of the planning need to be made visible by all those who are affected by it. Most organizations change, and so CASE tools should be used to make the plan easily maintainable. An information strategy planning methodology is needed that keeps pace with the changes. This chapter introduces the various types of planning tools that are useful in conducting an information strategy planning study.

The chapters in Part III of this book have been written with the assumption that appropriate CASE tools are used to maintain the information that is gathered using the methodologies we describe. If computerized tools are not used, these methodologies still apply, but much more tedious work is involved that results in large hand-drawn charts that are difficult, if not impossible, to keep up-to-date.

METADATA

The tools that are used to support the information strategy planning process operate on *metadata*. The term *metadata* means *data about data*. In Chapter 2, we defined the term *entity*, which we use to refer to something about which we store information. An example of a typical entity is *person*. We might store information about a person in a passport. The passport contains the person's name, address, age, and sex. Metadata would provide information about the data items themselves, for example,

- NAME   Type: alphabetic
                Size: up to 30 characters
                Purpose: attribute of PERSON

- AGE   Type: numeric
           Size: 3 characters
           Value: 1-120
           Purpose: attribute of PERSON

- SEX   Type: binary
           Size: one bit
           Values: 0 means MALE
                      1 means FEMALE
           Purpose: attribute of PERSON

The entity types maintained by a CASE planning tool are not things such as *customer, product,* or *machine tool;* they are instead data items that represent information about data, such as *goal, procedure,* and *attribute.* The data that is gathered during the information strategy planning study (metadata) can be stored in a database using CASE tools.

The same techniques that we use for modeling the enterprise itself can be used to model the planning data. The entity types used in the information strategy planning database represent planning information. They include the following:

- Entities concerned with the enterprise:
    Organizational unit
    Executive
    Location
    Goal
    Critical success factor
    Problem

- Entities concerned with activities or applications:
    Function
    Process
    Procedure
    Program
    Mechanism

- Entities concerned with data architecture:
    Subject area
    Entity type
    Relationship
    Attribute
    Data collection

- Entities concerned with planning:
    Project
    System
    Technology forecast
    Reason for distribution

Relationships among those entity types give information that is used in the strategic planning process.

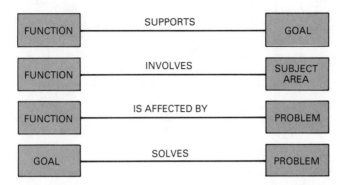

Using such relationships, an entity-relationship diagram can be built of the database needed for information strategy planning. Figures 6.1, 6.2, and 6.3 show portions of such an entity-relationship diagram. The database of metadata for information strategy planning has certain characteristics that are different from a typical production database. For example, the number of instances of each entity type are tens or hundreds, rather than thousands or hundreds of thousands. This is because there are a relatively small number of goals, organizational units, problems, procedures, and other such factors.

MATRICES   There is a great number of many-with-many relationships between the entities that make up the planning data model. Thus some of the important tools that are useful in planning take the form of matrices that allow us to view these many-with-many relationships directly, as shown in Figs. 6.4, 6.5, and 6.6. It is often useful during planning

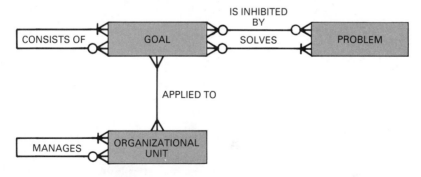

Figure 6.1   Relationships among goals, problems, and organizational units.

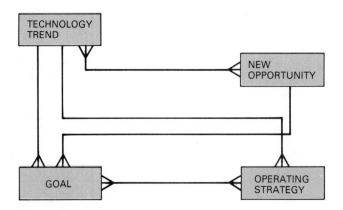

Figure 6.2   Relationships among technology trends, goals, opportunities, and operating strategies.

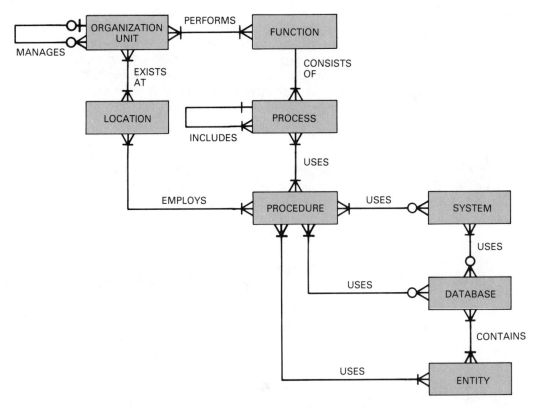

Figure 6.3   Typical planning database structure. (This is the structure of the data model maintained in the encyclopedia of a typical CASE tool.)

Processes	Employee	Contract Employee	Applicant	HR Compensation Regs, Plans, etc.	HR Benefits Regs & Plans	HR Staffing Requirements & Plans	Job Requisition	Stockholder	Boardmember	Misc. Contacts/VIPs	Financial Plans	Accounting Regs, Practices	Ledger Accounts	Customer Purchase Order/Invoice	Customer Payments	Other Income
	1	2	3	4	5	6	7	8	9	10	11	12	13	14	15	16
1 Evaluate Financial Proposals																
2 Estimate Near-Term Earnings														R		
3 Budget Finances	R	R		R	R						CRUD	R	CRUD			
4 Receive Funds												R		R	CRUD	CRUD
5 Pay Funds	R											R				
6 Report Finances	R											R	RU	R	R	R
7 Administer Taxes												R	R		R	R
8 Maintain Financial Reg, Policies											R	CRUD				
9 Audit Finances												R	R		R	R
10 Manage Financial Investments								CRUD				R				
11 Plan Human Resources	R	R				CRUD	CRUD		R		R					
12 Acquire Personnel	CRU	CRU	CRUD			R	R		CRU							
13 Position People in Jobs			R			R	RU		R							
14 Terminate/Retire People	RUD	RUD							RUD							
15 Plan Career Paths	RU			R	R	R										
16 Develop Skills/Motivation	RU	RU			R	R										
17 Manage Individual Emp Relations	RU	RU			R											
18 Manage Benefits Programs					CRUD											
19 Comply with Govt HR Regulations	R			R												
20 Maintain HR Regs, Policies				CRUD		CRUD										
21 Determine Production Requirement														R		
22 Schedule Production	R	R														

Figure 6.4 A matrix mapping processes against entities.

Tactical Goals

Organizational Units	Improve sales effectiveness (1)	Identify new target markets (2)	Improve market penetration (3)	Add distribution channels (4)	Address absenteeism problem (5)	Exploit new technology (6)	Improve information systems (7)	Streamline shop floor operations (8)	Enhance employee training (9)	Enhance customer support (10)	Improve product quality (11)	Expand product line (12)	Upgrade product warrantee (13)	Reduce inventory investment (14)	Reduce receivables to 45 days (15)	Improve cashflow management (16)	Locate venture capital (17)	Enhance corporate image (18)
1 Planning																		
2 Accounting															*	*		
3 Cash Management																*		
4 Investments																*		
5 Purchasing														*				
6 Facilities								*										
7 Human Resource Develeopment	*				*				*									
8 MIS																		
9 Legal													*				*	
10 Manufacturing					*						*	*		*				
11 Quality Assurance											*		*					
12 Packaging											*							
13 Materials Management							*								*			
14 Sales Regions	*											*				*		
15 Customer Services																		
16 Customer Education										*								
17 Order Processing	*			*								*						
18 Product Management			*			*						*						
19 Public Relations																	*	*
20 Market Research		*		*		*					*	*						
21 Distribution												*						
22 Engineering						*		*			*	*	*					
23 Research		*				*					*	*						
24 Prototype Manufacture						*		*			*	*						
25 Testing Laboratory						*					*	*	*					

Figure 6.5   A matrix mapping organizational units against tactical goals.

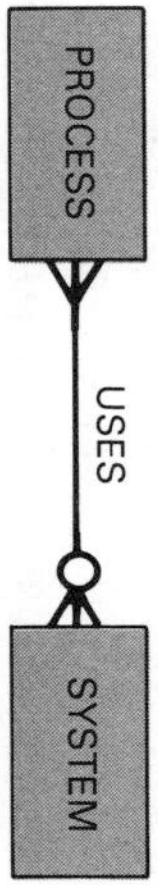

Figure 6.6 A matrix mapping business functions against current and existing systems.

PROCESS ⊱—USES—⊶ SYSTEM

C = Current   P = Planned   c/p = Current and Planned

SYSTEM \ PROCESS	Marketing			Sales Operations				Engineering			Production				Materials Management				Facilities Management			Administration			Finance			Human Resources			Management			
	Planning	Research	Forecasting	Territory Management	Selling	Administration	Order Servicing	Design and Development	Product Specification Maintenance	Information Control	Scheduling	Capacity Planning	Material Requirements	Operations	Purchasing	Receiving	Inventory Control	Shipping	Work Flow Layout	Maintenance	Equipment Performance	General Accounting and Control	Cost Planning	Budget Accounting/Tax Accounting	Financial Planning	Capital Acquisition	Funds Management	Personnel Planning	Recruiting/Development	Compensation	Business Planning	Organization Analysis	Review and Control	Risk Management
Customer Order Entry				c/p			c/p				c/p	c/p	c/p																		c/p			
Customer Order Control							C				C	C	C																					
Invoicing															C										C									
Engineering Control										P																								
Finished Goods Inventory															C	C	C					C												
Bills of Material									C	C	C				C							C	C											
Parts Inventory															C		C						C											
Purchase Order Control				C							c/p	c/p	c/p	C	c/p																			
Routings										C				C																				
Shop Floor Control										C				C			C																	
Capacity Planning												P	P	P																				
General Ledger																						P					P							
Expense																						C												
Product Costing										c/p				c/p			c/p					C	c/p											
Operating Statements																						C									C	C		C
Accounts Receivable																						C		C								C		C
Accounts Payable																						C				C					C			C
Asset Accounting																						C												C
Marketing Analysis				C	C		C																											C
Payroll																														C				

to show intersection data in the form of a matrix because it enables the user to see an overview of clustering or distribution. The sequence of items can be rearranged to display clusters, or computerized algorithms can be employed for clustering.

A CASE workstation screen is normally not big enough to show the whole matrix at one time, so a windowing mechanism is used to enable the view to scroll vertically or horizontally to display any given items mapped against one another. The intersection data is often small enough to be easily displayed, as in Fig. 6.4 showing processes (left) against the entities those processes use (top). Where the intersection data is not small enough to show on the matrix, the user might point to the intersection and display a separate window containing the intersection data.

HIERARCHIES

Some planning entities have a relationship with themselves. For example:

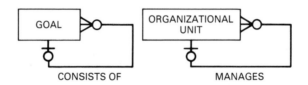

These recursive entity relationships can be drawn in the form of tree structures, for example, a hierarchy of goals or a hierarchy of organizational units (a conventional organization chart).

A CASE tool for analyzing and displaying information strategy planning data therefore is typically capable of displaying both matrices and hierarchies. It needs to display windows for entering or displaying intersection data on matrices and for entering and displaying information about metadata, such as goals, critical success factors, processes, organizational units, competitive threats, or whatever other entities form the metadata of strategic planning.

ENTITY-RELATIONSHIP DIAGRAMS

At an early stage of the information strategy planning study, entity-relationship diagrams are important tools that show the relationships between the entities in an enterprise. We introduced entity-relationship diagrams in Chapter 4, and we describe the methodology for creating them in Chapter 9. The planning tool needs to be able to represent such a diagram. The entities in an entity-relationship diagram are then mapped in matrices with processes, organizational units, locations, and so on. It is desirable that the data gathered during the information strategy planning study be applied during later stages of analysis, design, and construction. In these later stages, more detailed diagrams are used. The representation of this more detailed information needs to be a natural extension of the diagrams that are created during information strategy planning.

ANALYSES

Another group of planning tools constitute various types of analyses can be applied to the data that is gathered during information strategy planning. Some forms of analysis provide validation techniques to help ensure that the business model provides an accurate, consistent, and complete foundation for decision making. Other forms of analysis provide decision-support tools to assist in such matters as setting priorities for projects based on which factors have the most effect on meeting the corporate goals, clustering entity types into business areas, and examining the distribution of data or processing. Some types of analysis are as follows:

- **Exception Analysis.** Exception analysis uses rules to ensure the integrity of the data that is gathered during the planning process and to list any occurrences that do not meet the criteria. A check can be made that the required properties of the data are entered, for example, that all goals have a performance-ranking measurement and that all important associations have been entered. The lack of an association can be detected, for example, a goal that is not related to an organizational unit. Redundancies can also be detected, for example, two organizational units that perform the same function. Interesting facts of inconsistencies about the organization can be highlighted, such as entities that are required by critical processes but are not implemented.

- **Level Consistency Analysis.** This analysis verifies that associations between two hierarchies are logically consistent. It may locate associations at a high level that lack supporting links at detailed levels. It may detect parts of the organizational-unit hierarchy that do not have corresponding goals in the goal hierarchy.

- **Affinity Analysis.** If a numeric measure of affinity can be established between the objects in a set of objects, the objects can be clustered into groups to achieve greater efficiency. This can be done with entity types to study the grouping of entities into subject databases (discussed in Chapter 14). Clusters of entities or processes are sometimes a starting point for business area analysis or data modeling projects. When priorities conflict, comparing clusters from several affinity analyses provides insight into alternatives—highlighting problems that need compromises or technical solutions if one approach is chosen over others.

- **Project Action Analysis.** Project definitions can be defined with the help of affinity analysis. A project employs certain entity types and processes. The data must be created by certain processes. A project can relate to certain goals. It may be associated with multiple locations. Matrices showing these relationships are examined and adjusted as necessary.

- **Project Ranking Analysis.** The planning process can estimate how much various projects contribute to the accomplishment of specific goals. Planning tools can be used to rank alternate projects in terms of their value in meeting goals, and hence in terms of their effect on potential profit. Groups of projects may require shared databases. The combined value of implementing such databases can be assessed. New applications can be assessed in terms of the business problems they solve. Migration from old systems to new systems with better technology, better structuring, a greater level of automation, and lower maintenance cost, may be desirable. The implications of such migration can be examined with matrix manipulation, and the resources assessed. The value of migration in terms of solving business problems can be examined.

PART **II** METHODOLOGIES

7 THE INFORMATION STRATEGY PLANNING STUDY

As we discussed in Chapter 1, information is a corporate resource and should be planned on a corporatewide basis, regardless of the fact that it is used in multiple different computers, multiple departments, and sometimes even in multiple separate organizations. The information needs often remain the same when the enterprise itself is reorganized. The information architecture should therefore be designed independently of the current corporate organization. Implementation of the architecture will reflect the current organization and its concerns. These will affect the choice of which modules of the architecture are implemented first.

Beginning with Chapter 8, we examine in detail a number of methodologies that can be used in conducting an *information strategy planning (ISP)* study. Box 7.1 summarizes the major methodologies that are involved in the study.

TIME SCALE   The initial stages of information strategy planning ought to be completed in a period of about six months or less. In the case histories studied when writing this book, most were completed in six months but *only when a firm methodology was used*. When a firm methodology or firm management of the process was lacking, the attempt at strategic planning could ramble on for much longer and sometimes became discredited and disregarded. Because of the ongoing pressure to develop applications, information strategy planning needs to be tackled quickly and decisively.

Often, the effort is "90 percent complete" after six months. The remaining 10 percent involves subtleties and uncertainties about where to stop. It is important that the results are made *usable* after six months even if some of the subtleties are unresolved. If the detailed database design process is delayed until the information strategy plan is 100 percent complete, and data modeling itself

BOX 7.1 The methodologies of information strategy planning

- **Linkage Analysis Planning.** This methodology, discussed in Chapter 8, allows top management and senior information systems management to develop together, in a day or two, an overall strategic business vision. This vision then provides an overall framework within which the remaining steps of the information strategy planning process can operate.

- **Entity-Relationship Modeling.** This methodology, discussed in Chapter 9, maps the business functions hierarchically. It associates functions with organizational units, locations, and entities and documents the relationships between the entities that are identified.

- **Technology Impact Analysis.** This methodology is the subject of Chapter 10 and is concerned wth the extremely rapid evolution of technology and the business opportunities and threats created by it. It maps a taxonomy of new technology against the opportunities for new products, services, changes in corporate structure, and so on. Top management are often not fully aware of all the implications of advancing technology. This can result in lost opportunities or dangerous competition. Technology impact analysis attempts to identify and prioritize the opportunities and threats and bring them to the attention of executives who can take appropriate action.

- **Critical Success Factor Analysis.** This methodology, discussed in Chapter 11, is concerned with identifying those areas where "things must go right" if the enterprise is to succeed fully. [1] It is concerned with concentrating resources on the few most critical areas. It has proven to be a powerful way of improving corporate success. It identifies critical assumptions which need checking, critical information needs, and critical decisions for which decision-support systems are needed.

- **Goal and Problem Analysis.** This methodology, discussed in Chapter 12, creates a structured representation of the goals and problems of an enterprise, associates them with departments or organizational units, and with the management-by-objectives motivation of individual managers. Goals and problems are associated with information needs and information systems.

- **Business Area Identification.** The entity-analysis diagram is revised based on the results of the previous three methodologies and the entities are then associated with business functions and are placed into a matrix. This is discussed in Chapters 13 and 14. This matrix is clustered to find naturally cohesive groups of entities and functions. These naturally cohesive groups of entities then form the basis of the individual business areas. These business areas then become the focus of later business area analysis studies.

takes a long time, the total delay may be so great as to defeat the objectives of rapid application development. When CASE tools are used to support information strategy planning, detailed data modeling is often done while information strategy planning is in progress, and the CASE tools are often used to help in system design before the enterprisewide planning is complete. In other words, in practice the process is often more complex than the pure one-way, top-down procedure described in textbooks.

SEQUENCE OF ANALYSIS

Figure 7.1 shows how the methodologies of information strategy planning can be divided into two groups. The four methodologies that are associated with the top part of the information systems pyramid are those that are of most interest to senior management; they are directly involved in the management of the business. The steps in information strategy planning are ordinarily carried out in the following sequence, although the sequence of analysis can be varied according to the needs of the enterprise:

1. Perform linkage analysis planning to formulate a strategic business vision (Chapter 8).
2. Create an overview entity-relationship model of the enterprise (Chapter 9).
3. Perform technology impact analysis (Chapter 10).
4. Perform critical success factor analysis (Chapter 11).
5. Perform goal and problem analysis (Chapter 12).
6. Refine the entity-relationship diagram (Chapter 9).

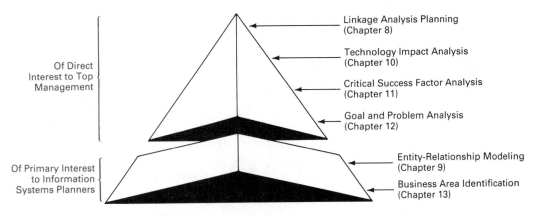

Figure 7.1 The top (strategy) level of the information system pyramid can be divided into two parts: one of direct interest to top management and one of primary interest to information systems planners.

7. Cluster entities into business areas (Chapters 13 and 14).

8. Establish priorities for business area analysis (Chapter 15).

The methodologies that are associated with the second level of the pyramid (see Fig. 7.1) are those that are of interest to information systems staff members. If the enterprise is lacking a clear strategic vision about where it is headed in the future, then the methodology of linkage analysis planning, which takes only a day or two, can help the planning group to articulate this vision. Then the more technical process of creating the overview entity-relationship modeling is generally done. After that the business-oriented stages of technology impact analyses, critical success factor analysis and goal and problem analysis are carried out. The reason for doing entity-relationship modeling early in the planning process is that a thorough understanding of the structure of the enterprise is desirable before detailed dialogs are conducted with top management that may lead to possible restructuring. The dialogs about goals and problems, potential impact of technology, and critical success factors are best carried out when the enterprise is understood in detail. After all the methodologies are applied, the modeling of the enterprise and its information needs will generally need to be refined.

METHODOLOGY ACTION DIAGRAMS

Appendix II contains a set of action diagrams that present the detailed steps that are involved in many of the methodologies we discuss in this part of the book. This appendix begins with an overview action diagram that describes the information strategy planning study as a whole. Appendix II can be consulted as the chapters in this part of the book are studied.

THE RANGE OF THE STUDY

In most enterprises, information strategy planning ought to be based on the entire enterprise, and in some cases the entire extended enterprise (see Chapter 7). There are major exceptions to this. Some enterprises consist of separate corporations with little or no similarity or connection. In these a separate study would normally be done of each corporation. There is often a temptation to limit the range of a strategic planning study to something less than the whole enterprise. This is usually due to the following concerns:

- The enterprise seems too big and complex.
- The enterprise is multinational, and it is difficult to coordinate a study in many countries.

- Different subsidiaries relate to fundamentally different types of business or markets.

- Different subsidiaries have different management philosophies or missions.

In general if one person manages an enterprise, an information strategy planning study ought to be done for that enterprise. *If it is too big to study, it is too big to manage.* The overview study of a vast corporation will quickly recommend fragmenting the study for practical reasons, but the fragments should be coordinated with an overview study.

One reason why separate or localized studies are done is that they fall under the jurisdiction of separate or localized information systems organizations. The existence of separate information systems organizations should not be a reason for limiting the definition of the enterprise and its business functions. The enterprise as a whole is the subject of strategic information planning. The enterprise *needs* a strategy for enterprisewide information systems.

Information strategy planning is a top-down definitional process that begins at the highest level and stops at the point where activities have an accurate generic definition. The enterprise is split into separate areas for study before detailed analysis of processes and data is done. No attempt is made to combine fundamentally different organizations, or business strategies, or markets into inappropriate common structures.

TOP MANAGEMENT INTEREST

It is often stated by strategic planners that they cannot get top management to take any interest in strategic information planning. This is usually because their approach is too technical. The types of analysis described in this book go to the heart of what top management is interested in: how the enterprise can be better run.

Linkage analysis planning can be very helpful in assisting the enterprise to formulate an overall strategic vision that guides the enterprise in establishing a clear direction for the future. Technology impact analysis surveys future technology and technological trends and asks how they can be used to run the enterprise better, to provide new opportunities, and to make a preemptive strike against competition. It asks how technology can cause new competitive threats. Critical success factor analysis determines what are those areas most critical for success in running the enterprise. It is designed to focus management's attention on the things most critical for them to accomplish. It identifies the critical decisions and critical information and ought to lead to the building of information systems that help in these areas. Goal and problem analysis is directly related to how the enterprise operates. It helps to provide a control mechanism throughout the enterprise and relates directly to the setting of objectives for individual managers.

Linkage analysis planning, technology impact analysis, critical success factor analysis, and goal and problem analysis can each be done relatively quickly with low resources. Linkage analysis planning takes only a day or two; the other three analyses can each be done with two skilled analysts interacting with top management for a month. The methodologies recommended in this book are not expensive to perform but can have a major effect on the management of the enterprise. Even if detailed design of databases and information systems were never done, the results of the studies described in this book would be likely to be very valuable in focusing the attention of executives on what can be improved in the enterprise.

RETHINKING THE ENTERPRISE STRUCTURE

While the information that is gathered during information strategy planning is of *direct* interest to top management, who participates directly in this process, top management should also be interested in the results of the design work that happens after the information strategy planning study has been completed. The analysis of corporate functions and data often results in a rethinking of the organization of the enterprise. Databases, networks, and desktop workstations provide the challenge of improving the procedures in an enterprise to such an extent that basic enterprise reorganizations are needed. The management structures of enterprises that use today's technology well are likely to be fundamentally different from existing management structures. New applications of advanced technology often lead the enterprise to new revenue sources, which often require new forms of management.

The first motor cars were called "horseless-carriages" and were the same shape as the carriage without a horse. Much later it became recognized that a car should have a different shape. Similarly, the first use of radio communication was called "wireless telegraphy" without the realization that broadcasting would bear no resemblance to telegraphy. Today we talk about the "paperless office" and "paperless corporation," but we build systems with screens and databases that duplicate the previously existing organization of work. It will be increasingly realized that we now have the technology to make *any* data available at *anybody's* desk and to provide major computational aids to decision making at that desk. We must ask the question: "Where should decisions *best* be made?" Answers to this question are likely to change the structure of the enterprise.

Senior management should regard enterprise modeling as a means not merely of studying the existing organization, but of asking how the organization should be changed. The analysts should be made to think creatively. It is easy for them to document today's paper flow, but the early stages of information strategy planning should not do that. They are concerned with what are the *fundamental* activities that must occur and what are the *fundamental* information needs. Rather than being concerned with today's documents, the analysts should ask: "What data is important now? What data will be important in the future?"

Enterprise modeling and the later data modeling, if done creatively, are likely to suggest structural changes, new procedures, or corporate reorganization. In most cases senior management could not care less about being involved in computerizing the existing procedures. However, if there is a threat of organizational changes, or a promise of better information sources, they usually want to know what is going on and be able to influence it. Often what senior management takes an active interest in is the ability to make decisions about how the business *should* be run. The analysis can be presented in such a light.

The detailed data modeling that is done after information strategy planning has been completed will be more fruitful *if it is accepted from the beginning that it is likely to change the corporate procedures or organization*. If this is understood, top management is likely to take more interest in the study. The study will be staffed differently, and its reporting procedures will be different.

EXTERNAL CONSULTANTS

It is often difficult for managers inside an enterprise to take a detached viewpoint. They spend most of their mental energies on specific problems and most of their business emotions on internal politics. A major new opportunity or application of technology is sometimes alien to the prevailing culture. The need to wind down or replace certain current procedures is usually far from apparent to people involved with those procedures. Intelligent external consultants can often see an organization's problems with clarity and may be highly inventive in pointing out new opportunities.

Manager of Corporate Planning:

Initial meetings were held with senior management and users to familiarize them with the concept, and later a more formal session by the consultant to introduce the detailed approach and methodology. This formal session was not a success. Essentially, it was a technical approach at too senior a level— a too technical level for the audience. Nevertheless, once we began the working sessions, involving the users on a regular basis, the whole project gained momentum and acceptance. A war room was set up and a coordinator appointed. In addition, two business analysts have been assigned to the project to assist users in the techniques at the formal user group sessions.

Some consultants are highly skilled with the methodologies we discuss in this book and can move quickly in implementing them. However, internal staff has the essential experience of the enterprise and its key players, and how it operates. Information strategy planning is often best performed by a two-person team, one being an external consultant, skilled and experienced with the methodologies, and the other being an internal person who knows the enterprise well and who has good rapport with top management. Sometimes different external consultants can be used with different portions of the methodology. Some are experienced with linkage analysis planning, some with critical success factor analysis, and some with entity-relationship modeling. The members of each two-person team should get along well together, move fast and professionally, have the full support of top management, and elicit all the help they need from diverse managers and staff.

It is important that the team members have the highest credibility and respect among the upper echelons of operating management. Such individuals can be identified in most organizations. They are the managers or analysts who are already in the highest demand for other pressing tasks. External consultants used should also have the highest credibility, which means a wide range of knowledge and experience in the subject area as well as an appropriate personality.

Top management should ensure the acceptability of the team and contribute to its success by formally announcing the program and endorsing the team.

TOP MANAGEMENT COMMITMENT

As we discussed in Chapter 1, information strategy planning must begin with top management sponsoring it and committing other senior executives to being involved in it. The study is designed to reflect their view of the business and should not begin without their commitment. Most of the input will come directly or indirectly from these senior executives.

The commitment ought to be to employ similar strategic planning techniques throughout the enterprise. In some organizations this commitment is made cautiously, in stages. Full commitment is often slow where (inadequate) older methodologies are entrenched. The results of portions of an information strategy planning study are likely to be presented to top management independently of the overall results. This is true particularly with linkage analysis planning, technology impact analysis, and critical success factor analysis. When the overall results are presented, a follow-on plan should be ready for approval.

THE FOLLOW-ON PLAN

At the conclusion of the information strategy planning study, individual areas of the business are identified for business area analysis studies. Although business area analysis is not part of information strategy planning, we introduce this important process in Chapter 16. The final stages of information strategy planning should list and prioritize areas of the enterprise that are likely candidates for business area analysis. It is likely that one business area will be analyzed *first*. As experience is gained in doing this, other business area analyses will follow. The first business area should be one where the payoff is high and one without excessive technical or political complexities.

Top management always asks how long the ongoing process of strategic planning will take. The team should have prepared an answer to this question, showing a buildup of business area analysis studies proceeding in parallel. The payoff in building certain critical systems should not be too far downstream.

The information strategy planning study almost always reveals certain system needs that should be filled *immediately* without waiting for a business area analysis to be completed. These are often critical decision-support systems and executive information systems. A quick-and-crude version of such systems may be implementable quickly using spreadsheet tools, decision-support software, or executive information system software. While there may be a business need to implement certain systems immediately, and this should be done, it should be stressed that the whole point of strategic information planning is to build an information systems *architecture* for the enterprise. This architecture will enable systems to be created, changed, and interlinked more rapidly when it exists. There is always some conflict between long-range architectural planning and immediate results.

Implementing all the information needs that an information strategy planning study identifies will take years. It is necessary to decide what to do first and, in general, to prioritize the stages of implementation. It is desirable that the components of the architecture that are implemented first should be those that solve immediate problems and have a rapid payoff. The implementations should proceed on a pay-as-you-go basis, usually with multiple implementations being done by different teams at the same time.

ONGOING REVIEWS

The information that results from the information strategy planning study is a valuable asset and should be updated periodically. The study should not be put on a shelf and forgotten. Information should be extracted from it to guide the business planning process on an ongoing basis. In conjunction with this, a periodic review of the strategic business vision, goals, problems, technology impact, and critical success factors should be done. Goals and problems should be reviewed when managers are counseled and appraised as part of the management-by-objectives procedure. The strategic business vision, technology impact, and critical success factors can be assessed annually as part of the business planning procedure. The linkage analysis planning and technology impact diagrams may have an ''owner'' who is responsible (among other things) for adding to them as new technologies, competitive threats, or opportunities become

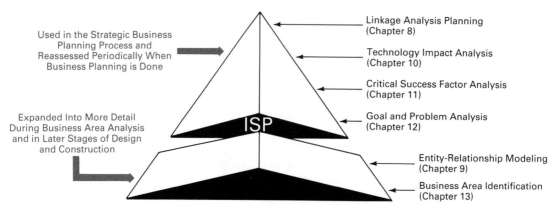

Figure 7.2 The management information gathered during information strategy planning is updated periodically, and the enterprise model is expanded into more detail during business area analysis and later stages of design and construction of information systems.

BOX 7.2 Potential benefits of information strategy planning

To Executive Management:

- An assessment of the opportunities from new technology.

- An assessment of the competitive threats from new technology.

- Adaptation of the strategic business plan to accommodate five-year technology trends.

- An assessment of the factors most critical for success.

- Translation of the critical success factors into actions in building information systems, decision-support systems and manager motivations, and control mechanisms.

- A defined logical approach to aid in solving management control problems from a business perspective.

- An evaluation of future information system needs based on business-related impacts and priorities.

- A planned approach that will allow an early return on the company's information systems investment.

- Information systems that are relatively independent of organization structure.

BOX 7.2 *(Continued)*

To Functional and Operational Management:

- An assessment of goals and problems and identification of computing facilities that can help with these.
- An assessment of the factors most critical for success.
- Translation of these factors into actions in building appropriate systems.
- A defined logical approach to solving management control and operational control problems.
- Top management involvement in establishing organizational goals and direction.
- Increased probability of having the most valuable systems built.
- Consistent data to be used and shared by all users.
- Systems that are management- and user-oriented rather than data processing–oriented.

To Information Systems Management:

- Effective communication with top management.
- Top management support and interest in systems.
- Better planning of systems that respond to business needs.
- A long-range planning base for data processing resources and funding.
- Agreed-on system priorities.
- Higher probability of delivering systems that are really useful.

apparent. This is a task that some technology enthusiasts enjoy. The models of the enterprise become more detailed as business area analysis studies are done. The information strategy plan is thus used and kept up-to-date as indicated in Fig. 7.2. Box 7.2 lists the potential benefits of information strategy planning.

REFERENCE

1. J. F. Rockart and C. V. Bullen (eds.), *The Rise of Managerial Computing* (Homewood, IL: Dow Jones-Irwin).

8 LINKAGE ANALYSIS PLANNING

For the information strategy planning process to be fully effective, it is important that top management form and clearly articulate a *strategic business vision,* which must be communicated to all the executives in the enterprise. This strategic vision provides a framework within which the strategic information planning process can operate. A methodology called *linkage analysis planning (LAP)* developed by Kenneth Primozic and Edward Primozic, both of IBM, is particularly effective in helping the senior executives of an enterprise to formulate this vision. The linkage analysis planning methodology is the subject of this chapter and is based on the work of the Primozics [1].

The changes that are occurring in the technology of information systems are having a major impact on the operations, marketing, and distribution strategies of all types of enterprise, in both the private and public sectors. These technological changes are key ingredients in the trends that are moving the business environment toward an information-based economy. It is critical that top management understand the capabilities of the new technologies that are beginning to be deployed. It is at the very top of the information engineering pyramid that the overall strategic vision must be formulated. A clear strategic vision allows the enterprise to establish the highest-level goals of the organization. After the strategic vision is established, the remaining steps of the information strategy planning study can allow the enterprise to identify the databases and information systems that will allow the organization to exploit technology as a strategic resource.

The strategic planning techniques that are discussed beginning with Chapter 9 are logical and left-brain–oriented. They concentrate on the steps that apply to the strategic planning of databases and information systems. While these techniques are important to strategic planning, they cannot be effective unless a clear strategic vision has been established and communicated to everyone in the enterprise. Formulating an overall vision of where the organization should be headed is largely an intuitive, qualitative, right-brain–oriented task. It is not a task that can be performed by the information systems executives alone. After the overall vision has been formulated, information systems practitioners can assist top management in applying the other methodologies as the information strategy planning study is conducted.

Brandt Allen, in the December 1982 issue of the *Harvard Business Review,* showed that many enterprises are outperforming their competitors by a wide margin due mainly to their ability to use new technology to construct information systems that are of strategic importance to the enterprise. These information systems are qualitatively different from the information systems that have been built in the past [2]. Allen stated

> Senior executives must become closely involved with their information systems to reassess and perhaps reorganize their computer resources. . . . Matters are at the crisis point in computing for many corporations. Technology, by itself, is not enough. . . . Key to these solutions is the formulation of a comprehensive strategy for the development of information resources within the company. . . . An unmanaged computer system can stop you dead.

Michael Porter and Victor E. Millar in a later *Harvard Business Review* article state [3]

> Every company must understand the broad effects and implications of the new technology and how it can create *substantial* and *sustainable* competitive advantages. (italics ours)

Porter and Millar then went on to identify three specific ways in which the technology affects competition:

- It alters industry structures.
- It supports cost and differentiation strategies.
- It spawns entirely new businesses.

It is of great importance for management in its strategic business planning to pick the right investments. In the information systems context this means that top management must choose the projects that offer the highest payoff. One of the tasks of strategic information planning consists of analyzing the business case for information systems investments. In doing this, top management must ask itself the following questions:

- What have we been spending for information systems? (Top management often does not know.)

- How do we stack up against the competition? (A difficult question to answer objectively, but the most important question that top management can ask itself in today's environment.)

- What impact do the current information systems have on the corporate management process? (In many enterprises, almost none.)

- Where in the enterprise should future information systems investments be made? (It often should not be in constructing systems similar to those that have been constructed in the past.)

- What are the priority projects and how much will each contribute to corporate growth, profitability, and in some cases survivability? (These decisions are too important to be made by the information systems department alone.)

Linkage analysis planning involves examining the key *linkages* that exist, both within the enterprise itself and between the enterprise and the organizations with which it interacts. Once top management understand the linkages, projects can be identified that can use the capabilities of advanced technology in gaining strategic business advantage.

LINKAGE ANALYSIS PLANNING SESSION

A linkage analysis planning session can be conducted in one or two days. The session must be attended by the senior business executives and also by the top executives in the information systems department. Top management must participate because it is they who fully understand the characteristics of the competitive arena. It is also important for information systems executives to participate because it is they who fully understand the technical environment. It requires the joint skills of top management and the information systems department to chart effectively the course that the enterprise must follow in exploiting technology to gain strategic advantage. Once the strategic vision has been formulated, information systems staff can then apply the other methodologies discussed in this book to validate the overall strategic plan and to determine the way in which the strategic plan should be implemented.

STEPS IN LINKAGE ANALYSIS PLANNING

In conducting linkage analysis planning, a number of techniques are employed in assisting the business executives and information systems managers to formulate and articulate the strategic vision. These techniques all help the group to assess the competitive position of the enterprise within its industry. The methodology of linkage analysis planning involves five major steps:

1. Analyzing the *waves of information systems growth* within the industry to determine how the information systems used by the enterprise today compare with those used by competition.

2. Analyzing the *experience curves* that exist within the industry to determine how the experience curves employed today by the enterprise compare with those of its major competitors.

3. Analyzing *industry power relationships* to determine the structure of the industry and to show how the industry can take advantage of technology and changes in power relationships.

4. Analyzing how the enterprise operates in the context of an *extended enterprise* that includes not only the enterprise itself but the organizations with which the enterprise interacts and does business.

5. Identifying the *electronic channel support systems (ECSS)* that are required for the enterprise to gain substantial and sustainable competitive advantage. (We discuss the characteristics of ECSSs later in the chapter.)

WAVES OF INFORMATION SYSTEMS GROWTH

The first step in linkage analysis planning involves analyzing the ways in which information systems have changed in the enterprise—and in the industry of which the enterprise is a part—as computer and communication technology has evolved and matured over time. Information systems have evolved differently in each industry and in each enterprise. It is important for senior executives to understand how the information systems of the enterprise compare with those of its competition. Information systems are evolving in a number of *waves*. Each successive wave is built on the previous ones.

Wave 1—Batch Systems

In the 1960s most enterprises automated their basic accounting and clerical operations using largely batch-oriented informations systems to improve the performance of such functions as

- Accounts receivable
- Accounts payable
- Payroll
- General ledger

First-wave systems concentrate on enhancing the productivity of individual business areas and are generally associated with clerical and administrative savings.

Wave 2—Online Systems

In the 1970s information systems being created were more sophisticated. They typically used online terminals to perform such functions as

- Asset turnover management
- Cash management
- Sales analysis

Second-wave systems concentrate on the effective use of corporate assets and with leveraging expenditures to enhance return on investment.

Most of the systems that were installed in the first two waves shared a single characteristic: They were designed to reduce the costs that were associated with performing earlier manual functions. While these systems are valuable, they do nothing to increase the revenue flowing into the corporation. Instead of making money, they simply save money.

Wave 3—Databases and Networks

Beginning in the 1980s enterprises started to install new types of systems that, instead of simply saving money, opened up new avenues for producing revenue. These information systems began to use technology to gain strategic advantage and often created entirely new businesses. These systems employ comprehensive communication networks and database techniques to perform such functions as

- Consolidation of financial functions
- Expansion of credit card services
- Hotel, travel, and theater ticketing
- Elimination of the middleman function in many enterprises
- Online catalog shopping

Third-wave systems concentrate on using technology to increase both market share and profitability.

Wave 4—Management Databases and Personal Computers

Even later in the 1980s, some forward-looking enterprises employed technology to create systems for improving the way in which top-level decisions are made concerning such things as

- Acquisitions
- Strategic planning
- Corporate transformation

Fourth-wave systems typically use advanced computer and communication technology, including relational databases and personal computers, to create systems to help top management improve the decision-making process.

Wave 5—People Systems

We are now beginning to see examples of a fifth wave in information systems growth, in which computer and communication technology is being used to reach the consumer directly. These types of systems use technology such as

- Home computers
- Full-motion video
- Touch screens
- Consumer databases

It is clear that these fifth-wave systems will ultimately be the most important to successful enterprises because they reach the ultimate consumer of the goods or services that the enterprise supplies. It is possible that the first organizations in an industry to put these types of systems into place will set the standards and establish the rules for survival in that industry.

PLOTTING WAVES OF INFORMATION SYSTEMS GROWTH

Figure 8.1 shows how we can plot these five waves of information systems growth. It is important for top management to ask itself how much of the information systems budget is being spent on systems in the two lowest waves and how much is being spent in the more important upper waves, where investments in information systems offer the opportunity for generating new revenue sources and significantly increasing profitability. Notice that the slopes of the curves toward the bottom of the chart in Fig. 8.1 are flatter than those at the top. This is because there is a

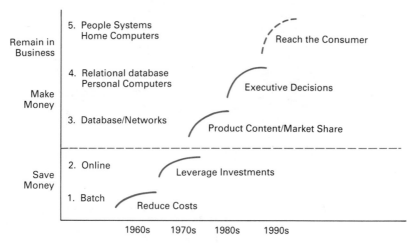

Figure 8.1 Waves of information systems growth.

declining marginal return on the investments made for information systems in the two lowest waves. The curves are steepest at the top, because these types of information systems have the biggest impact on the profitability of the enterprise. The biggest return on investment with first- and second-wave information systems comes as soon as the system is installed. Cost savings diminish after that. In today's environment, 60 percent to 70 percent of the information systems development budget is spent in maintaining and enhancing first- and second-wave systems for which the enterprise is no longer getting a big payback. However, it is important to note that effective below-the-line operational systems must exist and must continue to evolve for an organization to sustain an advantage over competition.

The top management of the enterprise must assess where the enterprise is in relation to the waves of information systems growth and to understand the trade-offs in investing above and below the line. Top management must also clearly understand the position of the industry as a whole and the position of the main competitors. Top management must determine when it will be necessary for the enterprise to cross from second-wave to third-wave, from third-wave to fourth-wave, and ultimately from fourth-wave to fifth-wave systems. Most companies are today at the top of the second wave. Most have not yet crossed the line from information systems that save money to systems that produce new revenue. Top management must realize that the leaders in some industries have crossed the line some time ago. To cross the line to revenue-producing information systems, top management must get involved in managing the new business environment that exists when strategic information systems are employed in running the business.

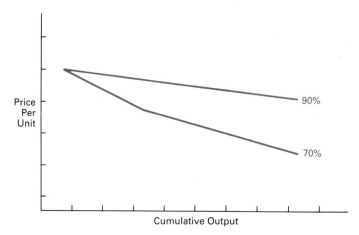

Price
Per
Unit

90%

70%

Cumulative Output

Figure 8.2   Experience curves.

**EXPERIENCE
CURVES**
Once the linkage analysis planning group has identified where the enterprise stands with respect to the waves of information systems growth, it must then determine where the enterprise stands with respect to the experience curve strategies that predominate in the industry. Experience curve strategies have traditionally been viewed from a cost or efficiency viewpoint. Experience curve strategies suggest that with any given level of technology, because of economies of scale, learning experiences, and production efficiencies, the cost of providing goods and services should decrease as volume increases. (See Fig. 8.2.) With this cost reduction in mind, we can examine a typical example.

Suppose that manufacturer A invests $100 million in a new plant aiming at a 90 percent experience curve. Manufacturer A then produces a product that cost $100 to manufacture on the first day. After the first million have been produced the cost is $90, after the second million, the cost is $81, and so on. Manufacturer B, on the other hand, invests $120 million in a new high-technology plant to produce a similar product, but aimed at a 70 percent experience curve. With a 70 percent experience curve, the product that initially costs $100 to make costs $70 after the first million and $49 after the second million. An enterprise whose product cost is $81 will find it difficult to compete with a competitor whose cost is $49. Most enterprises are on experience curves in the 70 to 90 percent range. Companies that are working with experience curves in the 90 percent range tend not even to measure the return. In practice, experience curves do not tend to be straight lines. Instead they tend to consist of connected curves, as in Fig. 8.3, with each new curve representing fundamentally different technology. It generally requires substantial investments and substantial risk in choosing the technology required to switch from one experience curve to another.

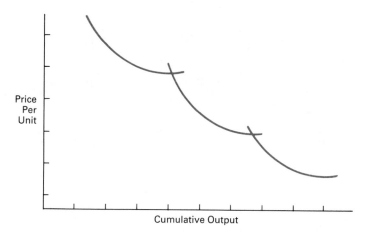

Figure 8.3   Changing experience curves.

The enterprise must determine where it stands with respect to the experience curves that predominate in the industry, where the competitors are, and what are the evolving technologies. The enterprise must then determine when it must switch from one experience curve to the next. If top management waits too long, and the competitors have already absorbed the new technology, the enterprise may not be able to catch up. In fact, the gap may already be so large that it may not be practical to close. In some cases, it may be more expedient to change the company name!

Figure 8.4 shows some typical experience curve charts for a few major industries. In the 1970s and 1980s many corporations changed experience curves to reduce costs and save money. Almost all enhancements in information systems have been aimed at lowering cost and maintaining quality. In today's environment, however, the emphasis has shifted. Corporations are now beginning to change experience curves again, but this time to gain strategic advantage, enter new markets, and change the rules of competition in the industry.

There are many false assumptions that can be made with respect to experience curves in an industry:

- Competitors are on the same experience curve as we are. (In many cases they are not; the industry leader may be on an entirely different experience curve.)

- Competitors have the same profit motive for the short run. (Industry leaders may take a longer view and may be willing to sacrifice short-term profits for long-range survivability.)

- Outside forces will not impact the cost curve. (Definitely not true in many environments.)

- Technology does not change. (Certainly false.)

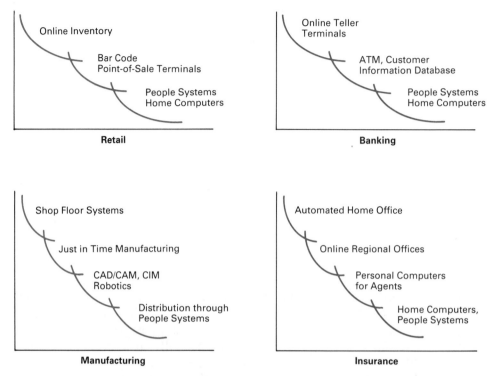

Figure 8.4 Typical industry experience curve strategies.

Analyzing the experience curves that exist in the information systems industry itself is useful in determining the kinds of computer and communication technology that are becoming available in today's environment. Figure 8.5 shows that for the first time we are beginning to use computers to store things other than words and numbers. In addition to words and numbers, we are now storing audio, graphics images, and full-motion video that allow the computer to represent concepts in the mind.

Information systems began by storing *data*. Database techniques allowed us to store data more efficiently and to begin retrieving *information*. An indication of this is that we no longer use the term *data processing department;* instead we now refer to the *information systems department*. Today, with advanced technology, such as relational databases, personal computers, expert systems, CD-ROM, video disk, touch screens, and so on, we are beginning to use computers to present *knowledge*. If the vision of top management does not encompass the new technologies, it will not be possible for information systems practitioners to exploit it, and the enterprise will be left behind when its competitors begin to take advantage of the new possibilities.

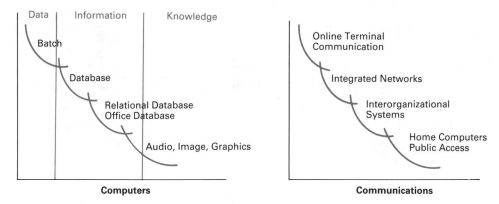

Figure 8.5   Information systems experience curve strategies.

INDUSTRY POWER RELATIONSHIPS   A third step in linkage analysis planning is to examine the power relationships that exist within a given industry and to determine how these power relationships are likely to change in the future. For example, Fig. 8.6 shows the relationships that might exist in a typical enterprise. This chart shows a chain that runs from the supplier to the manufacturer to the wholesaler to the retailer. A chart such as this begins to point out the key *linkages* that exist with the enterprise. It is a primary objective of linkage analysis planning to identify these linkages, to determine which of them are most important to the enterprise, and to anticipate how they are likely to change in the future.

A key question that must be asked in examining a chart of industry power relationships is "Who owns the chart?" If the chart in Fig. 8.6 represents the automobile industry, then the manufacturer can be perceived as owning the chart. If top management determines that the enterprise in question does *not* own the chart, it must then determine who the owner is, what the owner of the chart is doing, and what are the evolving rules of competition within the industry.

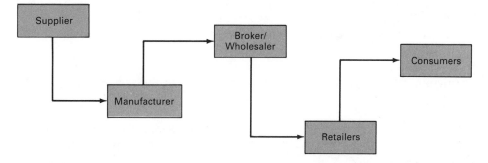

Figure 8.6   Industry power relationships.

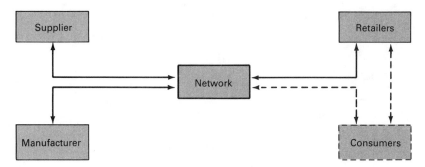

Figure 8.7 Changes in industry power relationships.

An important step in analyzing an industry's power relationships is to determine how the power relationships and, therefore, how the linkages in the chart, are likely to change in the future. For example, Fig. 8.7 shows the relationship that might exist when a network is employed that allows the organizations on the chart to communicate directly. Such a network is an example of what the Primozics call an *electronic channel support system*. They refer to such systems as *channel* systems because they are designed to cure problems in the distribution channels of the enterprise.

In this example, the ECSS would permit the manufacturer to begin using "just-in-time manufacturing." It might also allow techniques such as "just-in-time distribution" to the retailer. Future technological enhancements might allow the consumer to be reached directly. Such changes in industry power relationships often have significant impacts on the players on the chart. For example, in this case the use of the network facilitates a more streamlined and effective distribution network.

Another key question that must be asked in analyzing industry power relationships is: "How might the enterprise form strategic alliances that can be advantageous?" If organizations can join forces to cause changes in industry power relationships, these alliances must be anticipated by top management. Strategic alliances that might be detrimental to the enterprise must also be anticipated, and top management must address today's and tomorrow's power relationships and weigh the trade-offs, benefits, exposures, and investments accordingly.

There are a number of additional questions that top management can ask in attempting to understand the linkages that exist in the industry. These questions include

- What are we doing, and what should we be doing, relative to gaining substantial and sustainable competitive advantage, given the existing industry power relationships?

- Are we changing the industry? Are we leaders in the industry, or simply reacting to changes caused by others? Are we installing electronic channel support systems or are they being installed by our competitors? If our competitors are installing them, we will be able to compete in the future?
- Are we differentiating ourselves and our products from others?
- Are we entering new markets?

By examining and clearly understanding industry power relationships top management can begin to have an understanding of how the enterprise must operate in the context of an *extended enterprise*.

THE EXTENDED ENTERPRISE

Top management has traditionally viewed the enterprise using the management triangle, with top management at the top of the triangle, middle management in the center, and operational management at the bottom. This traditional view of the organization is shown in Fig. 8.8. However, businesses no longer fit the classical model of a chief executive officer directing internal corporate operations, such as manufacturing or purchasing, without regard to customers, suppliers, competitors, and technology.

The new economic realities demand that businesses define themselves in the context of an *extended enterprise* that comprises not only the enterprise itself but also the organizations with which it interacts. (See Fig. 8.9.) The next step in linkage analysis planning is to construct a chart of the extended enterprise and to determine which linkages are most critical. Perceiving the business as an extended enterprise requires a clear understanding of two fundamental insights:

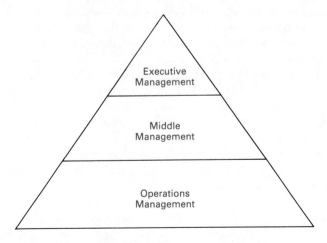

Figure 8.8 Classical management triangle.

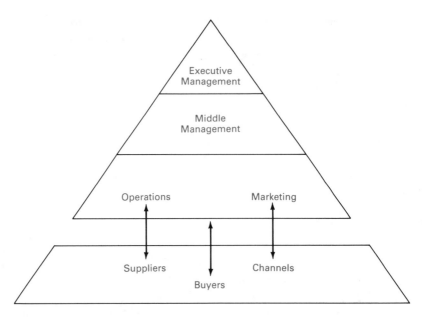

Figure 8.9 Extended enterprise.

First, the success of the enterprise depends on the existing and potential relationships that exist among workers, managers, suppliers, competitors, and distribution channels. Second, the information content of products and services in most industries is steadily increasing. Many industries continue to price products and services and develop strategies based on the cost of raw materials, manufacturing, and transportation. This is done not realizing that in many instances over 70 percent of the final cost of goods and services delivered to customers is dependent on information. Long-term success will be determined by how well the enterprise is able to capture, manipulate, exchange, and manage this information and to use it as a strategic tool.

Figure 8.10 shows the overall environment that might apply to an enterprise in the automotive industry. By examining industry power relationships and the linkages that exist, we might picture the extended enterprise as shown in Fig. 8.11. Such a chart allows us to begin seeing which linkages are the most important. It also allows top management to ask questions about how it can enhance market share in important supporting industries, such as auto financing and auto insurance, and how can the consumer be better served in the future (touch screens, automated ordering, etc.).

To have a clear view of the extended enterprise, top management must understand the technical environment as well as the business environment. This makes it possible for the enterprise to identify and form the strategic alliances or pick the most effective projects in which to apply technology to compete effectively in the future.

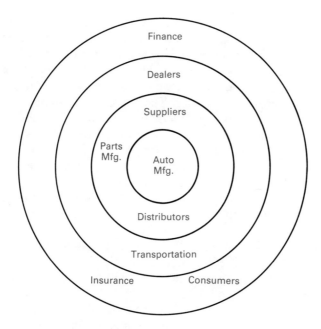

Figure 8.10 Automobile manufacturing industry.

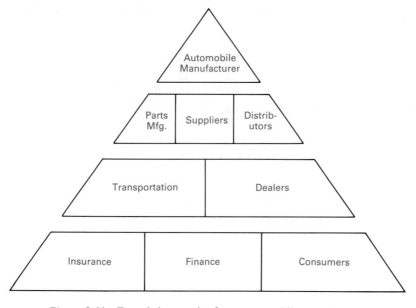

Figure 8.11 Extended enterprise for an automobile manufacturer.

ELECTRONIC CHANNEL SUPPORT SYSTEMS

Having a clear view of industry power relationships and of the structure of the extended enterprise, top management can begin to identify the new types of electronic channel support systems that will be required. As we pointed out earlier, an ECSS typically spans traditional company boundaries. The appropriate use of an ECSS can significantly enhance a company's productivity, flexibility, and ability to compete. In the future, companies that choose not to install these types of systems may be unable to compete with businesses that do. It is the job of top management to identify the ECSSs that will be required for the enterprise to remain in business. This important task cannot be delegated to the information systems department alone. It requires insights at the highest levels in the organization.

Information systems to support the extended enterprise should focus on better serving the customers of the enterprise. A successful electronic channel support system can make it very difficult for a competitor to attract the interest of customers because the ECSS may provide unique services not available elsewhere. In many cases, companies find it difficult to compete with the company that first installs such a system.

As stated at the beginning of this chapter, for the information systems planning process to be fully effective it is important that top management have a clearly articulated strategic business vision. It is the ultimate goal of linkage analysis planning to help articulate this vision and identify the electronic channel support systems that will be important for the organization in the future.

REFERENCES

1. Contact your local IBM marketing office for additional information on the linkage analysis planning methodology developed by Kenneth and Edward Primozic.

2. Brandt Allen, "An Unmanaged Computer System Can Stop You Dead," *Harvard Business Review,* November–December 1982.

3. Michael E. Porter and Victor E. Millar, "How Information Gives You Competitive Advantage," *Harvard Business Review,* July–August 1985.

9 ENTITY-RELATIONSHIP MODELING

An important step in the information strategy planning process is to create an overview entity-relationship model of the enterprise. We begin this process by identifying organizational units, locations, functions, and entities. In performing this step, we identify where functions are carried out, what types of entities they use, how they relate to the organization chart, what organizational units are in what locations, and so on. We then create an overview entity-relationship diagram that models the enterprise.

It is important that the overview entity-relationship model should not be too detailed. It is desirable to establish a broad overview in a fairly short time. Detail will be added during individual business area analysis studies. The top level might be thought of as being like an author planning a book and creating its table of contents. The author surveys the overall contents of the book, divides it into parts and chapters, and then decides which chapters should be tackled first. Similarly, at the overview-modeling stage we scope out the overall structure and information needs of the enterprise, divide it into areas, and then put together a plan for analyzing each area in detail.

Many strategic planning studies for computing have in the past sat on shelves in binders and fallen out of use. A key objective of effective information planning is to make the strategic planning representation alive, have it reviewed as part of the business planning cycle, and keep it updated so that it continues to be a valuable corporate resource.

Help from senior management and end users is generally essential in creating the enterprise model. *Only they* know how the enterprise really works.

Manager of Corporate Planning:

At first, even though we thought that users might need to be involved, we expected that the computer analysts would be able to play a greater part. As it turned out, this was not so because the computer analysts did not know the business in sufficient detail to perform the task of defining entities for the model. It was soon clear that users needed to play a much greater role than we had at first envisaged.

The enterprise modeling process often reveals redundancies and anomalies in the corporate organization of which top management are unaware. The strategic planning efforts described in this book have often led to corporate reorganization, not merely the reorganization of information systems.

Manager of Corporate Planning:

One of the main observations I have of this methodology is that even if a physical implementation does not take place, it is a worthwhile exercise in terms of modeling a business. The benefits become clear as you progress through the project in that a better understanding by more people across the operation exists and that organizationally a company can change to support the functions of the company.

THE ORGANIZATION CHART

The first step of enterprise modeling is to create an up-to-date organization chart. Figure 9.1 shows a typical organization chart. For a large enterprise, the organization chart has many boxes on it. To be handled conveniently, it needs to be subdivided in some way (as do many of the other large diagrams we will use). To be able to view different portions of such a large chart conveniently, a CASE tool can be used to maintain it. Notice that two of the upper boxes on Fig. 9.1 have three dots before their text. The three dots mean that *more* of the chart is available to be displayed. To display it the user points to the boxes in question and uses a command such as EXPAND. Similarly, a section of a hierarchical chart can be shrunk to one box by using a command such as CONTRACT.

Figure 9.2 shows an organization chart represented in the form of an action diagram. An action diagram is more compact than the type of chart shown in Fig. 9.1, but managers are more familiar with conventional organization charts. It is often useful to present information in familiar ways until managers gain experience with newer methods.

OBJECTS

The boxes of the organization chart are called *objects* about which we may store data. If we are using in-

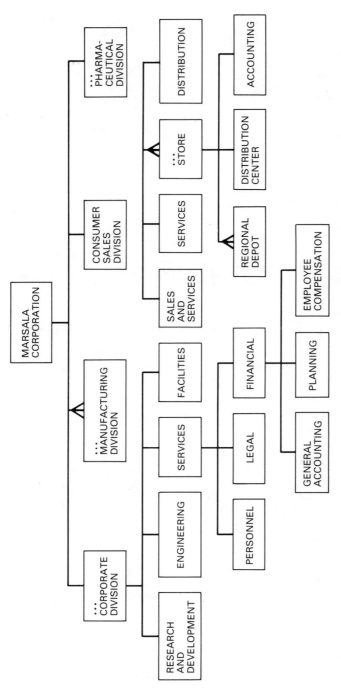

Figure 9.1 An organization chart for the Marsala Corporation. Three dots in several of the blocks indicate that these can be expanded to show more details of those organizational units.

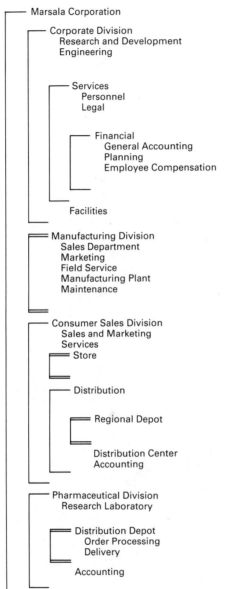

Figure 9.2 An action diagram showing an alternative method of displaying an organization chart in Fig. 9.1.

formation engineering techniques for the creation of systems, an object is an entity about which data is stored in the encyclopedia. (See Chapter 2.) In this chapter, we refer to four types of objects:

- **Organizational Unit.** A division, department, or functional area of the enterprise that is individually managed and distinct from other organizational units.
- **Function.** A group of activities that together support one aspect of furthering the mission of the enterprise.
- **Location.** A place at which functions are performed.
- **Entity.** A person, thing, or abstract concept about which we store data.

Throughout the information strategy planning process, we collect information about each object that we identify during enterprise modeling. For example, where the object is *organizational unit,* we may collect information about who manages a particular organizational unit. We may also want to collect related information, such as location, goals, or critical success factors for that organizational unit.

LOCATIONS

An enterprise may have offices, factories, warehouses, and so on at many locations. A particular organizational unit, too, can exist at multiple locations. We can represent this on a diagram showing a many-with-many relationship between the objects *organizational unit* and *location:*

The diagram states the following two facts about the relationship between organizational units and locations:

- An organizational unit is *based at* one or many locations.
- A location is the *site of* one or many organizational units.

Whenever a many-with-many relationship exists between two types of entities, as in the previous example, we can draw a matrix showing which entities are associated with which:

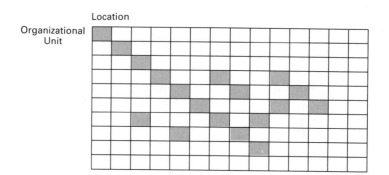

Figure 9.3 is an actual matrix, created during enterprise modeling for a medium-sized corporation, showing how organizational units are mapped against locations.

ENTERPRISE FUNCTIONS

After establishing the organization chart, the next step in modeling an enterprise is to create a chart decomposing the business functions the enterprise performs. A *business function* is a group of activities that together support one aspect of furthering the mission of the enterprise. They have names that often end in "ing," for example, *purchasing, receiving, financial planning*.

Business functions are sometimes grouped into *functional areas* as shown in Fig. 9.4. Functional areas refer to the major areas of activity; in a corporation they might be engineering, marketing, production, research, and distribution. One medium-sized manufacturing company listed its functional areas as follows:

- Business planning
- Finance
- Product planning
- Materials
- Production planning
- Production
- Sales
- Distribution
- Accounting
- Personnel

	Home Office	Manufacturing Plant	Sales Headquarters	Santa Clara Sales Office	Chicago Sales Office	New York Sales Office
	1	2	3	4	5	6	7
1 President		*					
2 Finance & Admin.		*					
3 Production			*				
4 Sales				*			
5 Marketing			*				
6 Research & Development		*					
7 Planning		*					
8 Accounting		*					
9 Cash Management		*					
10 Investments		*					
11 Purchasing			*				
12 Facilities		*					
13 Human Resource Development		*					
14 MIS		*					
15 Legal		*					
16 Manufacturing			*				
17 Quality Assurance			*				
18 Packaging			*				
19 Materials Management			*				
20 Sales Regions				*			
21 Customer Services			*				
22 Customer Education				*			
23 Order Processing				*			
24 Product Management				*			
25 Public Relations				*			
26 Market Research				*			
27 Distribution			*				
28 Engineering			*				
29 Research			*				
30 Prototype Manufacture			*				
31 Testing Laboratory			*				

Figure 9.3 A matrix mapping organizational units against locations.

Functional Areas	Functions
Business Planning	Market Analysis Product Range Review Sales Forecasting
Finance	Financial Planning Capital Acquisition Funds Management
Product Planning	Product Design Product Pricing Product Specification Maintenance
Materials	Materials Requirements Purchasing Receiving Inventory Control Quality Control
Production Planning	Capacity Planning Plant Scheduling Workflow Layout
Production	Materials Control Sizing and Cutting Machine Operations
Sales	Territory Management Selling Sales Administration Customer Relations
Distribution	Finished Stock Control Order Serving Packing Shipping
Accounting	Creditors and Debtors Cash Flow Payroll Cost Accounting Budget Planning Profitability Analysis
Personnel	Personnel Planning Recruiting Compensation Policy

Figure 9.4 Typical corporate functional areas decomposed into high-level functions.

Each functional area may be subdivided into a number of functions, as illustrated in Fig. 9.4. Box 9.1 shows examples of typical functional decomposition that has been performed for various industries.

PROCESSES   Enterprise functions can be further subdivided into *processes* (see Fig. 9.5, p. 156). Whereas a *function* is ongoing and continuous, a *process* relates to a specific act that has a definable

BOX 9.1 Examples of function decomposition by industry

Insurance

Management Planning

Corporate direction planning
Long-range planning
Business planning
Acquisition/ventures planning

Product Management

Managing the book of business
Product service monitoring
Product reevaluation

Control and Measurement

Financial planning
Operational planning
Performance evaluation

Product Development and Maintenance

Product design
Pricing
Product goals and measurement
Product implementation

Facilities, Equipment and Supplies

Facility planning
Facility services management
Equipment and supplies management
Warehousing and distribution

Merchandising

Lead development
Selling
Customer qualification

Risk engineering
Establishing and maintaining customer record
Billing and collections
Customer servicing

Product Service

Insurance
Insurance claim evaluation and disposition
Noninsurance processing service
Noninsurance professional service

Financial

Cash management
Asset accounting
Expense allocation
Claim reserves
Tax processing
Corporate books and ledgers administration
Investment management

Administration

Legal services
External relations
Advertising
Auditing
Information development
Operational support
Work force management
External services management
Systems planning
System development/maintenance and operations

(Continued)

BOX 9.1 *(Continued)*

Finance

Management Planning and Control

Objectives planning
Forecasting alternatives
Measurement and control
Organization
Policy setting
Resource allocation
External relations

Product Development

Review and approval
Resource evaluation
Strategy development
Education development
Pricing

Marketing

Market definition
Market research
Advertising and promotion
Public relations
Product implementation
Competitive analysis

Money Management

Investment management
Money market instruments

Customer

Investigation and acceptance
Account establishment
Account control
Account maintenance
Account termination

Funds Transfer Services

Letter of credit
Money transfer
Bond transfer
Stock transfer
Loan
Deposit/withdrawal checking
Collections
Lock box
Automatic dividend reinvestment
Foreign exchange
Cash management

Trust

Accounting service
Asset management

Operations

Communications
Data processing
Transaction servicing
Inquiry servicing
Collections
Mail

Finance

Budget planning and control
Financial analysis
Asset management
Liability management
Capital management
Financial reporting

BOX 9.1 *(Continued)*

Finance *(Continued)*

Personnel

Planning
Recruiting and hiring
Training
Wage and salary administration
Employee relations
Benefits management
Career development
Retirement or separation
Government compliance

Legal

Litigation
Tax consequence advising

Process (Chemical)

Planning

Strategic planning
Market research
Technical feasibility
Economic analysis
Forecasting
Resource requirements

Product Development

Exploration
Engineering development
Licensing
Engineering design
Construction

Marketing

Sales forecasting
Advertising/promotion
Pricing

Contracts review
Legislation impact analysis
Legal compliance review

Administration

Accounting
Audit
Facilities
Regulatory compliance
Taxes
Payroll
Security

Selling/contracting
Order entry
Customer service
Sales analysis

Manufacturing

Production forecasting
Scheduling
Inventory
Plant operations
Packaging
Warehousing
Shipping
Maintenance
Quality control
Product cost control

Distribution

Carrier and rate negotiations
Supply/demand planning

(Continued)

BOX 9.1 *(Continued)*

Process (Chemical) *(Continued)*

Distribution *(Continued)*

Order processing
Rating and routing
Terminal operations
Warehouse planning/operations
Fleet planning
Fleet operations
Inventory control

Financial

Financial planning
Financial analysis
Capital transaction and control
Budgeting
General accounting

Cost accounting
Taxes
Government report
Payroll

Administration

Personnel development
Salary and benefits administration
Labor and personnel relations
External affairs
Legal
Insurance
Information services
Facilities services

Process (Paper)

Product Development

Product design
Raw material requirements
Facility planning
Market forecast
Financial requirements
Market planning

Marketing

Sales planning
Product plan
Sales analysis
Order entry
Customer services
Pricing

Production

Requirement planning
Production scheduling

Raw material planning
Receiving
Production reporting
Quality control
Inventory
Shipping
Maintenance

Engineering Support

Project engineering
Environment
Energy requirements
Standards
Material handling

Financial

Cash management
Budgeting
Capital expenditures

BOX 9.1 *(Continued)*

Process (Paper) *(Continued)*

Financial (Continued)

Cost analysis
Financial reporting
Payroll
Customer billing
Accounts receivable and pay-
   able
Audit

Administration

Purchasing
Personnel services

Manufacturing

*Product Development and
Application*

Technology development
Product application
New product
Old product
Application engineering
Specifications
Drafting and records
Product performance

Product Planning

Determination of business case
Evaluation of business case

Marketing

Marketing planning
Market research, market devel-
   opment
Pricing
Publications, advertising, pro-
   motions

Traffic
Salary administration
Information services
Legal
Stockholder relations
Public affairs

Industry Relations

Labor relations
Personnel development
Safety

Sales analysis and forecasting
Warranty policy and other soft-
   ware
Market operations
Distribution network
Field sales and services
OEM sales and service
Order entry

Financial Management

Funds management
Cash
Short-term financing
Long-term financing
Financial control
Budget/expense
Managerial accounting
General accounting
Bookkeeping
Internal control

(Continued)

BOX 9.1 *(Continued)*

Manufacturing *(Continued)*

Administration

Legal
Public relations
Security
Governmental reporting
Office management

Planning, Control, and Measurement

Fiscal year business plan
Annual operating plan
Quarterly operating plan
Reporting and control

Personnel Management

Planning
Acquiring
Development and administration
Reporting
Termination

Operations Control

Master production plan
Transportation planning
Performance reporting
Inventory control

Capacity Management

Determination of optimum capacity
Capacity allocation
Acquisition of capacity

Material Acquisition

Vendor evaluation
Order control
Receiving and inspection

Plant Operations

Planning, schedule, and control
Performance reporting
Expediting
Planning of material, manpower
Order processing—plant order boards
Product and process specifications
Execution
Order release
Dispatching
Storage/warehousing
Quality
Preventive maintenance
Material transfer—to/from supplier/customer

Distribution

Buying

Vendor selection
Requirements
When to buy

Allocation
Sales planning
Inventory control
Pricing
Markdowns

BOX 9.1 *(Continued)*

Distribution *(Continued)*

Selling

Presentation
Display
Work force planning
New item introduction
Advertising
Customer service

General Operations

Purchasing
Facilities maintenance
Security
Public relations
Audit
Inventory control
Physical inventory control

Management and Financial Control

Budgets
Cash management

Government

Judicial

Prosecution
Defense
Court procedures
Control
Civil

Public Facilities

Definition
Construction

Profit planning
Measurement and control
Capital expenditure planning
Credit granting
Financial negotiation
New business

Administration

Accounts payable
Accounts receivable
Payroll
Statistical and financial report-
   ing
Audit
Merchandise processing
Personnel/training

Maintenance
Property management

Public Protection Process

Enforcement
Confinement
Rehabilitation
Prevention
Inspection

(Continued)

BOX 9.1 *(Continued)*

Government *(Continued)*

Finance

Taxing
Licensing
Accounting
Collections
Funds management
Payroll
Purchasing

Personnel

Recruiting/hiring/terminating
Career development
Job classification
Labor relations
Compensation and benefits
Employee/position management

Management

Conflict
Measurement and control
Policy determination
Budgeting
Security/privacy
External relations
Record keeping

Education—University

Student

Promotion/recruiting
Evaluation and admissions
Class registration
Academic and career advising
Financial aid
Student activities/life
Student services
Student status/archives

Community Service

Library
Public records
Election administration
Cultural and recreational support
Environmental control

Public Aid Process

Eligibility determination
Financial assistance
Work force
Social services
Residential care

Health Services

Admissions
Inpatient care
Outpatient care
Education and research
Emergency care
Community health services

Credit Instruction

Curriculum development
Scheduling instructional resources
Teaching and learning
Evaluation and measurement

BOX 9.1 *(Continued)*

Education—University *(Continued)*

Research and Artistic Creativity

Project identification and definition
Procurement of resources
Project execution
Evaluation
Dissemination of results

Public Services and Extension

Activity development
Administrative and logistical services for clientele
Resource procurement and organization
Activity delivery
Activity evaluation

Financial Management

Income acquisition
Stewardship of funds
Receipting and disbursement of funds
Cash management
Protection against financial liabilities
Financial services
Financial record keeping

Institutional Planning and Management

Goals development
Strategic planning (long term)

Tactical planning (short term)
Allocation of resources
Monitor and control
Internal communications

Physical Plant Management

Program statement
Design
Construction and procurement
Maintenance/operation
Disposition
Protection
Rental property management

Goods and Services

Assessment of needs
Acquisition
Inventory of expendables
Inventory of nonexpendables
Distribution

Alumni Affairs

Tracking
Programs and services
Institutional evaluation

External Communication and Relations

Publicity
Negotiation
Public service
Extrauniversity affiliation

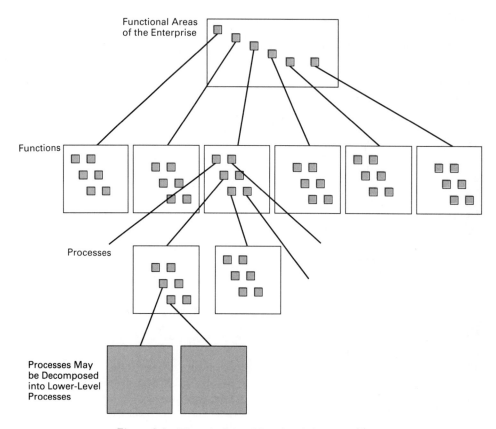

Figure 9.5   The principle of functional decomposition.

start and stop. A process has identifiable inputs and outputs. The name of a process should begin with an action verb such as:

- Create purchase requisition
- Select supplier
- Follow up order
- Prepare information for accounts payable
- Analyze supplier performance

Decomposition of business functions and processes should be done independently of how the enterprise is split into departments. The organization may change its reporting structure periodically, but it still has to carry out the same functions and processes. Some corporations reorganize traumatically every two years or so, like the government of Bolivia. The identification of functions and processes should represent fundamental concern for how the corporation operates, independently of its current organization chart (which is often misleading).

Manager of Corporate Planning:

The processes that occur here are mostly ill defined. They have evolved and developed over a period of time as a result of attempts to respond to a changing environment. Often, functions will overlap and organizational structures designed for a simpler operation no longer fit the bill. When looking at an integrated information system, therefore, we quickly realized that we needed to analyze the business, its processes, and the overall operation as well as identify the links between functions and the degree of dependency between them.

Functions and processes are concerned with *what* has to be done to operate an enterprise, not with *how* it is done. *Procedures* are concerned with *how it is done. Procedures change as technology changes. There are multiple types of procedure that could* be used to accomplish given processes. Whereas the procedures may be scrapped or changed, the functions and processes still have to be carried out to run the enterprise. Box 9.2 summarizes the characteristics of functions and processes.

Figure 9.6 shows functions decomposed into processes and some processes decomposed into lower-level processes. It is important to note here that information strategy planning concentrates on functions, not on processes or procedures:

- Functions are determined during information strategy planning.

- Processes are analyzed during business area analysis of a specific business area.

- Procedures are designed after business area analysis when specific information systems are designed.

An analyst may write a definition of a function and store it. For example, an analyst may define *inventory management* as "the function of controlling the receipts and withdrawals of raw materials, parts, and subassemblies from the stores and accounting for the stock." There may or may not be a separate department to accomplish this function; it is a function that may apply to several departments. The stores may be split or combined, but the *function* remains the same.

BOX 9.2   Characteristics of functions and processes

Functions are determined during information strategy planning; *processes* are analyzed during business area analysis. *Procedures* relate specifically to *how* a process is carried out. These are designed when individual information systems are designed.

Functions

- An enterprise *function* is a group of activities which together support one aspect of furthering the mission of the enterprise.
- A function is ongoing and continuous.
- A function is *not* based on organizational structures.
- A function categorizes *what* is done, not *how*.
- Examples of functions are *advertising, account control, shipping, labor relations*.

Processes

- A *process* is a specified activity that is repeatedly executed in an enterprise.
- A *process* can be described in terms of inputs and outputs.
- A process has a definable start and stop.
- A process is *not* based on organizational structures.
- A process identifies *what* is done, not *how*.
- The name of a process should start with an action verb, for example, *create requisition, reorder parts, assemble orders*.

LIFE CYCLE OF FUNCTIONS   The products and services created by an organization, and also the services needed to support them, tend to have a four-stage life cycle: planning, acquisition, stewardship, disposal. Figure 9.7 illustrates some of the types of function at each stage in the cycle. In attempting to identify functions, it sometimes helps to think through all the stages in the life cycle of each type of product, service, or resource. This can be done with money, personnel, raw materials, parts, finished goods, capital equipment, buildings, machinery, fixtures, and so on.

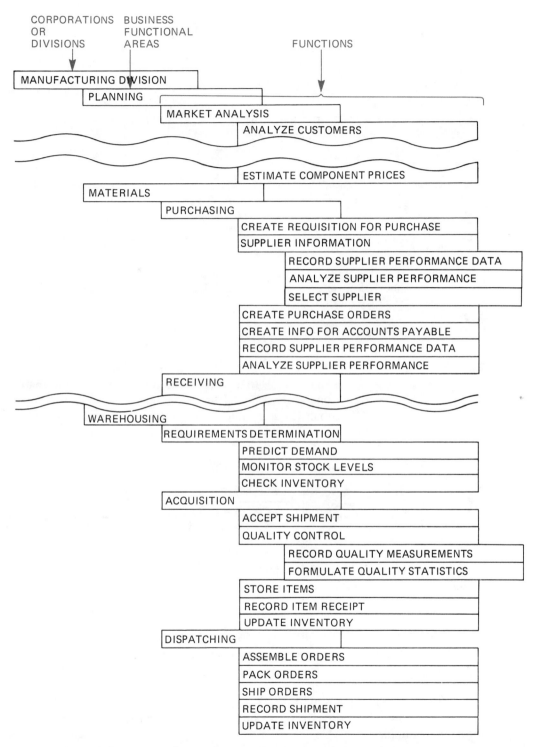

Figure 9.6 An enterprise chart showing functional areas, functions, and processes. The name of a function should be a noun or gerund. The name of a process should normally begin with an action verb. Procedures (not necessarily computerized) are designed to implement the processes.

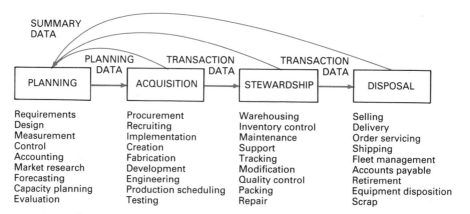

Figure 9.7 The functions that apply to products, services, or resources tend to be in the sequence of a four-stage life cycle: planning, acquisition, stewardship, and disposal.

Requirements	Procurement	Warehousing	Selling
Design	Recruiting	Inventory control	Delivery
Measurement	Implementation	Maintenance	Order servicing
Control	Creation	Support	Shipping
Accounting	Fabrication	Tracking	Fleet management
Market research	Development	Modification	Accounts payable
Forecasting	Engineering	Quality control	Retirement
Capacity planning	Production scheduling	Packing	Equipment disposition
Evaluation	Testing	Repair	Scrap

MAPPING OF FUNCTIONS TO ORGANIZATIONAL UNITS

An organizational unit carries out several functions, and a given function may be performed by more than one organizational unit. We thus have a many-with-many association between functions and organizational units:

This diagram states the following two facts about the associations between organizational units and functions:

- An organizational unit *carries out* one or many functions.
- A function *is performed by* one or many organizational units.

As with all such many-with-many associations a matrix can be drawn and filled in to show which organizational units perform which functions, as in the following example:

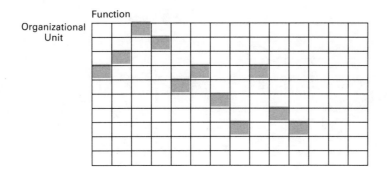

Similarly, functions can be mapped against geographical locations:

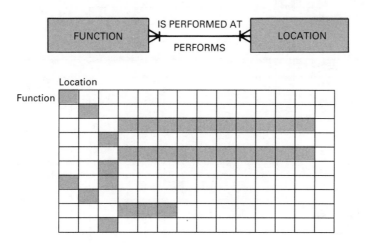

**MAPPING
EXECUTIVES TO
FUNCTIONS**

On the organization chart, managers are shown as having a one-with-one association with organizational units. In principle, then, the matrix of organizational units and functions could be directly converted into a matrix that maps *managers* against functions. In practice, however, managers also carry out informal activities that are not identified on the organization chart. Indeed, in some enterprises the organization chart *hides* the true power structure of the enterprise.

EXECUTIVE	Marketing: Planning	Research	Forecasting	Sales Operations: Territory Management	Selling	Administration	Order Servicing	Engineering: Design and Development	Prod. Spec. Main.	Information Control	Production: Scheduling	Capacity Planning	Material Requirements	Operations	Materials Mgmt: Purchasing	Receiving	Inventory Control	Shipping	Facilities Mgmt: Workflow Layout	Maintenance	Equipment Performance	Administration: General Accounting	Cost Planning	Budget Accounting	Finance: Financial Planning	Capital Acquisition	Funds Management	Human Resources: Personnel Planning	Recruiting/Development	Compensation	Management: Business Planning	Organization Analysis	Review and Control	Risk Management
Vice President of Finance	RA																					A/E	A/E	A/E	A/E	A/E	A/E							RA
Controller						I					I	I			I							RA/E	RA/E	RA/E	RA/E	RA/E	RA/E							RA
Personnel Director																						I	I	I	A/E	A/E	A/E	RA/EW	RA/E	RA/E				
Vice President of Sales	RA/EW		RA/E	RA/E	RA/E	RA/E	RA/E				I				I																I		I	
Order Control Manager			E	I	I	I	RA				I	I			I																			
Electronic Sales Manager	I		E	RA	RA	RA	RA																											
Electrical Sales Manager	I		E	RA	RA	RA	RA																											
Vice President of Engineering			I					RA	RA	RA									RA															
Vice President of Production											RA	RA	RA	RA	RA	RA	RA	RA	RA	RA	RA	I	I	I										
Plant Operations Director											I	RA	RA	RA	I	I	RA	RA	I	I	I													
Production Planning Director								I	I	I	RA	RA	I	I	I	I																		
Facilities Manager	I								I	I	I	I	I	I					RA	RA	RA							I			I			
Materials Control Manager									I			I	I	I	RA	RA	RA	RA	RA	RA	RA	I	I	I				I						
Purchasing Manager												I		I	RA	RA	RA	RA					I											
Division Lawyer	RA	I							I	I															RA	RA	RA					RA	RA	RA
Planning Director	RA	I	I					I	I		I	I		I								I	I	I	RA	RA	RA				I	I	RA	I

R: Responsibility A: Executive or policy making authority
I: Involved E: Technical expertise W: Actual execution of the work

Figure 9.8 A matrix mapping business functions against the executives in an enterprise.

Strategic Planning Consultant:

The company has a detailed list of F&Rs [functions and responsibilities]. The problem is: They are not followed. Getting agreement as to who really has what responsibility, and who belongs to what data, was very difficult.

A separate matrix is often created that documents the true relationships between executives and business functions. Figure 9.8 is an example.

Recording the type of involvement an executive has with a business function can be done with the following codes:

- R —Direct management *responsibility*.
- A —Executive or policymaking *authority*.
- I —*Involved* in the function.
- E —Technical *expertise*.
- W—Actual execution of the *work*.

These codes are entered into the matrix. I (Involved) may only be used when R (Responsible) or A (Authority) are not present. Some executives have the four codes R, A, E, and W; some have two or three codes; some have only one.

The codes used vary somewhat from one enterprise to another. In some studies two versions of the chart are drawn—one to document the current situation and another to describe an ideal or target situation.

A HIGH-LEVEL ENTITY CHART

At the highest-level overview of data, we identify broad data subjects, such as:

- Sales regions
- Customers
- Orders
- Products
- Parts
- Materials
- Vendors
- Employees
- Capital equipment

Identifying these broad data subjects is the first step in identifying the subject databases we discussed in Chapter 5.

For each data subject, we identify *entities*. As we mentioned earlier, an entity is any person or thing, real or abstract, about which information is stored. For example, the following lists some typical entities that are associated with sales regions, customers, and orders:

- **Sales Regions**
  Sales region name
  Branch office
  Salesperson
  Annual quota

- **Customers**
  Customer name
  Address
  Contact

- **Orders**
  Customer order
  Order item
  Invoice
  Payment
  Receivable
  Ledger entry

Entities can be associated with functions:

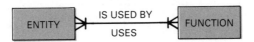

This diagram states the following two facts about the associations between entities and functions:

- An entity *is used by* one or more functions.
- A function *uses* one or more entities.

Similarly, an entity is associated with organizational units and locations:

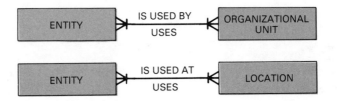

As before, a matrix can be drawn and filled in to show which entities are associated with which organizational units and locations.

RELATIONSHIPS BETWEEN ENTITIES

Organizational units and functions are arranged hierarchically. One organizational unit manages zero or many other organizational units and is managed by zero or one organizational units:

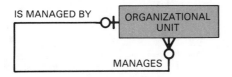

One function is composed of zero or many other functions and is part of zero or one function:

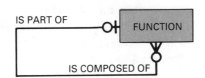

The associations among different types of entities are not necessarily hierarchical. Entities can have many-with-many associations with one another:

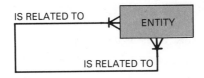

PLANNING DATA MODEL

By combining all the many-with-many relationships that we have discussed thus far, we arrive at the model shown in Fig. 9.9, in which there are six many-with-many relationships between our four objects. All relationships can be read in both directions, but we have given only one label to each to avoid cluttering the diagram. Any of the six relationships can be represented in the form of matrices.

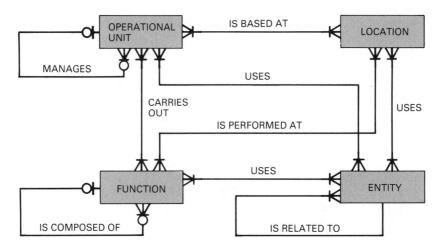

Figure 9.9 An entity-relationship model of the planning data described in this chapter. A matrix can be generated for each of the six many-with-many relationships shown on the chart. To avoid clutter the relationships are labeled in one direction only.

CREATING THE ENTITY-RELATIONSHIP MODEL

As entities are identified, they are placed into an entity-relationship diagram, if possible using a CASE entity-relationship modeling tool. Each relationship between two entities is given a name. Often a name is required in each direction:

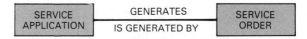

This diagram states two facts about the associations that exist between service applications and service orders:

- A service application generates a service order.
- A service order is generated by a service application.

The relationship line should document the cardinalities in both directions, as discussed in Chapters 3 and 4:

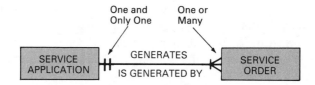

There are sometimes two or more relationships between two entities. Such relationships have different names. Sometimes an entity has a relationship with *either* one entity *or* another:

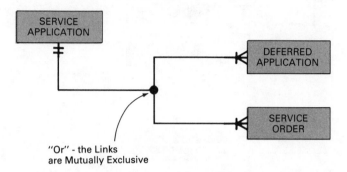

The next chart is an example of a simple entity-relationship diagram that documents the following facts about *customers, orders, order-lines,* and *products:*

A customer *places* one or more orders.

An order *has* one or more order-lines.

An order-line *relates to* one and only one product.

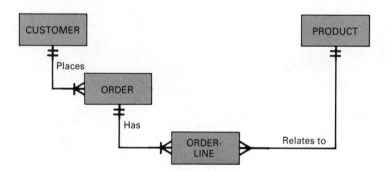

This representation is a statement about the fundamental nature of the data concerning customers, orders, order-lines, and products. It is independent of current procedures, systems, or departmental structures. The systems and procedures may be drastically redesigned, and the departments that use them reorganized, but the foregoing statement about customers, orders, order lines, and products will remain valid.

Figure 9.10 shows a portion of an entity-relationship diagram for a telephone company.

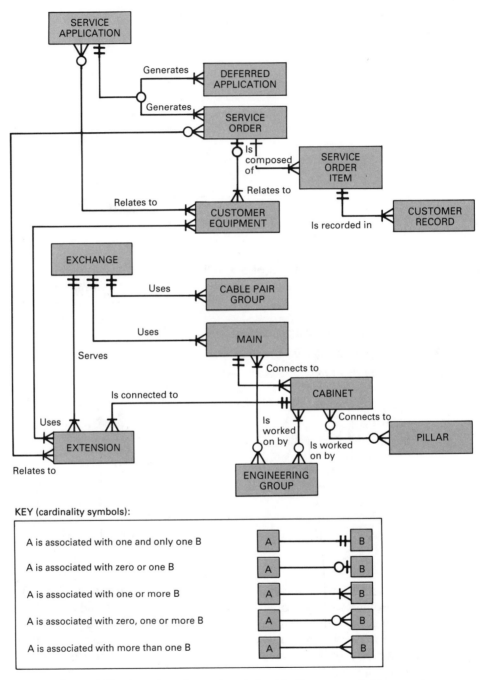

Figure 9.10 A portion of an entity-relationship diagram for a telecommunications company.

AVOIDANCE OF TOO MUCH DETAIL   As we discussed in Chapter 8, information strategy planning creates an overview of the enterprise that acts as a logical framework into which further analysis and design of data and procedures can fit. An important objective is to do this fairly quickly, maintaining the interest of senior management. Some strategic planning efforts have attempted to identify data *attributes* as well as *entities* and even to normalize the data. To create a normalized data model takes *much* longer than merely identifying entities and their relationships. It is important to complete the identification of entities and their relationships quickly. It is important to complete the information strategy planning study quickly and not bog down in too much detail. Detail such as normalization of data does not interest senior management. This detail follows in the business area analysis studies that each analyze a coherent portion of the enterprise.

In an attempt to move quickly, some strategic planning studies have avoided building an entity-relationship diagram. They have merely identified the entities. The entity-relationship diagram has been left until the later detailed data modeling. In the author's view it helps to build an entity-relationship diagram at this stage *if an appropriate CASE tool is used*. The entering of relationships takes little time and helps to validate the identification of entities. It sometimes provokes the discovery of entities that have been missed. It helps later in the splitting of entities and business functions into separate groups to identify business areas.

PROPERTIES OF THE ENTERPRISE MODEL   The enterprise model should have the following properties:

- **Completeness.** The model should present a complete list of the functional areas, functions, and activities that constitute the enterprise.

- **Appropriateness.** The model should be a reasonable and useful way to understand the enterprise. The functions or activities identified at each level of analysis should seem natural and correct to the management involved.

- **Permanence.** The model should remain true and valid as long as the enterprise's statement of purpose remains true. Some enterprises reorganize themselves periodically. Some have periodic management upheavals. But in spite of these, the same functions must be carried out. The model should survive reorganizations and be independent of whether the data is stored in files, in databases, or on paper.

10 TECHNOLOGY IMPACT ANALYSIS

It is the job of top management to perceive the enterprise not as it is today but as what it can become in the future. The view of what the enterprise can become is often reflected in a financial model that projects the revenues and expenses five or more years into the future and breaks them into detail. There are many assumptions inherent in such a model and they need to be documented and as far as possible validated. Over a five-year span a corporation may introduce many new products or services and change or drop existing ones. The view of the future affects many of the current plans and expenditures. A major data processing system or corporate network takes two or more years to build, so it needs to be built with a view of future needs. Much of the planning of information systems needs to be long-range planning.

During the coming years great changes in technology will occur. We can expect to see new technology coming into use at a furious rate. New technology offers new business and management opportunities and poses new competitive threats. At a time of great technological change, there are many bankruptcies and takeovers among corporations that did not have enough foresight or did not act on their foresight. Top management is often unaware of all the critical changes in technology and the business opportunities they present, and often opportunities are missed or corporations find that competition is overtaking them.

Appendix II contains an action diagram that lists the detailed steps in performing a *technology impact analysis* study. Technology impact analysis employs a hierarchical list of technological changes and relates these to business and management opportunities and competitive threats.

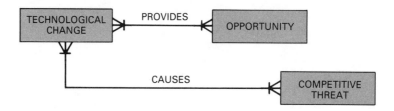

These changes relate to organizational units, goals, and problems; as shown here:

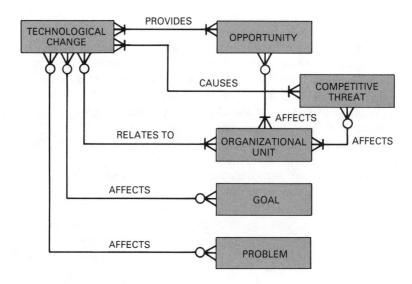

A TECHNOLOGY ACTION DIAGRAM

A taxonomy of technological changes is hierarchical and can be conveniently represented on an action diagram, as in Fig. 10.1. Box 10.1 shows a more detailed action diagram of information technology. The group responsible for strategic planning should maintain such an action diagram. The action diagram in Box 10.1 relates only to information technology. Others may be maintained relating to molecular biology, medicine, materials, and so on, as appropriate to the enterprise in question. The list of technological changes needs modifying frequently, so it should be maintained on a medium that makes the updating of a taxonomy easy. A CASE action diagramming tool is ideal for this purpose.

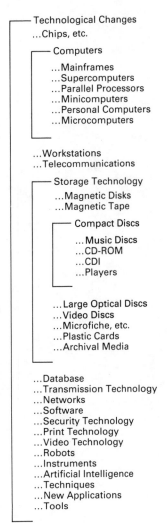

Figure 10.1 An overview action diagram of technological changes.

BOX 10.1 A detailed action diagram of technological changes

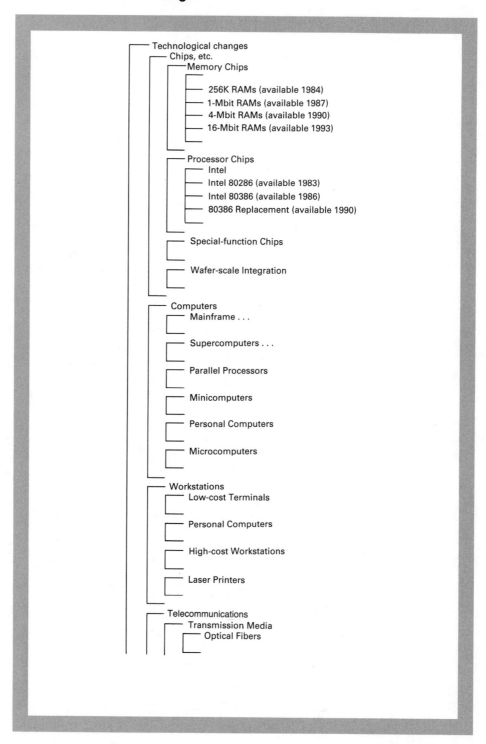

Technological changes
Chips, etc.
Memory Chips

256K RAMs (available 1984)
1-Mbit RAMs (available 1987)
4-Mbit RAMs (available 1990)
16-Mbit RAMs (available 1993)

Processor Chips
Intel
Intel 80286 (available 1983)
Intel 80386 (available 1986)
80386 Replacement (available 1990)

Special-function Chips

Wafer-scale Integration

Computers
Mainframe . . .

Supercomputers . . .

Parallel Processors

Minicomputers

Personal Computers

Microcomputers

Workstations
Low-cost Terminals

Personal Computers

High-cost Workstations

Laser Printers

Telecommunications
Transmission Media
Optical Fibers

BOX 10.1   *(Continued)*

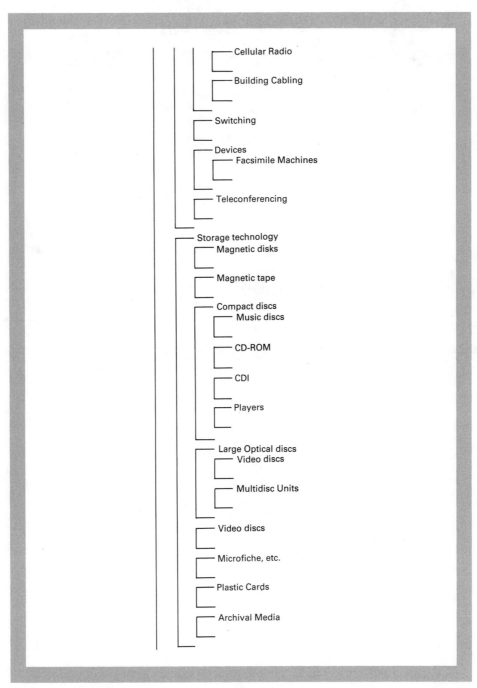

- Cellular Radio
- Building Cabling
- Switching
- Devices
  - Facsimile Machines
- Teleconferencing
- Storage technology
  - Magnetic disks
  - Magnetic tape
  - Compact discs
    - Music discs
    - CD-ROM
    - CDI
    - Players
  - Large Optical discs
    - Video discs
    - Multidisc Units
  - Video discs
  - Microfiche, etc.
  - Plastic Cards
  - Archival Media

(Continued)

BOX 10.1 *(Continued)*

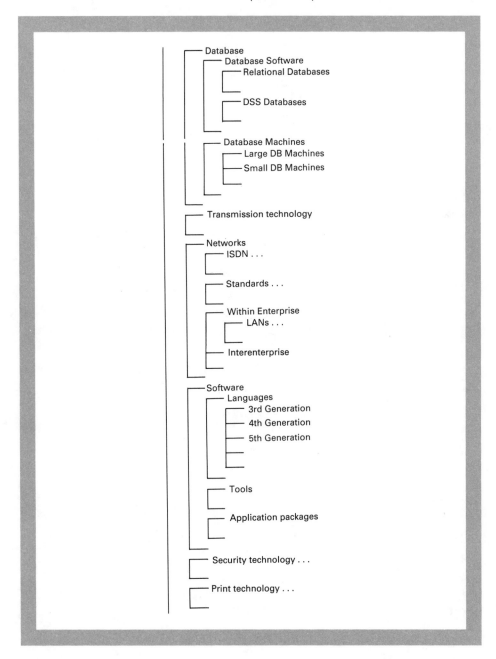

BOX 10.1   *(Continued)*

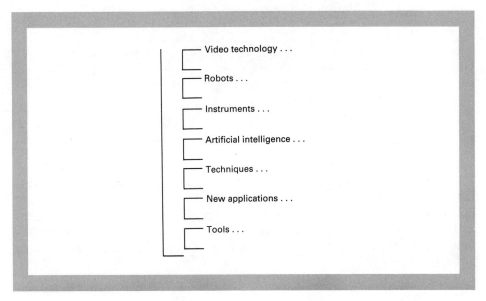

Note: The notation of three dots (...) indicates a line that can be expanded to reveal a greater level of detail.

BUSINESS AND MANAGEMENT OPPORTUNITIES

An enterprise should develop its own list of business and management opportunities that result from technological changes. The list of technological changes is directly related to the list of opportunities. Most of them result from competition using the technology in the same way but perhaps with better marketing, greater capital, or different corporate alliances.

Box 10.2 shows a list of typical opportunities relating to information technology. Again an action diagram editor can be used to maintain such a hierarchical taxonomy. The action diagram of technological changes can be mapped against the action diagram of business opportunities:

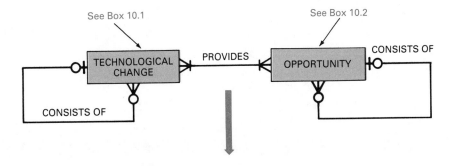

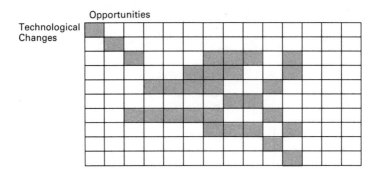

Because the lists of technologies and opportunities are large, it is desirable that an appropriate CASE tool be used so that the corresponding matrix should be contractable and expandable so that individual areas of interest can be conveniently displayed for study. An appropriate computerized tool allows opportunities and competitive threats to be related to the organizational units affected by them.

BOX 10.2   An action diagram of business and management opportunities

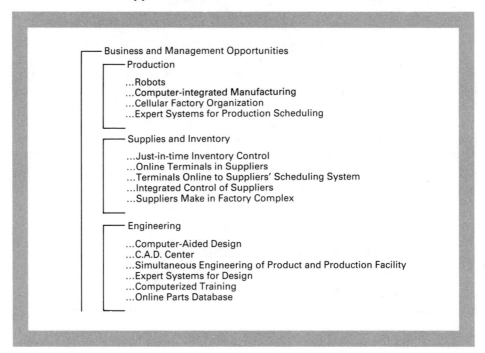

BOX 10.2   *(Continued)*

Marketing

...Telemarketing
...Online Catalog
...Expert System for Setting Discounts
...Computerized Mailing
...Customers Online to Marketing Database
...Terminals in Agents
...Terminals in Retailers
...Customer Corporations Online
...Dealers: Smaller, Larger Number, Online
...Worldwide Sales/Marketing Network

Sales

...Salespeople with Portable Terminals
...Expert Systems for Salesmen
...Expert System for Order Configuration
...CDI for Training
...Videotapes for Training
...Screen Order Entry

Products

...Product Redesign for Robot Fabrication
...Intelligence in Products
...New Products
...Product Versions for International Sales

Services

...Toll-Free Number for Customer Service
...Online Services
...Service Using Expert Systems
...Strategic Alliances
...New Service Areas

Internal Systems

Office Automation

...Electronic Conferences/Meetings
...Electronic Mail Network
...Facsimile Machines
...In-House Electronic Publishing

Paperless Accounting Systems

...Interactive Screen Entry of Accounting Data
...Financial Support Software
...Accounting Online to Financial Models
...Budget System Online
...Link to Executive Information System

...Information System Network
...Electronic Training
...Selling Execs Processing Power

(Continued)

BOX 10.2 *(Continued)*

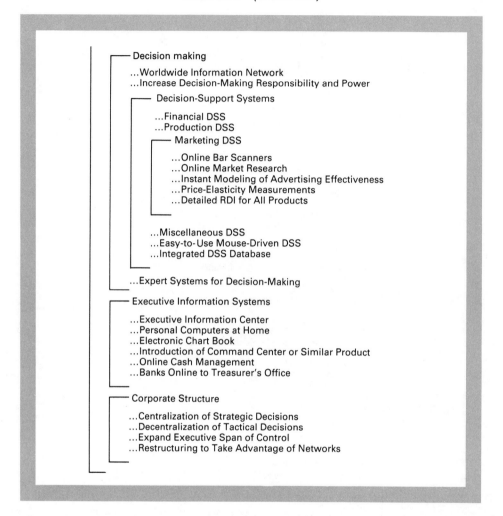

Note: The notation of three dots (...) indicates a line that can be expanded to reveal a greater level of detail.

EFFORT REQUIRED Technology impact analysis can be done fairly quickly and inexpensively. Two analysts who are alert to new technology can complete such a study in three weeks or so. It is often desirable that one of the two is from a consulting firm that has done such studies before. The return on this investment is often very high. It is a form of analysis that every major corporation should do.

The work may start by using existing action diagrams of technology trends and business/management opportunities, such as those in Boxes 10.1 and 10.2. The action diagrams can be added to and edited to meet the needs of the enterprise in question.

The identification of trends, opportunities, and threats can be done in initial brainstorming sessions. These often have five or so participants and a neutral moderator who organizes the session. A typical session lasts for a couple of hours and attempts to produce ideas in an uninhibited fashion. A principle of such a session is that to encourage the accumulation of ideas, no one can be criticized for suggesting an ill-thought-out or impractical idea. The maximum stimulation of inventive discussion about the future is required. The technology impact analysts will digest the ideas after the session, select those that seem appropriate, and add them to their action diagrams. The analysts then generate the matrices that map technology against opportunities and threats.

TIME SCALE   Some of the technologies and opportunities are immediate, some short term, and some longer term. The intersections of the matrices can show this by marking them with a time-scale code:

0 — Immediate.

1 — One year away.

2 — Two years away.

3 — Three years away.

and so on.

PRIORITIES   The opportunities and threats can be ranked on a priority scale:

A — Very critical. Immediate implementation is needed.

B — Critical. Should be implemented with some urgency.

C — Should be implemented with medium priority.

D — Required but with no urgency.

E — Desirable but not absolutely required.

The matrix intersection may thus have both a time-scale indicator and a priority indicator.

MANAGEMENT INTERVIEWS

When a rich set of technology trends, opportunities, and threats has been recorded, the analysts interview appropriate managers, sometimes adding to their lists. They then attempt to determine which of the opportunities and threats are potentially important. The matrices are adjusted and appropriate segments of them printed.

When the analysts are satisfied with their conclusions so far, the results should be presented in senior management meetings. There is usually heated discussion at this stage about the opportunities and threats. The priority codes may be adjusted. Action should be demanded on any items that remain in the top three priority categories. Memos should be created detailing the actions to be taken.

PERIODIC REVIEW

The action diagrams and matrices remain valuable on an ongoing basis. They should be maintained in a computer, and they should be reviewed periodically. When this is done, they usually grow as more technology trends unfold and become better understood, and more ideas occur about corporate opportunities. The information gathered during technology impact analysis is of great value to any corporation wanting to control its destiny in an era of powerful rapidly changing technology.

11 CRITICAL SUCCESS FACTOR ANALYSIS

The computer systems of the past have inundated executives with reports. The typical executive is overwhelmed with too much information and asks: "Why do I have to wade through all these reports and yet I can't find most of the information I need to manage the business well?" Many functional managers have an interest in feeding information to a general manager. The general manager is flooded with reports and yet cannot find the most critical pieces of information that are needed to detect and solve problems. Computerized systems, if not planned well, can have the negative effect of causing an overload of not-very-useful information. This problem is felt by high executives in all industries, and often their frustration level is high.

In spite of this, if you ask executives what information they need, they tend to ask for everything. If you ask what decisions they make, they can provide a daunting list. In practice, there are a small number of pieces of information that are particularly critical to an executive's job and a relatively small number of decisions that are especially important. A technique used with great success in a growing number of corporations analyzes the *critical success factors (CSFs)* of the enterprise and the executives that manage it.

John F. Rockart [1, 2] originally developed the critical success factor approach as a means of understanding the information requirements of a chief executive officer. The approach has subsequently been applied to the enterprise as a whole and has been extended into a broader planning methodology [3]. It has been made the basis of several consulting practices [4] and has achieved major results where it has been used well. Some large consulting firms have made critical success factor analysis an integral part of their strategic information planning methodologies [5], and this is clearly where it belongs.

Rockart defined critical success factors as "those few critical areas where things must go right for the business to flourish" [2]. A corporate president can be asked to identify a handful of factors of paramount importance for the corporation to succeed fully—aspects of running the business that must be done well if overall success is to be achieved. The president can be asked to describe the factors *most* critical for success. Most corporate presidents find this question interesting and relevant, and, after thinking about it, produce a good answer.

> *J. R. Daniel (Subsequently Managing Director of McKinsey & Company):*
>
> In most industries there are usually three to six factors that determine success; these key jobs must be done exceedingly well for a company to be successful. [6]

Once the critical success factors for the enterprise as a whole are determined, a lower-level set of critical success factors can be established for each member of the top management team. What are the critical success factors for the vice-president of marketing, the vice-president of production, the vice-president of information systems, and so on? When these critical success factors are determined, those for the next level can be established. In this way critical, success factors can be found for all the executives, and the motivations of the executives can be related to the achievement of the success described in the critical success factors.

Consultants with much experience in critical success factor analysis have developed interviewing techniques for establishing the most appropriate critical success factors for an enterprise. When a critical success factor is established, *measurements* must be determined so that executives can *monitor* continually whether the success in question is being achieved. Regular reports are needed. A monitoring process should alert managers to slippage below the desirable levels. That which is monitored tends to improve.

An appealing feature of critical success factor analysis is that it can be done quickly with little resources. Two skilled interviewers working for three weeks or so have done a good job of critical success factor analysis in some corporations. It requires three hours or so of time of the executives interviewed. For this relatively low investment, results have been achieved that fundamentally improve the management processes and lead to far more effective information systems.

EFFECTS OF CRITICAL SUCCESS FACTOR ANALYSIS

Critical success factor analysis tends to have two effects on individual executives. First, it helps them focus on those activities that are most important. In writing his classic work *On War* for the German general staff, Baron von Clausewitz stated that the most effective general concentrates his forces on the few significant battles. A less effective general scatters his forces throughout the entire battle area. Similarly, effective executives concentrate their efforts on the critical success factors. Second, it helps them think through their information needs. It helps information system planners to identify critical information and get it to executives who need it, along with appropriate decision-support tools and resources. It helps in the planning and prioritizing of the decision-support systems that must be built.

Good managers, like good generals, have *implicit* critical success factors that they employ, usually subconsciously. Critical success factor analysis makes these implicit critical success factors *explicit*. The interviewing technique turns a spotlight on them, refines them, possibly adds to them, and enables managerial priorities to be set more knowledgeably. Critical success factor analysis is extremely valuable in enabling a corporation to be managed better, independently of its use in building better computer systems. Results from the critical success factor interviews are immediately useful. They can be used long before the requisite information systems can be built. They make human control mechanisms better and cause an enterprise to focus on what is most critical. With them, allocation of resources can be improved, particularly executives' time. But the computer can turn critical success factor analysis into a control mechanism that pervades the whole enterprise and enables business strategy planning to be translated into strategic information planning.

DEFINITIONS

Classical management literature differentiates between a *mission*, a *strategy*, an *objective*, and a *goal*. Critical success factors are different from all these. We will use the following definitions in this book:

- **Mission.** The *mission* of an enterprise is the highest-level statement of objectives. It gives a broad description of the purpose and policy of the organization.

- **Strategy.** A *strategy* in an enterprise is a pattern of policies and plans that specifies how an organization should function over a given period. A strategy may define areas for product development, techniques for responding to competition, means of financing, size of the organization, image that the enterprise will project, and so on.

- **Objective.** An *objective* is a general statement about the direction a firm intends to take in a particular area without stating a specific target to be reached by particular points in time.

- **Goal.** A *goal* is a specific target that is intended to be reached by a given point in time. A goal is thus an operational transform of one or more objectives.

- **Critical Success Factors.** *Critical success factors* are the limited number of areas in which satisfactory results will ensure competitive performance for the individual, department, or organization. Critical success factors are the few key areas where "things must go right" for the business to flourish and the manager's goals to be attained.

The goals of managers are the targets they shoot for. The critical success factors are the factors that most affect their success or failure in the pursuit of these goals. A goal is an overall objective; a critical success factor is what has to be done to achieve that goal. Goals represent *ends;* critical success factors represent *means* to those ends.

The mission-and-purpose statements of an enterprise are often quite different from the critical success factors. The former represent long-range vision or an end point that the corporation wishes to achieve. The goals of an enterprise might include statements such as "growth of 30 percent per year," "increase market share to 40 percent," "excellence of medical care" (in a hospital), and so on. The critical success factors relate to the conduct of current operations and the key areas in which high performance is necessary. They give the measures that are necessary in a control system for top management. They need careful and continuous measurement and management attention if the organization is to be successful.

A critical success factor at one level may become a *goal* at a lower level. For example, a critical success factor at the top level may be *retain top-quality managers.* For the personnel department this becomes a goal, and the critical success factors needed to achieve this goal are established, for example, establish an appraisal scheme to recognize executive talent, establish a scheme to develop executive loyalty, measure the effectiveness of bonus/incentive plan.

In a business, the critical success factors relate to those aspects of the corporation that will ensure competitive performance. They differ greatly from one type of business to another. They differ from one *time* to another. Changes in the external environment can cause changes to the critical success factors. For example, a petroleum crisis can change the critical success factors in the automobile industry. As a small corporation grows, it needs to shift gears and accurately identify new critical success factors.

EXAMPLES OF CRITICAL SUCCESS FACTORS

Box 11.1 gives examples of top-level critical success factors that have been identified for a few industries. Some critical success factors are common to an entire industry; others are unique to particular corporations. Figure 11.1 shows critical success factors that have been identified for the medical clinic industry and shows critical success factors for three particular clinics having different characteristics [7].

Critical success factors vary with the situation of a particular corporation

BOX 11.1   Examples of business critical success factor lists

Automobile Industry

- Fuel economy
- Image
- Efficient dealer organization
- Tight control of manufacturing costs

Software House

- Product innovation
- Quality of sales and user literature
- Worldwide marketing and service
- Ease of use of products

Prepackaged Food Corporation

- Advertising effectiveness
- Good distribution
- Product innovation

Seminar Company

- Obtaining the best speakers
- Identification of topics
- Mailing list size and quality

Microelectronics Company

- Ability to attract and keep the best design staff
- Government R&D support
- Support of field sales force
- Identification of new market needs

Life Insurance Company

- Development of agency management personnel
- Advertising effectiveness
- Productivity of clerical operations

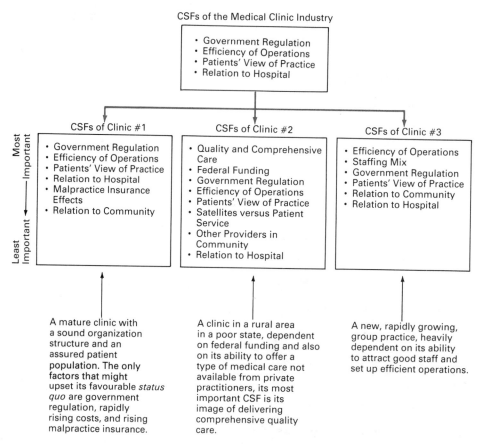

CSFs of the Medical Clinic Industry

- Government Regulation
- Efficiency of Operations
- Patients' View of Practice
- Relation to Hospital

Most Important ←————→ Least Important

CSFs of Clinic #1

- Government Regulation
- Efficiency of Operations
- Patients' View of Practice
- Relation to Hospital
- Malpractice Insurance Effects
- Relation to Community

CSFs of Clinic #2

- Quality and Comprehensive Care
- Federal Funding
- Government Regulation
- Efficiency of Operations
- Patients' View of Practice
- Satellites versus Patient Service
- Other Providers in Community
- Relation to Hospital

CSFs of Clinic #3

- Efficiency of Operations
- Staffing Mix
- Government Regulation
- Patients' View of Practice
- Relation to Community
- Relation to Hospital

A mature clinic with a sound organization structure and an assured patient population. The only factors that might upset its favourable *status quo* are government regulation, rapidly rising costs, and rising malpractice insurance.

A clinic in a rural area in a poor state, dependent on federal funding and also on its ability to offer a type of medical care not available from private practitioners, its most important CSF is its image of delivering comprehensive quality care.

A new, rapidly growing, group practice, heavily dependent on its ability to attract good staff and set up efficient operations.

Figure 11.1 Critical success factors for the medical clinic industry in the 1970s and for three specific clinics studied by Gladys G. Mooradian [7]. Ten years later, malpractice insurance effects had become a major critical success factor, along with controlling costs, which had risen to a much higher level.

within an industry. It might be a new corporation trying to carve a foothold in an established industry. In this case a critical success factor is the creation of products that are perceived by the customers as being of better value, in some way, than those of the established corporations. It may depend on searching for a gap in existing product lines or creating something that adds value to existing product lines.

New critical success factors may have increased importance at certain times. For example, two corporations may merge, and for a period, a critical success factor is the integration of their product lines and sales forces. A problem may arise such as a major product line being made obsolete by competition or a particular product gaining a bad reputation. Recovery from these situations may be a critical success factor. Sometimes new critical success factors arise from external causes, such as a petroleum crisis, a local war removing strategic mineral sources, a new union contract, or the effect of new legislation.

As we mentioned earlier in this chapter, critical success factors are normally established first for the enterprise as a whole or for the chief executive office. They are then developed for the level below that—the major divisions of an enterprise. Figure 11.2 shows critical success factors for a group of chain stores at the top level and at the level of six vice-presidents. Critical success factors can then be developed for managers at the level below this.

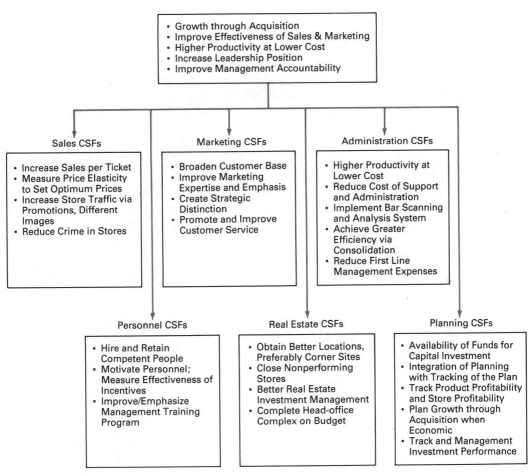

Figure 11.2 The corporate critical success factors and critical success factors at one level down in a chain store operation. Critical success factors can also be established for managers a level below these.

NOT WHAT THE DESIGNER EXPECTED

Often, a chief executive's choice of critical success factors is not what an information system designer would have anticipated. For example, the following is a list of critical success factors that was developed by the president of a major oil company [1]:

1. Organizational decentralization so that diversification can better take place in order to provide a broader earning base for future decades when petroleum supplies diminish

2. Liquidity (to facilitate acquisitions)

3. Relations with government

4. Societal image

5. Success in new venture

An information system designer often has a different view of what information is needed. It is essential therefore that the top management team be involved with the identification of critical success factors using a methodology such as that described in this chapter.

CHARACTERISTICS OF CRITICAL SUCCESS FACTORS

Critical success factors are quite different from "key indicators" that have been used by some earlier information system planners. They are not a standard set of measures that can be applied to all corporations. As we have indicated, they are specific to a *particular* situation at a *particular* time. They have diverse measures. Some are evaluated with soft subjective measures. Some are evaluated through information not currently gathered in an explicit way.

Most critical success factors are *internal,* but some are *external.* Internal critical success factors relate to actions that can be taken within the corporation, such as improving product quality or lowering inventory costs. External critical success factors relate to factors in the outside world, such as company acquisitions or acquiring financing.

Critical success factors can be categorized as those that involve *monitoring* and those that involve *building. Monitoring* critical success factors involve the scrutiny of existing situations, for example, tracking employee morale or monitoring the quantity of defect reports. *Building* critical success factors relate to changing the enterprise or future planning, for example, improving the product mix or setting up franchise operations. Managers who spend most of their time fire-fighting have mostly *monitoring* critical success factors. Managers who are mostly concerned with planning have *building* critical success factors. Most managers have a mix of building and monitoring critical success factors.

Some top-level critical success factors, as we said, are characteristic to an

Figure 11.3   The hierarchical nature of critical success factors.

industry. Rockart quotes four critical success factors shared by all those corporations in the supermarket industry [1].

- Product mix
- Inventory
- Sales promotion
- Pricing

Every supermarket firm must be concerned about these four. Some firms may have critical success factors unique to their particular needs, for example, create marketing distinction or grow through acquisition.

Critical success factors can be thought of as being in a hierarchy. Some relate to an industry as a whole, some to the individual corporation, some to a particular organizational unit, and some to an individual manager (Fig. 11.3).

Rockart lists five sources of critical success factors [2]:

- **The Industry.** Some critical success factors arise from the characteristics of the industry itself.
- **Competitive Strategy or Industry Position.** A corporation may have a particular niche or role within an industry. It may have unique strategies to grow faster than its competition in the industry.
- **Environmental Factors.** Environmental changes occur, such as an increase in interest rates or changes in regulation. The corporation must take advantage of these if possible.
- **Temporal Factors.** These relate to short-term situations, often crises, such as a major accident, bad publicity, cash shortage, executive loss, or loss of a

market segment because of the sudden appearance of competitive products. Critical success factors relating to such crises may be important but short lived.

- **Managerial Position.** Some critical success factors relate to a particular manager. Certain jobs have certain critical success factors associated with them.

MEASURES

It is necessary to measure critical success factors so that progress in achieving them can be tracked. Only very rarely do traditional financial accounting systems provide the required data. Sometimes cost accounting systems provide useful data, but often the need for improved cost accounting is revealed in the critical success factor analysis. A substantial proportion of the data needed cannot be provided as a *byproduct* of conventional information systems. It must be specifically collected from other sources. It may then be stored in specially structured databases. Some of the required data comes from external sources.

Many critical success factors require data from multiple logical files that may be widely dispersed, for example, comparative profitability of products, bid profit margin as a ratio of profit on similar jobs, or risk assessment in contracts by examination of experience with similar customer situations. These types of measures require database systems and high-level database languages that can assemble and manipulate the requisite data.

A small proportion of the critical success factors require subjective assessment rather than being easily quantifiable. Some factors can have only *soft* measures; however usually there is some means of creating numeric measures. Top executives are used to this and spend much time with subjective judgments and measurements. Objective measures can often be found, but it takes considerable thought. Sometimes, considerable discussion is needed of how the factors will be measured. At others times there is too much data, and discussion relates to how the data can be appropriately summarized.

In some cases the discussion of how to measure a critical success factor results in several different measurements. For example, one organization needed to measure its technological reputation with customers. It developed seven possible measures of this. A simple numeric measure was the ratio of bids made to orders received. This had other factors affecting it, such as sales aggressiveness. Most soft measures took the form of the results of person-to-person interviews. Several measures were used to measure the one factor. It was decided to initiate a process of top executives interviewing customers because this was a highly critical success factor.

In the same organization the *morale of key scientists and engineers* was considered a critical success factor because of the importance to the company of these individuals. Measures of this ranged from numeric data such as turnover, absenteeism, and lateness to feedback from informal management discussions with the scientists and engineers. More formal employee assessment interviews could also be used with the manager rating the employee on a morale scale.

Some critical success factors have revealed the need to build new, often small, information systems. Today these can usually be created quickly using existing software and personal computers or possibly nonprocedural database languages running on a mainframe.

STRATEGIC PLANNING TOOL

Ideally, a CASE tool for strategic planning should be used to store the critical success factors. Figure 11.4 shows the data model that might be used to maintain critical success factors in a CASE planning tool.

Each manager who manages an organizational unit typically has from three to seven critical success factors. Whereas a goal may relate to multiple organizational units (and hence to multiple managers), critical success factors are determined for specific managers and their performance in achieving them should be measured.

REPORTING

To track the achievement of critical success factors a reporting system needs to be designed. This involves the design of appropriate databases. Executive information systems for monitoring critical success factors should be developed in prototype form. There is likely to be much evolution of the prototype.

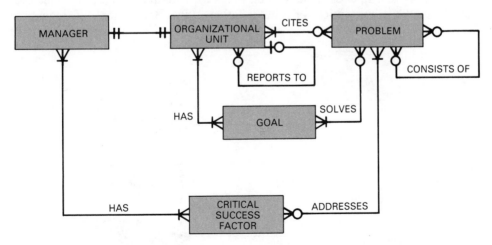

Figure 11.4   An entity-relationship model of goals and critical success factors. (This is the structure of the data model maintained in the encyclopedia of a typical CASE tool.)

| CRITICAL INFORMATION, ASSUMPTIONS, AND DECISIONS | Associated with the development of critical success factors, three lists should be produced: the *critical information set,* the *critical assumption set,* and the *critical decision set.* Figure 11.5 shows the relation- |

ships that exist among critical success factors, critical information, critical assumptions, and critical decisions. These lists are impor- tant input to the building of strategic data models, as shown in Fig. 11.6.

Critical Information

Certain information must be available to track the critical success factors. This information should be modeled as part of the overall entity-relationship model- ing. A list of critical information is created during the critical success factor analysis. Some of this information is internal. Some can be extracted from ex- isting information systems. Some has to be specially developed. Some is infor- mation that exists externally and can be purchased. Some is external information that may be hard to obtain.

Critical Assumptions

Underlying the goals and critical success factors of an enterprise are certain *assumptions.* The validity of these assumptions often changes with time. It is desirable to record the assumptions so that their validity can be discussed. Sometimes, to check the validity of the critical assumptions, certain information is needed. This becomes part of the *critical information set.* Box 11.2 illustrates some typical examples of critical assumptions.

Critical assumptions include such items as assumptions about competitive activities, the future price of oil, inflation, the effectiveness of incentive

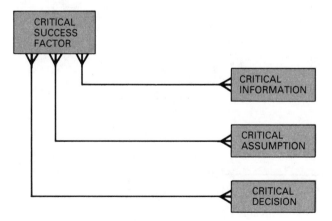

Figure 11.5   An entity-relationship model of critical success factors, critical information, critical assumptions, and critical decisions.

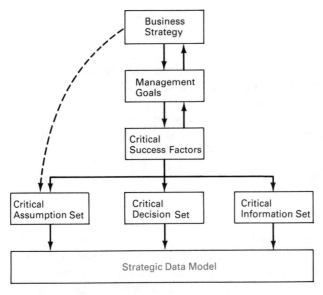

Figure 11.6 The critical assumption set, critical decision set, and critical information set provide inputs to the strategic data model.

BOX 11.2 Examples of critical assumptions that underlie critical success factors

- Acquisition is the primary path to growth for convenience stores.
- Technology will improve productivity by 50 percent over the next three years.
- It will be two years before IBM markets a competing product.
- Quality store managers
  Are detail oriented.
  Work well with others.
  Have high energy.
  Are able to develop people.
  Have good communication skills.
  Meet budgets.
- A 10 percent increase in price will reduce unit sales by 5 percent (this type of assumption should be represented with a price elasticity curve).
- We should grow through acquisition where economically feasible.
- The price of crude oil will rise by $5 in the next year.
- Expansion programs will be funded by cash flow.
- Technology dissemination will cause increased competition from small companies.
- Cash flow is the most significant restriction to growth.
- The defined risk posture is appropriate to the objectives for growth.

schemes, customer reaction to a new product, political factors, social trends, and so on. These change with time. Experience indicates that a key to adapting the critical success factors with time lies in understanding the assumption set that underlies the critical success factors. [3] The critical assumptions need to be analyzed and monitored. A change in the business strategy may cause a change in the critical assumption set that in turn changes the critical success factors. Executive information systems are sometimes designed to help track the critical assumptions. This ability is often *implicit* in the design; it should be made explicitly.

Critical Decisions

Certain *decisions* are particularly critical in the running of an enterprise. When critical success factors are developed, it is desirable to determine what are the particularly critical decisions that must be made. This leads to the building of decision-support systems. In many cases actions can be taken quickly in information centers to provide aids for decision making; in some cases major decision-support system projects are necessary. Box 11.3 lists typical examples of critical decisions.

In some cases top executives take more interest in the critical assumption set than the critical decision set. Much decision making, and the use of decision-support systems, is delegated to lower-level managers or staff. High-level executives may use executive information systems but less commonly use decision-support systems. Decision-support systems are used in great detail lower in the organization. High executives sometimes obtain critical information at the touch of a button, but do not often manipulate the information in a decision-support fashion. The critical *assumptions,* however, are regarded as part of the *judgment* that high executives are paid for.

ONGOING
UPDATING

As we have indicated, critical success factors change with time. New factors become important when competition changes or when external factors change. For example, the decline in oil prices in 1986 dramatically changed the critical success factors of oil companies. For some oil companies ''corporate survival'' became a critical success factor in 1986. Critical success factors may also change somewhat when the management team changes, because different executives have different views of what is critical and take different thrusts against competition.

In the following pages we describe a methodology for developing critical success factors. As with technology impact analysis, Appendix II contains an action diagram that details the procedure for critical success factor analysis. Like all the action diagrams of procedures contained in Appendix II, it should

BOX 11.3   Examples of critical decisions that are associated with critical success factors

- Determine the most profitable new product features.

- Determine priorities between development and acquisition.

- Determine appropriate debt/equity ratio.

- Determine which products should be dropped/replaced.

- Determine allocation between expenditures and debt retirement.

- Determine optimal advertising and promotion expenditure.

- Decide which properties to sell, acquire, or retain.

- Determine balance of entrepreneurial activity and controlled activity.

- Determine areas of maximum competitive advantage.

- Restructure worldwide maintenance competitive advantage.

- Restructure MIS activities on the basis of fourth generation methodologies.

- Determine whether new head office complex should be built.

- Determine lease/purchase ratio for products.

- Should one objective be to have earnings parallel cash flow?

- Adjust rewards/incentives for key personnel.

- Determine maximum acceptable level of project risk.

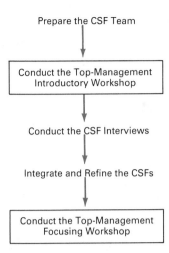

Figure 11.7 A methodology for developing critical success factors. This methodology is shown in more detail in an action diagram in Appendix II.

be adjusted to fit specific circumstances. The main stages in the procedure are shown in Fig. 11.7.

A key part of the methodology for critical success factor analysis is a *top management focusing workshop*. This workshop generates what is often a heated discussion of the enterprise and what is critical. The focusing workshop may be held, not once, but periodically to review the critical success factors and update them as appropriate. Apart from modifications that result from changes in the enterprise and its world, modifications may be made as a result of experience with the critical success factors and their consequent building of executive information systems and decision-support systems.

Reviewing the *critical assumption set* regularly can provide early warning that a change has occurred and the critical success factors need modifying.

CRITICAL SUCCESS FACTOR ANALYSIS TEAM   Analysis and recording of the critical success factors in an enterprise are sometimes done by the team that does the overall information strategy planning. In other cases it is done by a specialized team. Some consultants have considerable expertise and experience in interviewing executives to establish critical success factors. Often the best arrangement is a two-person team in which one member is an external consultant skilled at this process and the other is an internal analyst who will maintain the critical success factor model when the external consultant has gone. The skill of the interviewers is critical. They should have as deep as possible an understanding of the industry, the enterprise, and the jobs of the executives they interview.

The critical success factor team has a unique opportunity to communicate with top management to achieve a better understanding of the corporation and its critical information needs. It must be well prepared for this opportunity. The team should know the industry problems, issues, newsmakers, and its competitive drives. It should understand the corporation well, its industry positioning, its product thrust, its structure, and its politics.

PREPARATION
FOR THE STUDY

In preparing to conduct the critical success factor analysis, the team needs to study the recommended methodology and understand the interviewing techniques that are employed. The team members should make themselves as familiar with the industry as possible, reading appropriate articles in *Forbes, Business Week, Fortune, The Wall Street Journal,* and so on, and perhaps reading market studies of the industry. One or more team members should be selected because of their knowledge of the industry.

The team members should study the enterprise. They can study its annual reports, internal documents, organization charts, and job descriptions. An appropriate CASE tool can be used to facilitate the drawing of an organization chart. At least one member of the team should be familiar with the enterprise as a whole, its politics and top personalities. The strategy, opportunities, environment, and current problems should be discussed in detail among the team members. As part of its own preparation the team should record what it perceives to be the goals, problems, critical success factors, and critical success factor measures for the enterprise. This is done as an exercise prior to the first top management workshop and should not be allowed to bias the collection of goals, problems, critical success factors, and other factors, as stated by management. The team members should spend time with top management, making themselves as familiar as possible with the current strategies, viewpoints, politics, and opportunities.

INTRODUCTORY
WORKSHOP

Before the management interviews begin, an introductory workshop should be conducted with a small top management group. In this workshop the team presents the critical success factor procedure and explains to top management why it is valuable. The team makes top management aware that a rethinking of the enterprise is likely to ensue, not merely the planning of information systems.

In the introductory workshop the goals and major problems of the enterprise are discussed and recorded. A list is established of the managers who should be interviewed in the following weeks. It is extremely important that top management agrees to give full support to the interviewers. Active involvement of a key member of top management should be solicited. A date is then set for the focusing workshop when the results of the critical success factor interviews will be reviewed and debated. This second workshop is very critical.

SETTING UP THE INTERVIEWS A letter is sent to each of the interviewees explaining the nature and purpose of the interviews and indicating the support of top management. A date is set for the interview. The interviews should progress from the lowest-level managers to the highest level. Much information and experience will be gathered in the lowest-level interviews that will help in the higher-level ones. The interviewee is provided with an outline of the interview and some information about the critical success factor technique. A copy of this chapter might be useful for this purpose.

PREPARATION FOR THE INTERVIEW Before conducting a critical success factor interview, the interviewers need to be as thoroughly prepared as possible. They should assume the role of the interviewee. They should list his or her probable goals, problems, critical success factors and critical success factor measures, critical assumptions, critical decisions, and critical information. There may be much discussion of these. This is done as an aid to preparing for the interview and should not be allowed to bias the real interview when it occurs.

Some corporations have elicited the critical success factors of an individual manager in a single interview. Others have used *two* interviews. With the two-interview approach, the first interview is a preliminary one that sets the manager thinking about critical success factors. The second interview, a few days later, is used to record the manager's thoughts and discuss them. We describe the one-interview approach here, which is faster.

Detailed discussion of the critical success factors that are gathered follows in a top management review workshop. Other interviews are needed when the activity moves to the later stage of defining and producing prototypes of information systems that are required for critical success factor reporting. The interview may begin with a general discussion of the interviewee's views of the enterprise. Information may be gathered in this discussion that will help in the other critical success factor interviews. The interviewers should then establish that the manager understands the critical success factor procedure and the purpose of the interviews. They should explain that earlier information systems failed to meet the needs of management and that the critical success factor procedure is intended to establish the most important information needs of management and help in identifying the most useful decision-support systems and executive support systems.

When the manager has had any questions about the purpose of the interview satisfied, the interviewer should ask the manager to describe the mission and role of that manager's organizational unit. The interviewer will sense to what extent the manager ''adds value'' to the information handled by that department. Does the manager perceive the role of the organizational unit to change the enterprise or simply to carry out procedures developed by past managers?

The manager should be asked to identify individual goals and possibly the goals of the organizational unit. The time span of the goals should be noted. Very long-term goals have little effect on the current critical success factors. Goals that should be accomplished within a year or so are those that are important in critical success factor analysis.

Many managers have written goals that were established in a counsel-and-appraisal interview or in a formal management-by-objectives procedure. Managers are often measured on the accomplishment of these goals. The list is recorded by the interviewers, and the interviewers ask the manager if there are any additional goals that are not on the list—goals that are less formally stated. The informal goals can be important input to the critical success factor planning process. Occasionally they are more important than the formally written goals.

Next the manager may be asked what problems the enterprise or that organizational unit has. Sometimes the goals relate to the *solution* of these problems; sometimes the problems *inhibit* the achievement of the goals.

Now the interview focuses on the most important subject—developing the critical success factors. Sometimes the manager may have already done some homework and may produce a written list of critical success factors; sometimes the interviewers have had to elicit them with discussion. Rockart recommends three questions that are helpful for zeroing in on critical success factors [2]:

1. What are those things you see as critical success factors for your job at this time?

2. In what one, two, or three areas would failure to perform hurt you the most? Where would you hate to see something go wrong?

3. If you were isolated from the business for two weeks, with no communication at all, what would you most want to know about the business when you came back?

In practice, good interviewers employ a variety of cross-checking questions as the interview proceeds. They need to be helpful but not put words into the manager's mouth. They should *draw out* critical success factors, not tell the manager what the critical success factors should be. The interviewer must avoid "leading the witness." This is more difficult if the manager has not thought about the concept and hence needs illustrations, anecdotes, and prompting. For this reason managers must be encouraged to do their homework prior to the interview.

The interviewers should check the list in the following ways to ensure that the interview has not had a limited focus:

- Have *external* critical success factors been considered as well as *internal* critical success factors? For example, critical success factors relating to interest rates, the price of oil, competitive thrusts, new technology, and regulatory issues.

- Have *building* critical success factors been considered as well as *monitoring* critical success factors? For example, new product designs, uses of new technology, restructuring the procedures or the organization.

- Have *short-term* factors been considered, such as current crises, accidents, cash shortages, competitive announcements?

- Have critical success factors been considered that relate to
  The position or viewpoint of the manager in the enterprise
  The activities of competition
  The industry in general

- Is the list restricted to critical success factors that have *hard* measures? Some important critical success factors have *soft* measures.

- Is the list limited to critical success factors that are appropriate for computerization? The objective is to elicit *all* information needs.

- Is the same critical success factor stated in multiple ways? Aggregate the critical success factor list to help prevent this redundancy.

- Are past and future concerns also examined? Often a manager gets stuck discussing in multiple ways an area that is of particular concern at the moment.

SETTING PRIORITIES FOR CRITICAL SUCCESS FACTORS

Sometimes additional insight can be obtained by asking which of the critical success factors are most important and prioritizing them. Absolute priorities are not essential and would often be difficult to establish. Prioritization does help to focus on the most important concerns.

DETERMINING MEASURES FOR CRITICAL SUCCESS FACTORS

It is essential to be able to measure a critical success factor. The appropriate measures should be discussed in the interview and sources of data identified to establish the measures. Often multiple measures are used for one critical success factor. The interviewee may indicate measures that are used now but are unusual. It is useful to establish measures at this point because these may be important in the establishment of data models. The final determination of measures may wait until a later stage when prototypes of information systems or decision-support systems are created.

Often the establishment of measures leads to the need for a specific database. For example, in a large chain of convenience stores a critical success factor was the optimal pricing of the goods. A difference in price of a few cents could often make a large difference in sales and profit. Optimal pricing required the measurement of price elasticity. This could be done by installing bar-scanning equipment in the stores and experimenting with price changes to establish how sales of different goods responded to price changes, and so establishing points on a price elasticity curve. This price elasticity data was not measured prior to the establishment of the critical success factor.

COORDINATING THE RESULTS

When the interviews are complete the team should coordinate and refine the results. The critical success factors lower in the hierarchy should relate to the critical success factors higher in the hierarchy. A coordinated listing should be produced and distributed to the managers involved. Further dialog with them may produce more refinements before the top management review workshop.

From the coordinated critical success factors, a critical information set, a critical decision set, and a critical assumption set should be established. Different managers and different organizational units have *some* critical information needs and critical decision sets in common. Decision-support systems should be built that serve the needs for more than one organizational unit. For example, several organizational units may determine that it is critical to hire and retain competent, quality people. A central personnel system concerned with finding, measuring, motivating, and compensating good people may serve many organizational units.

The listing of critical success factors, critical information, critical decisions, and critical assumptions should be circulated prior to holding the top management focusing workshop.

TOP MANAGEMENT FOCUSING WORKSHOP

The workshop in which top management reviews the critical success factors is a particularly important meeting. One vice-president of finance commented about it:

This is the key meeting. The interviews are merely a preliminary, a "softening-up" process in which managers get an initial opportunity to think deeply about the corporation, as well as to develop relationships with the consultants. [8]

It is vital that the participants study the critical success factors, think about them, and make notes prior to this meeting. In this focusing meeting, management should be ready for a vigorous discussion of what can make the company succeed. The debate is often heated. Differing individual perspectives and de-

	Better Real-Estate Management	Relationship with Dealers	Response to Government Regulation	Availability of Funds for Capital Investment	Customer Image of Company	Hire and Retain Quality Competent Managers	Improve Management Accountability	Higher Productivity at Lower Cost	Improve Marketing Skills and Emphasis	Growth through Acquisition
Collins					2	4		5	3	1
Jones			4		2			1		3
Weston		3			1			4		2
Goldberg				2	3			4		1
Zeldin			5		1			3	4	2
McFaddon			4		2			3	1	
Kopley			1				5	4	2	3
Ness	4		5		1			3		2

Numbers Indicate Priority Given by
Executive to CSF

Figure 11.8 Critical success factors obtained by interviewing the top executives are combined to identify corporate critical success factors.

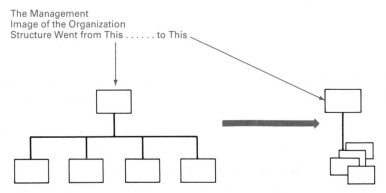

The Management
Image of the Organization
Structure Went from This . . . . . . to This

Figure 11.9 The focusing session enables top management to see the interconnectedness of the critical success factors and critical decisions.

sires emerge. Untangling the differences and focusing on the core needs of the business is an exciting process to most high-level executives.

A matrix like that in Fig. 11.8 can be presented to the participants, showing the critical success factors listed by different executives showing the priorities they placed on them. A matrix displayed using a CASE tool can be adjusted during the workshop with the objective of reaching consensus about the corporate critical success factors. Seeing the critical success factors in black and white is very different from an intuitively-felt set of notions about the business. Sometimes it is a revelation. Some critical success factors are a surprise to some executives. The objective of this meeting is to achieve top management consensus about what are the critical success factors.

Rockart and Crescenzi [8] quote one executive as saying

> During the meeting our concept of our organization structure went from an organization chart that looked like that on the left [of Fig. 11.9] to one that looked like that on the right. This is important. It affected our system's design enormously. More importantly, it has affected the way we manage the business.

IMMEDIATE SYSTEM PROTOTYPING

In general, we advocate a progression through the stages of information strategy planning, business area analysis, and then design and construction. However, when the critical success factors of top management are identified, it is desirable that these should be employed *immediately*. Extraction of the required data for tracking the critical success factors may be done quickly, and this data summarized appropriately and made available in executive information systems.

When *critical decisions* are identified it is desirable to build a decision-support system as quickly as possible. Much decision-making can be supported with relatively simple tools, such as conventional or multidimensional spreadsheet tools running on a personal computer. Some decisions need highly sophisticated systems that take much longer to develop. In many cases a simple tool is a valuable stopgap until a sophisticated system can be built.

When executive information systems or decision-support systems are planned, prototypes should be created quickly. Often much modification of the prototype is done. Iteration through multiple prototypes is common. Prototyping of such systems related to critical success factors should be done quickly. It is clearly urgent to get critical success factor information to executives who need it. Later, as the more comprehensive analysis and design is done, the early, quick-and-dirty, systems will evolve into more elegant integrated systems.

INPUT TO STRATEGIC PLANNING Once an enterprise is being managed with the help of critical success factors, consideration of these factors should be an ongoing input to the top management planning process. They should be reviewed at strategic business planning sessions. In some corporations the top critical success factors are reviewed at board meetings. Board members review them before the meeting and discuss whether they are still appropriate or whether new ones are necessary. Critical success factors, and their associated information systems and decision-support systems, then become a vital part of the ongoing process of management.

REFERENCES

1. John F. Rockart, "Chief Executives Define Their Own Data Needs," *Harvard Business Review,* March–April 1979.

2. Christine V. Bullen and John F. Rockart, *A Primer on Critical Success Factors,* Center for Information Systems Research, Working Paper No. 69, Sloan School of Management, M.I.T., Cambridge, MA, June 1981.

3. John C. Henderson, John F. Rockart, and John G. Sifonis, *A Planning Methodology for Integrating Management Support Systems,* Center for Information Systems Research, Working Paper No. 116, Sloan School for Management, M.I.T., Cambridge, MA, September 1984.

4. Consulting practices include Index Systems, Arthur Young and Company, McKinsey & Company, James Martin Associates.

5. Arthur Young and Company employs an integrated information engineering methodology that includes critical success factor analysis, with software built by KnowledgeWare, Inc., Atlanta, GA.

6. J. Ronald Daniel, "Management Information Crisis," *Harvard Business Review,* September–October 1961.

7. Gladys G. Mooradian, *The Key Variables in Planning and Control in Medical Group Practices,* Masters Thesis, Sloan School in Management, M.I.T., Cambridge, MA, 1976.

8. John F. Rockart and Adam D. Crescenzi, "Engaging Top Management in Information Technology," *Sloan Management Review,* Vol. 25, no. 4 (1984), pp. 3–16.

12 GOAL AND PROBLEM ANALYSIS

An enterprise has certain goals. An important part of the information strategy planning process is *goal and problem analysis,* in which the analysts identify the goals of the enterprise and put them in writing. If everyone understands the goals clearly, the enterprise is more likely to achieve them. One of the most common forms of human folly is to lose sight of the goals. Goals are used in a control mechanism for the enterprise. They set targets, and the success in progressing toward those targets is measured. If part of the enterprise falters in its achievement of goals, this needs to be detected and corrective action taken as quickly as possible.

Goals should be worded so as to express a *precise* course of action. "Be a market leader" is a vague goal. Goals should be precise where possible. Goals should focus on *results*. They should be decomposable into work that has to be done. Goals should be *measurable*. In some cases the measure is binary—either the goal has been achieved or not, for example "Hire a new chief engineer." Where possible, a hard measure should be applicable. In some cases a soft measure has to be used, for example, with "Improve market image of the enterprise." The extent to which such a goal has been met can be established with market research interviewing techniques.

When high-level goals are identified, these can be broken down into lower-level goals that apply to lower-level departments (see Fig. 12.1). Goals are thus associated with the organizational units of an enterprise:

As with other many-with-many associations, this can be represented as a matrix:

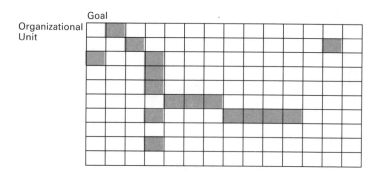

The following repeats the definitions from Chapter 11 for the terms *mission, strategy, objective,* and *goal:*

- **Mission.** The *mission* of an enterprise is the highest-level statement of objectives. It gives a broad description of the purpose and policy of the organization.

- **Strategy.** A *strategy* in an enterprise is a pattern of policies and plans that specifies how an organization should function over a given period. A strategy may define areas for product development, techniques for responding to competition, means of financing, size of the organization, image that the enterprise will project, and so on.

- **Objective.** An *objective* is a general statement about the direction a firm intends to take in a particular area without stating a specific target to be reached by particular points in time.

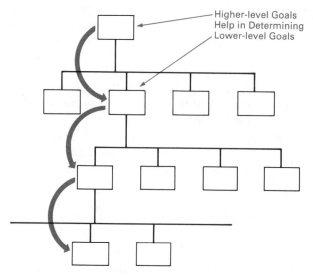

Figure 12.1   Related goals are established throughout the organization chart.

- **Goal.** A *goal* is a specific target that is intended to be reached by a given point in time. A goal is thus an operational transform of one or more objectives.

The following show possible mission, strategy, objective, and goal statements for a regional airline:

- **Mission.** Profitably serve the public by providing air transport in the eastern one-third of the country.
- **Strategy.** Improve our route structure.
- **Objective.** Develop a more profitable route structure.
- **Goal.** Eliminate by year end all routes with an average seat occupancy less than 40 percent.

PLANNING HORIZON

Different goals can have different planning horizons. It is useful to categorize them as *tactical* and *long term*. *Tactical* goals relate to short-term tactics and have a planning horizon of about a year, occasionally two years. *Long-term* goals relate to a planning horizon of five years or so, occasionally longer.

Strategic information planning in business should be done separately for the tactical and the long-term horizon. Tactical planning focuses on questions such as

- What is the target revenue and profit for the next fiscal year?
- What are sales quotas for the next fiscal year?
- What products will be introduced by the end of the next fiscal year?
- How many new sale representatives should be recruited?

Tactical planning creates budgets and quotas and builds these into a financial model for the next fiscal year. It tracks the sales and expenses, compares them to the targets, and makes whatever adjustments are needed to achieve the target revenue and profit.

Long-term planning focuses on questions such as

- What is the target revenue five years from now?
- How will that growth be achieved?
- How should the product line evolve over the next five years?
- What will make us a market leader (or survivor) five years from now and what actions must we take to ensure that?

In general, long-term planning creates a scenario for a time five years or so in the future and asks: "How do we get from here to there?" The question, *"How do we get from here to there?* is the crucial question of strategic planning.

The military asks what battlefield information systems will be needed eight years from now (there will be many) and what networks, data models, and standards will be needed so that they can intercommunicate.

Most corporations build a long-term financial model that attempts to forecast revenues and expenses over a period of five years or more and asks how the products and customer base must evolve to achieve the desired long-term growth.

It is useful to represent goals hierarchically. A high-level goal can be broken down into low-level goals of greater detail. Sometimes a *long-term* goal is regarded as a high-level goal and *tactical* goals are lower-level short-term goals needed to achieve this long-term goal. The enterprise *mission* statement can be regarded as the highest-level objective.

Box 12.1 lists the goals of an electronics manufacturer. There are 4 long-term and 18 tactical goals. At the top of the list is the corporate mission statement. The goals listed in Box 12.1 can be represented hierarchically. An action diagram editor is a useful tool for doing this. Figure 12.2 shows the goals defined in Box 12.1 represented in the form of an action diagram. Figure 12.3 is a matrix mapping the tactical goals of Fig. 12.2 against the organizational units of an enterprise.

The goals of a high-level organizational unit need to relate to the goals of its subordinate organizational units:

Level	Goals
Corporate	Purpose and Mission Corporate Objectives
Division	Division Goals
Department	Department Goals
Work Center	Work Center Goals
Individual	Individual Goals

BOX 12.1   Goals of an electronics company

Goal: Be a Market Leader

Definition: Attain and achieve market leadership position in all phases of the business.
Planning Horizon: PE, Permanent.

Goal: Increase Sales

Definition: Increase sales by 30 percent per year.
Planning Horizon: ST, Strategic.

Goal: Increase Productivity

Definition: Increase manufacture of video display to meet increased sales without sacrificing product quality or increasing costs.
Planning Horizon: ST, Strategic.

Goal: Become Number 2 Workstation Vendor

Definition: Grow to become the second largest workstation vendor.
Planning Horizon: ST, Strategic.

(Continued)

BOX 12.1 *(Continued)*

Goal: *Finance Product Development*

Definition: Generate sufficient funding for complete product development from both internal and external sources.
Planning Horizon: ST, Strategic.

Goal: *Improve Sales Effectiveness*

Definition: Shorten sales cycle to an average of 90 days. Provide better support so personal sales contacts are more productive.
Planning Horizon: TA, Tactical.

Goal: *Identify New Target Markets*

Definition: Locate new uses for video displays. Find customers who can be served by expanding or modifying current plant and equipment.
Planning Horizon: TA, Tactical.

Goal: *Improve Market Penetration*

Definition: Increase market share to 35 percent by making workstations the dominant force in the marketplace.
Planning Horizon: TA, Tactical.

Goal: *Add Distribution Channels*

Definition: Augment internal sales force with external distribution channels. Identify foreign distributors for market expansion in Europe and South America.
Planning Horizon: TA, Tactical.

Goal: *Address Absenteeism Problem*

Definition: Improve working conditions and morale to reduce absenteeism in the plant to 1.5 percent of working days.
Planning Horizon: TA, Tactical.

Goal: *Exploit New Technology*

Definition: Take advantage of advances in new technology to improve product quality and reduce manufacturing costs by 16 percent.
Planning Horizon: TA, Tactical.

BOX 12.1 *(Continued)*

Goal: *Improve Information Systems*

Definition: Reduce database redundancy by data modeling. Standardize choice of DSS software. Increase 4GL penetration to 45 percent of systems.
Planning Horizon: TA, Tactical.

Goal: *Streamline Shop Floor Operations*

Definition: Simulate alternative layouts of equipment and manufacturing operations. Modify so as to maximize efficiency.
Planning Horizon: TA, Tactical.

Goal: *Enhance Employee Training*

Definition: Develop new employee training programs and set up ongoing monitoring to assure prescribed procedures are being followed.
Planning Horizon: TA, Tactical.

Goal: *Enhance Customer Support*

Definition: Maximize repeat purchases by making sure customers are making the best use of our products. Establish ''hot line'' for emergency problems that require immediate response.
Planning Horizon: TA, Tactical.

Goal: *Improve Product Quality*

Definition: Design and build products with less than 0.05 percent defect rate and with extended durability. Products should also be visually attractive.
Planning Horizon: TA, Tactical.

Goal: *Expand Product Line*

Definition: Produce a wider variety of goods using video display to support market expansion strategy.
Planning Horizon: TA, Tactical.

Goal: *Upgrade Product Warranty*

Definition: Extend warranty to two full years.
Planning Horizon: TA, Tactical.

(Continued)

BOX 12.1   *(Continued)*

Goal: *Reduce Inventory Investment*

Definition: Plan manufacturing and raw material delivery schedules so that less than two weeks' inventory are on hand at any time.
Planning Horizon: TA, Tactical.

Goal: *Reduce Receivables to 45 Days*

Definition: Improve collection procedures so that receivables are reduced to an average age of 45 days.
Planning Horizon: TA, Tactical.

Goal: *Improve Cash Flow Management*

Definition: Plan investment strategy of cash-on-hand so that a maximum return is earned, yet ensuring that adequate supplies of cash are available to meet expenses.
Planning Horizon: TA, Tactical.

Goal: *Locate Venture Capital*

Definition: Prepare prospectus to attract investment from venture capitalists to expand research and manufacturing facilities. Contact all known investors in high-tech manufacturing and design.
Planning Horizon: TA, Tactical.

Goal: *Enhance Corporate Image*

Definition: Raise level of general awareness in the marketplace of Paloma Displays. Ensure that the company receives all possible favorable publicity.
Planning Horizon: TA, Tactical

Figure 12.4 shows a top-level goal of a government Department of Education being broken into lower-level goals for its organizational units.

The highest-level objectives must address the questions (stressed by Drucker in his book *Management* [1]) of

- What is our business?
- What will our business be?
- What should our business be?

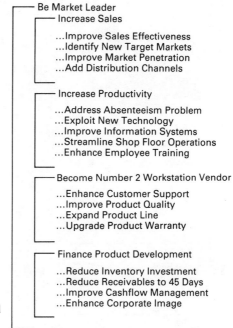

Figure 12.2 A hierarchy of goals represented in the form of an action diagram.

These are questions that top management should ask continuously, to understand the business better and to manage it more effectively. Continual top management questioning about what the business should be is vital.

Of primary importance in defining the business objectives are questions about the customers and their needs:

- Who are the customers?
- Where are they?
- What are their needs?
- What will they buy and why?
- At what price?
- How do we reach them?

An organization's customers are its reasons for existence. A government department's customers might be taxpayers or they might be welfare recipients. An organization that does not translate its customers' needs directly into a hierarchy of goals can develop forms of internal politics that serve no real external purpose. (This is commonplace in practice.)

To meet the needs of the customers, various resources are needed: human resources, production resources, capital, equipment, materials, and so on. Goals must be set that relate to the optimal supply, use, and development of resources.

	Improve Sales Effectiveness	Identify New Target Markets	Improve Market Penetration	Add Distribution Channels	Address Absenteeism Problem	Exploit New Technology	Improve Information Systems	Streamline Shop Floor Operations	Enhance Employee Training	Enhance Customer Support	Improve Product Quality	Expand Product Line	Upgrade Product Warranty	Reduce Inventory Investment	Reduce Receivables to 45 Days	Improve Cashflow Management	Locate Venture Capital	Enhance Corporate Image
	1	2	3	4	5	6	7	8	9	10	11	12	13	14	15	16	17	18
1 Planning																		
2 Accounting															*	*		
3 Cash Management																*		
4 Investments																*		
5 Purchasing														*				
6 Facilities								*										
7 Human Resource Development	*				*				*									
8 MIS																		
9 Legal													*				*	
10 Manufacturing					*						*	*		*				
11 Quality Assurance											*			*				
12 Packaging											*							
13 Materials Management								*						*				
14 Sales Regions	*											*			*			
15 Customer Services																		
16 Customer Education										*								
17 Order Processing	*			*								*						
18 Product Management				*		*						*						
19 Public Relations																	*	*
20 Market Research		*		*		*					*	*						
21 Distribution												*						
22 Engineering						*		*			*	*	*					
23 Research		*				*					*	*						
24 Prototype Manufacture						*		*			*	*						
25 Testing Laboratory						*					*	*	*					

Figure 12.3 A matrix mapping the tactical goals of an enterprise against its organizational units.

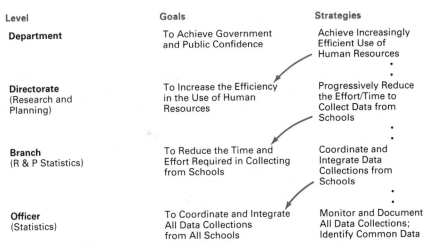

Level	Goals	Strategies
Department	To Achieve Government and Public Confidence	Achieve Increasingly Efficient Use of Human Resources
Directorate (Research and Planning)	To Increase the Efficiency in the Use of Human Resources	Progressively Reduce the Effort/Time to Collect Data from Schools
Branch (R & P Statistics)	To Reduce the Time and Effort Required in Collecting from Schools	Coordinate and Integrate Data Collections from Schools
Officer (Statistics)	To Coordinate and Integrate All Data Collections from All Schools	Monitor and Document All Data Collections; Identify Common Data

Figure 12.4   An example of goal definition and refinement for a department of education.

SOURCES OF GOALS

Goals can be found written in a variety of documents in an organization, for example,

- Business plans
- Information technology plans
- Information plans
- Annual reports
- Executive reports and memos
- Management-by-objectives documentation

During goal and problem analysis, the information strategy planning team should seek out these written sources of goals before conducting interviews with management to elicit their statements of goals. If the enterprise uses management-by-objectives and performs appraisal interviews with managers, the findings of these activities are a particularly fertile source of goals. It is often desirable that managers set their own individual goals and that these should relate to the hierarchy of goals in the enterprise. The goals of the enterprise need to be reassessed periodically.

PROBLEMS

Every enterprise has *problems* that make it more difficult to achieve the *goals* that have been set for the organization. Sometimes a goal relates to the solution of a particular problem.

Problems should be recorded along with goals. When attention is focused on a problem, the problem is more likely to be solved.

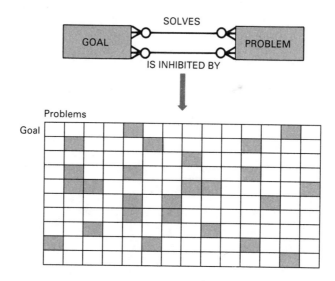

Like goals, problems can be mapped against organizational units:

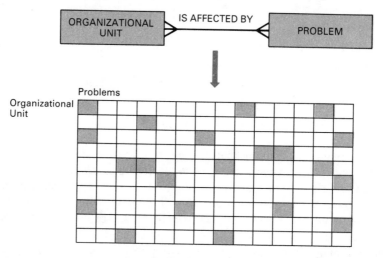

When executives are interviewed during information strategy planning, they should be asked about problems as well as goals. What problems prevent them meeting the goals that are important? What possible solutions are there to the problem? What information systems facilities would help them to meet a particular goal and what would help them deal with a particular problem?

Figure 12.5 gives a list of problems quoted by a production executive. For

INTERVIEWEE: J. McDONALD
ORGANIZATIONAL UNIT: PRODUCTION
INTERVIEWED BY: KEN WINTER
DATE: 6.6.88

PROBLEM	SOLUTION	CRITICALITY RATING	INHIBITS GOAL:	CAUSED BY PROCESS:	IMPACTS PROCESS	REQUIRES ENTITY/SYSTEM
Lack of effective production planning impairs efficiency	Better production planning system	5	• Reduce manufac-turing cost per item • Reduce inventory investment	• Plan production • Shop floor control		Better production planning system
Smaller, more frequent orders; Higher costs of handling; Smaller batches	Order trend analysis; Better prediction; Better system for batching small orders; Longer lead times	4	• Reduce inventory investment • Reduce manufacturing cost per item		• Plan production • Customer relations	• Orders • Order forecasts
Inability to look at enough alternatives for shop floor layout	Shop floor simulation	4	• Reduce manufac-turing cost per item • Reduce inventory investment	• Plan production		System for simulating shop floor operation
Lack of ability to identify, promote and retain top quality people	• Better information on personnel resources • Better incentive schemes • Improve morale	3	• High efficiency production	• Personnel compensation		• Measurement of morale • Rating of production personnel
Lack of "what-if" capability on cost sheets	Online cost-sheet analysis	3	• Reduce manufacturing cost per item			Spread sheet for "what-if" cost estimates

Figure 12.5 A form used in executive interviews to document problems and solutions.

each problem, it lists the possible solutions to the problem, the criticality of solving the problem, the processes involved, and the system or information requirements.

CRITICALITY RANKING

Both goals and problems should be given a criticality ranking. A scale of five is appropriate for this:

5 — Critical to the operation of the business, for example, legal compliance. Must be performed with rigid timetable.

4 — Critical to the undisrupted operation of the business, for example, payroll.

3 — Required to support the business, for example, management and financial reports.

2 — Required to support the business; however, the importance and timetable for the activity is lower than 3, for example, regular scheduled reports.

1 — Desirable, but not absolutely required to support the business.

EXECUTIVE INTERVIEWS

The heart of goal and problem analysis is interviews with key executives, to understand their perspectives about the business, their information needs, and the problems they have. The interviews should validate the goals of the enterprise and the matrices that model the enterprise. After each interview the information collected should be coordinated and analyzed, ideally with the help of CASE technology.

The executives interviewed will normally be no more than two levels below the president of the company. They will be responsible for the major functions of the enterprise; that is, director of finance, manager of production planning, purchasing manager, director of marketing. In a typical study about 20 such interviews are conducted, although the number varies greatly with the size and requirements of the business. Typically an interview takes two to four hours, and only two are scheduled per day.

The executive sponsor of the study normally helps to determine the list of executives who are interviewed. Some may be interviewed for political reasons. Executives omitted in the interviews could be resentful and oppose the conclusions of the study. Higher-level executives should usually be interviewed last because the interviewers' techniques improve with practice and because doubts or suspicions about the results of earlier interviews can be resolved by questioning top management.

An introductory meeting with all the interviewees should be held before the interviewing begins. At this meeting the executives are introduced to the concepts of the matrices and diagrams used and are given relevant lists of processes, definitions of goals, and matrices that they can examine and validate. They are asked to think about their goals and problems in preparation for the interview. They are asked to think about what systems or information could help to solve their problems.

The interviews for validating the overview model of the enterprise may also validate the goals and problems. Combining these interviews lessens the executive time involved and helps to integrate the overall results.

The purposes of the interviews are the following:

1. To validate the overall model of the enterprise that has been created.
2. To agree on the goals of each organizational unit.
3. To determine current problems.
4. To discuss current problems.
5. To determine information needed by individual executives and to place a value on each piece of information.
6. To determine and prioritize the need for future systems.
7. To gain executive rapport and involvement.

BOX 12.2 Typical interview questions for goal and problem analysis

1. What are your responsibilities? Are they different from those indicated on the organization chart?

2. What are the basic goals of your area?

3. What are the three greatest problems you have had in meeting these goals? (Not only current problems but problems of the recent past.)

4. What has prevented you from solving them?

5. What is needed to solve them?

6. What value would better information have in these areas (in person-hours saved, dollars saved, better opportunities, etc.)?

7. In what other areas could the greatest improvements be realized, given better information support?

8. What would be the value of these improvements?

9. What costs may be incurred by inaccurate or untimely information?

10. What is the most useful information you receive? (The best aspects of current systems must be retained.)

11. What would you most like to receive?

12. How would you rate your current information support with respect to types of information, timeliness, accuracy, adequacy, cost, consistency, ease of use, or clarity of presentation?

13. How are you measured?

14. How do you measure your subordinates?

15. What other kinds of measurement are you expected to make?

16. What kinds of decisions are you expected to make? What computer aids might help in your decision making?

17. What major changes are expected in your area in the next year? Next two, four, or six years?

18. What do you expect, and what would you like, to result from this study?

19. Any additional views or comments? (Often a good way to terminate an interview.)

Typical questions that might be asked in executive interviews are listed in Box 12.2. Wherever appropriate the answers to the questions should be quantified, expressed in value ranges, or broken down into items that can be quantified. The interviewer should use a standard form for recording the information from each interview. The form in Fig. 12.5 is an example. If possible, the information collected from the interviews should be digested, structured, and entered into a computer using a CASE tool.

In some cases the problems expressed in the interviews are *perceived* ones that may or may not be *real* ones. Perceived problems are traced back to root causes and forwarded to quantifiable effects, if possible. As far as possible, *real* problems should be the ones that are recorded. Each executive is given a copy of what *is* recorded related to his or her interview or area and is asked to confirm it.

CATEGORIZATION OF PROBLEMS

Recorded problems can be categorized as follows:

A. Problems that do not affect information systems. These are given to the executive who sponsored the study.

B. Problems related to *current* information systems.

C. Problems related to *planned* information systems.

D. Problems that could be aided by information systems that are *neither in existence nor, at present, planned*.

A code for this categorization can be recorded with the problem description.

LINK TO SYSTEMS AND ENTITIES

Goals and problems should be associated with systems and entities, where relevant. Matrices can show the relationships of goals and problems to relevant systems and entities. Figure 12.6 is a matrix mapping the tactical goals listed in Fig. 12.2 with the entities of an enterprise.

It is often the case that the information needed to help achieve a goal or solve a problem *already exists* in the databases of the enterprise, but that it is not being put to use. The matrix analysis often shows that it is desirable to extract the relevant information and make it available to managers in spreadsheets, decision-support systems, or executive information systems.

Appendix II contains an action diagram that documents the overall procedure that should be followed in performing an analysis of goals and problems.

	1	2	3	4	5	6	7	8	9	10	11	12	13	14	15	16	17	18
	Improve Sales Effectiveness	Identify New Target Markets	Improve Market Penetration	Add Distribution Channels	Address Absenteeism Problem	Exploit New Technology	Improve Information Systems	Streamline Shop Floor Operations	Enhance Employee Training	Enhance Customer Support	Improve Product Quality	Expand Product Line	Upgrade Product Warranty	Reduce Inventory Investments	Reduce Receivables to 45 Days	Improve Cashflow Management	Locate Venture Capital	Enhance Corporate Image
1 Employee	*				*			*	*	*								*
2 Contract Employee																		*
3 Applicant																		
4 HR Compensation Regs, Plans, etc.																*		*
5 HR Benefits Regs & Plans					*				*									
6 HR Staffing Requirements & Plans					*			*										*
7 Job Requisition																		
8 Stockholder																		
9 Boardmember																		
10 Misc. Contacts/VIPs																		
11 Financial Plans																	*	
12 Accounting Regs, Practices																*	*	
13 Ledger Accounts																*	*	
14 Customer Purchase Orders/ Invoice	*		*					*		*		*		*	*	*		
15 Customer Payments															*	*		
16 Other Income															*	*		
17 Company Purchase Orders														*		*		
19 Company Bills																*		
19 Company Checks/ Payments																*		
20 Stocks & Bonds																*		
21 Loans																*		
22 Bond Accounts																*		
23 Product Plans		*				*											*	
24 Production Procedures		*	*			*		*	*		*		*					
35 Principles of Terminology		*				*		*	*		*	*						
26 Raw Materials														*				
27 Utilities																		
28 Supplies														*				
29 Products	*	*	*	*		*		*	*	*	*	*	*	*			*	*
30 By-Products																		
31 Bill of Materials						*		*	*	*	*	*	*	*				
32 Work in Progress								*	*		*			*		*		
33 Facility Plans	*		*															*
34 Facility Procedures								*	*		*							
35 Facility Standards									*		*							
36 Land																		
37 Sites								*	*									
38 Buildings								*	*									
39 Vehicles								*	*					*				
40 Equipment						*		*	*					*				
41 Tools								*	*		*							
42 Furniture & Fixtures																		
43 Business Plans, Proposals	*	*	*			*											*	
44 Organizational Units	*							*	*	*						*	*	*
45 Committees & ???????																		
46 Vendor		*		*							*		*			*	*	
47 Vendor Contracts				*							*	*	*			*		
48 Customer	*	*	*								*		*			*	*	*
49 Customer Contracts	*	*	*								*				*			
50 Market Profiles	*	*	*	*		*						*	*					*
51 Competitors	*	*	*	*		*						*	*					*
52 Unions					*													
53 Governments																		
54 Technical & Educational Groups						*												
55 Financial Institutions																*	*	*

Figure 12.6 A matrix mapping tactical goals against entities used in monitoring those goals.

PERIODIC REEXAMINATION The goals and problems of an enterprise need to be reexamined periodically. An overall review should be done once a year to help ensure that information systems are evolving in an appropriate fashion.

Counsel-and-appraisal interviews should be conducted with all managers periodically as part of the management-by-objectives process. A purpose of these interviews is to reestablish the goals of individual managers and to track their progress in meeting these goals. The compensation and other incentives of the managers should relate to their success in meeting the agreed-on goals. Some organizations conduct management-by-objectives interviews once a year, some once every six months, and some once every three months. At this time the goals and problems that have been identified by the analysis of goals-and-problems process should be examined and updated.

If a CASE tool is used to support the information strategy planning process, the goals and problems that were identified for the department in question could be easily summarized and printed inspection and any anomalies noted. Similarly, at business planning meetings, the information concerning the area being discussed could be printed for review.

REFERENCE

1. Peter F. Drucker, *Management* (London: Heinemann, 1974).

13

BUSINESS AREA IDENTIFICATION

After the analyses described in Chapters 10, 11, and 12 have been completed, the information gathered generally causes changes to be made in the entity-relationship diagram that was created during enterprise modeling. In many enterprises, the completed entity-relationship diagram will contain 100 to 400 entities. Since each entity will eventually be described by 8 to 40 attributes, the overall entity-relationship model is typically too large to be implemented in the form of a single database. The design job would be too complex to complete in a reasonable amount of time. Thus, the next step in information strategy planning is to decide how to identify individual business areas. These business areas become the subjects of later business area analysis studies.

THE ENTITY/ FUNCTION MATRIX The first step in identifying business areas is to take the entities and functions that were identified during entity-relationship modeling and transfer them to a matrix diagram that maps functions against entities. An entity-function matrix is shown in Fig. 13.1. The analyst fills in the intersections of this diagram to indicate which functions create, read, update, and delete each entity. The codes C, R, U, and D are entered, as appropriate, at the intersections:

- C — Create
- R — Read
- U — Update
- D — Delete

The analyst should be asking at this stage what entities are used in conjunction with each function. In the early stages of the analysis the analyst usu-

Data Subjects:	Financial Planning	Accounting	Financial Control	Staff Organizations	Training	HR Programs	Production Planning	Research and Development	Purchasing	Production	Product Planning	Marketing	Order Processing	Business Management	Vendor Relations
Employees	R	R		CRUD	RU	R							R		
HR Plans, Procedures, Regs				CRUD	R	CRUD	R				R			R	
Financial Plans, Procedures, Reg	CRUD	RU	CRUD	R			R				R			R	
Financial Income	R	CRUD	R								R			R	
Financial Outflow	R	CRUD	R											R	
Financial Investments	R	CRUD	CRUD											R	
Product Plans, Procedures, Regs	R			R	R		R	R			CRUD	R		R	
Product Materials		R					R	CRUD	RU	RU		R			
Finished Products		R					R	CRUD		RU	R	R	RU		
Facility Plans, Procedures, Regs	R			R			R	R		R	R			CRUD	
Company Locations		R		R	R				R	R				CRUD	R
Equipment		R					RU	CRUD		R	R			R	
Org. Plans, Procedures, Regs	R	R	R	CRUD	R						R			CRUD	
Vendors		R							R					R	CRUD
Customers	R	R									R	R	CRUD	R	

Figure 13.1 A matrix mapping functions against data subjects.

ally discovers entities not yet on the list. These are then added to the entity-relationship diagram and function decomposition diagrams and are then added to the matrix. Again a CASE tool is a great help, as new diagrams can be automatically generated each time new information is added.

The matrix diagram can automatically highlight problems. For example, it is easy to spot an entity that is not created by any function or a function that does not use any entity. The matrix diagram can also highlight situations that should be examined because of potential problems, for example, an entity that is apparently created by more than one function.

VALIDATING THE MATRIX

The items on the matrix can be grouped together in a variety of ways. The analyst uses the matrix to validate the design and check its completeness. Appropriate CASE tools allow rows and columns to be resequenced in a variety of ways to help in the validation.

Functions can be originally sequenced in accordance with the functional decomposition chart, in which functions are grouped that have the same parent. Using CASE tools, the analyst can highlight a function or a group of functions and ask that the associated entities be displayed together. The group is then checked for completeness. Similarly, the analyst can highlight an entity or related group of entities and ask that the associated functions be displayed together. The analyst can highlight a related group of entities on the entity-relationship diagram and see this grouping on the matrix with their associated functions.

The entity-relationship diagram, function decomposition diagram, and entity-function matrix form an interlinked set of diagrams that when used together enable a person to check the completeness and validity of the analysis. They enable the analysis to be discussed with management.

OTHER MATRICES

Two other matrices may be created and manipulated with a similar CASE tool. The organization chart can be mapped against the functions or the entities. The analyst can map functions against the departments on the organization chart, again checking for completeness and validity. Entities can be mapped against departments. The *create, read, update,* and *delete* codes can be automatically transferred from the function/entity matrix to the department/entity matrix. The analyst can gain an understanding of the extent to which departments share the use of data or are in conflict in ownership of data or in the right to update it. When top management examines the mapping of the organization chart against the functions or entities, they sometimes become persuaded that the organization chart needs modifying.

In some strategic planning studies the executives who are interviewed are themselves listed on a matrix like the one in Fig. 8.8. If a function/entity matrix exists, the information in an executive/function matrix can be converted into a matrix mapping the executives against the data they are involved with. The executives in question can assist in validating the analysis.

CLUSTERING THE MATRIX

A function/entity matrix should be clustered to show what functions and data fit naturally together. These groupings form the basis for identifying *business areas* that will be examined in more detail during business area analysis. The groupings may form the basis of new information systems and help determine what functions a specific system will perform and what data it will use.

Two types of computer algorithm can be used to cluster a function/entity matrix. The one we examine in this chapter is called *life-cycle clustering*. To perform life-cycle clustering, we prepare a list of functions that are arranged in the sequence of a natural life cycle and then cluster the entities that are created by each function. In many cases, this simple form of clustering is all that is necessary to identify business areas.

In Chapter 14, we examine a procedure called entity-activity analysis. Entity-activity analysis uses a more detailed form of clustering called *affinity anal-*

ysis clustering. Affinity analysis clustering can be used to identify subject data-bases, which can help to refine the business area groupings that are identified using the techniques of this chapter.

Fig. 13.2 shows another function/entity matrix. High-level groupings of entities are shown, sometimes referred to as *data subjects* or simply *subjects.* In performing life-cycle clustering, the functions are listed *in the sequence of the life cycle of the product,* first planning the business, then obtaining the financing, then undertaking the market study, and so on, until finally the product is

Data Subjects:

Functions:	Customer	Budget	Financial	Vendor	Procurements	Materials Inventory	Fin. Goods Inventory	Orders	Costs	Sales	Sales Territory	Payments	Planning	Employee	Salaries	Facilities	Work in Progress	Machine Load	Open Requirements	Shop Floor Routings	Product	Product Design	Parts Master	Bill of Materials
Market Analysis	R									R	R		R								R			
Product Range Review											R		R											
Sales Forecasting	R	C								R	R		C								R			
Financial Planning	R								R				C											
Capital Acquisition	R	C											C											
Funds Management	R	R																						
Product Design													R								C	C	C	
Product Pricing	R									R											C			
Product Spec. Maint.																					R		C	C
Materials Requirements				R														C			R		R	R
Purchasing				C	C																R		R	
Receiving				R	R	R															R		R	
Inventory Control						C											R							
Quality Control					C																			
Capacity Planning				R													R	C	R	R				
Plant Scheduling				R													R	C	R	R	R			
Workflow Layout																	C		C	R				
Materials Control				R													R			R				R
Sizing and Cutting																	R	C	R					R
Machine Operations																	R	C						
Territory Management	C									R	R													
Selling										C	C													
Sales Administration								R			R													
Customer Relations	R							R		R														
Finished Stock Control							C										R				R			
Order Servicing	R							C													R			
Packing								R													R			
Shipping																					R			
Creditors & Debtors	R			R								R												
Cash Flow	R			R	R			R	R			R			R	R								
Payroll													C	R	R									
Post Accounting					R				C				C											R
Budget Planning	C	R								R	R		R			R								
Profitability Analysis										R	R													
Personnel Planning			R											C	C									
Recruiting			R											R	R									
Compensation Policy			R											R	R									

Figure 13.2 A matrix mapping functions against data subjects.

delivered; then the accounting is completed. The personnel function is not directly related to the product life cycle, so it is listed last.

To cluster the items in Fig. 13.2, we change the sequence of the entities. A ''C'' in Fig. 13.2 indicates that a given function *creates* or *updates* a given entity. An ''R'' indicates that it *reads* but does not modify that entity. The

Data Subjects:

Functions:	Planning	Budget	Financial	Product	Product Design	Parts Master	Bill of Materials	Open Requirements	Vendor	Procurements	Materials Inventory	Machine Load	Work in Progress	Facilities	Shop Floor Routines	Customer	Sales	Sales Territory	Fin. Goods Inventory	Orders	Payments	Cost	Employee	Salaries
Market Analysis	R			R												R	R	R						
Product Range Review	R																				R			
Sales Forecasting	C	C		R												R	R	R						
Financial Planning	C	R																			R			
Capital Acquisition	R	R	C																					
Funds Management		R	R																					
Product Design	R				C	C	C																	
Product Pricing		R		C																	R			
Product Spec. Maint.				R		C	C																	
Materials Requirements				R		R	R	C	R															
Purchasing				R		R			C	C														
Receiving				R		R			R	R	R													
Inventory Control											C		R											
Quality Control										C														
Capacity Planning							R	R				C		R	R									
Plant Scheduling				R								R	C	R	R									
Workflow Layout				R										C	C									
Materials Control				R		R		R					R											
Sizing and Cutting				R		R					R		C											
Machine Operations											R		C											
Territory Management																C		R		R				
Selling																	C	C						
Sales Administration																		R		R				
Customer Relations																R	R			R				
Finished Stock Control				R									R						C					
Order Servicing				R															R	C				
Packing				R																R				
Shipping				R															R					
Creditors & Debtors									R										R		R			
Cash Flow									R	R			R						R	R	R	R		R
Payroll																					C		R	R
Cost Accounting							R			R											C	C		
Budget Planning	R	C	R										R							R		R		
Profitability Analysis				R																R		R		
Personnel Planning				R																			C	C
Recruiting																							R	R
Compensation Policy				R																			R	R

Figure 13.3   The entity that is created or updated by the first function is moved to the left. Then the entity created or updated by the second function is moved to the left and so on. The ''C's'' are now arranged on a top-left-to-bottom-right diagonal.

entity that is created or updated by the first function is moved to the left. Then the entity (if any) created or updated by the second function is moved to the left. This continues for all entities. The resulting matrix, shown in Fig. 13.3, has its "C's" arranged on a top-left-to-bottom-right diagonal.

The functions and data can now be grouped into major system areas by boxing the groupings as shown in Fig. 13.4. The analyst may examine the

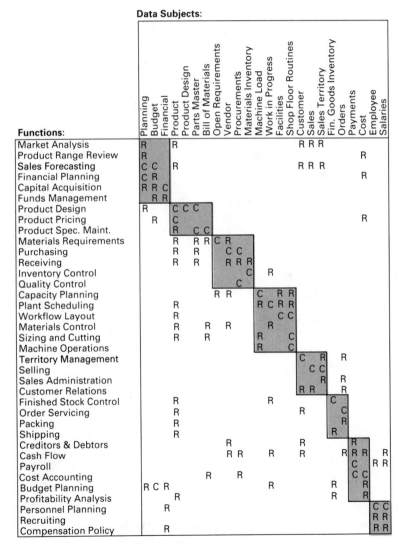

Figure 13.4 Functions and data subjects are clustered into natural groupings.

groupings that result, again endeavoring to validate the functions and entities. The boxes represent logical information subsystem groupings with responsibility for creating and maintaining the various classes of data. A variety of subjective considerations may cause the analyst to adjust the groupings. Groupings such as those in Fig. 13.4 identify the business areas of the enterprise and also the various subject databases that those business areas require.

In Fig. 13.5 names are given to the clusters of functions. When a use of

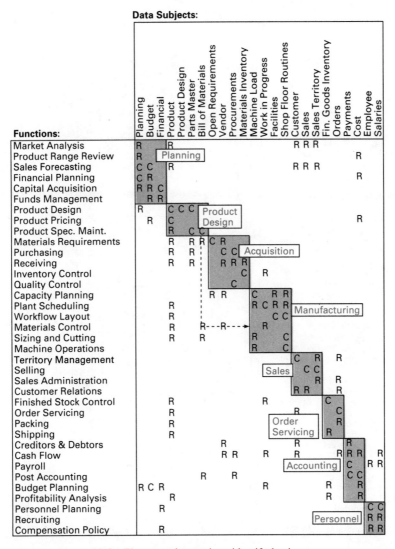

Figure 13.5   The natural groupings identify business areas.

data falls outside any box in Fig. 13.5, the functions in the box must access a database elsewhere, or else data must flow from one subsystem to another. The dashed line in Fig. 13.5 illustrates this. The *materials control* function uses *bill of materials* data. This data may be passed from the *product design* subsystem to the *manufacturing* subsystem. Many such data flows could be drawn among the subsystems of Fig. 13.5 as shown in Fig. 13.6.

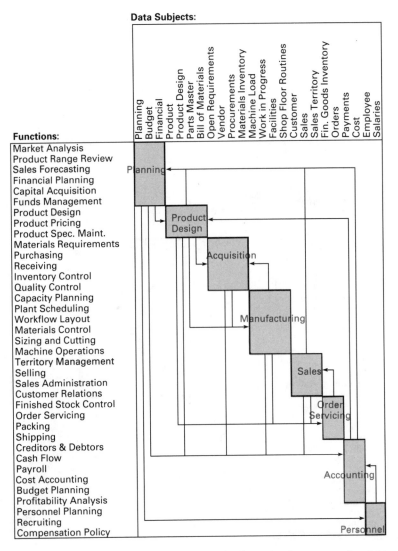

Figure 13.6 Arrows are added to show the dependencies among the eight subsystems.

BUSINESS AREAS   A business area is a naturally cohesive grouping of business functions and data that forms the basis for business area analysis. The clusters discussed in this chapter can be adjusted by hand to meet a variety of constraints.

A business area should be

- One with clear-cut definable boundaries.
- Small enough that business area analysis can proceed quickly.
- Large enough to take advantage of shared databases in a natural coherent way.
- Nonoverlapping with other business areas (i.e., not sharing business functions).
- Generally not updated by other business areas, although some data will be passed among business areas.

BUSINESS SYSTEMS   A business area contains several business systems. A business system also consists of a cluster of naturally cohesive entity-types and processes. Natural business systems may be identified at the same time that business areas are determined. The boundaries of a natural business system will be determined with more precision when business area analysis is done. A natural business system should not span two business areas.

We can thus have two clusterings of the business function/entity–type matrix: one into natural business systems and one into business areas ready for business area analysis.

DEPENDENCIES AMONG FUNCTIONS   The functions in an enterprise are highly interdependent. One function uses data that is generated by other functions. Dependencies among functions can be drawn on a *dependency diagram*. A dependency diagram uses round-cornered boxes to show functions (or processes). A dependency between two functions is drawn as a line with an arrow connecting the two boxes. The following diagram means that function B is dependent on function A:

If function A does not take place, then function B cannot take place. The most common reason for the dependency is that function A generates or updates data which is required by function B. The data may pass directly from function

A to function B, or function A may update database records that are used by function B.

Some corporations doing information strategy planning draw the dependencies among functions; others do not. Process dependency diagrams are an essential part of business area analysis, but they are not always necessary to achieve the objectives of information strategy planning. The essential information needs of an enterprise can be determined without drawing dependency diagrams. However, function dependency diagrams can clarify the overview model of the enterprise.

An entity/function matrix such as Fig. 13.5 could be *automatically* converted into a dependency diagram showing the dependencies among the eight subsystems on the diagram. Fig. 13.6 shows the dependencies.

THINKING ABOUT THE CORPORATE STRUCTURE

In most corporations, entities and business functions have never been charted. When they are listed and related to the data they use, it is usually clear that much duplication exists. Each area of an enterprise tends to expand its activities without knowledge of similar activities taking place in other areas. Each department tends to create its own paperwork. This does not matter much if the paperwork is processed manually. However, if it is processed by computer, the proliferation of separately designed paperwork is harmful because it greatly increases the cost of programming and maintenance.

When information strategy planning lists the entities and business functions, it should minimize the duplication. Charts mapping entities against functions that use those entities reveal duplication in functions and often suggest desirable ways of reorganizing business functions. Proper application of information strategy planning and business area analysis has led to substantial reusable designs and reusable code in organizations. This can greatly reduce the costs of programming and maintenance.

A computerized enterprise ought to have different procedures from an enterprise with manual paperwork. A corporation with workstations on all knowledge workers' desks, connected by a corporatewide network to databases, ought to have different procedures from a corporation with batch processing. The entry of data into a workstation replaces the need to create multiple copies of forms that flow among locations. Information becomes instantly available, and procedures should be changed to take advantage of this. In some enterprises the overview modeling began as a technique for examining *existing* procedures and evolved into a technique for examining what procedures *ought* to be. The following quotation from interviews about the processes are typical of what is discovered:

First, we found that the existing procedures were horrifyingly redundant. Every O and M guy in the business had invented his own bits of paper. You had numerous different forms where one computerized form would suffice. But, unfortunately, each different department had its own different structured analyst who had cast the redundant methods into different COBOL programs. These, collectively, had become a maintenance nightmare.

Second, we found that it was more than just redundant paperwork. The procedures and the flow of work had anomalies, sometimes weird, expensive anomalies. For the last 20 years new procedures have kept springing up like mushrooms in the night. In some cases management had a vague sense that the anomalies were there, but they could only comprehend trees not the forest.

Third—and it took months before we dared to express this heresy—the management structure itself was wrong. It needed a thorough reorganization of the departments and even divisions in order to get tight control and high administrative productivity. This perception could only come through a functional analysis of the entire organization.

Senior functional management said they could not afford the time to participate in the entity analysis, so they gave me their senior clerks. A very senior, senior clerk, who gloried in the title "provider," learned to map data and normalize it.

One day he asked me to talk with him and the planning manager because he had something important to say. He went in and said to the planning manager, "Our OPAS meeting is wrong!"

Now OPAS is the *holy of holies* in this company. In the head office every Monday morning the priesthood gathers—the senior functional managers who decide *what* should be *where* in the three plants, in *what proportion* with *what priorities* and *what yield*.

This senior clerk could now see that the output of the cold reduction mill becomes feed to the slitting mill, the output of that went into the next process, and so on, and the OPAS decisions near the head of this were screwing up export orders about 13 stages down the track.

He grabbed the planning manager, and the planning manager wasn't even prepared to listen. But he wove the argument and the net and caught the manager within it. There was a draft of cold air of "Why's?" which blew all the way up to the OPAS meeting. They are questioning head office moves, on the one hand, and incentives, on the other, and how export orders affect the planning.

All of this happened because a senior clerk saw that he had a funny thing in his relational map. When he traced it through, it shouldn't have been there.

They are making sure *that* senior clerk doesn't annoy that particular
functional manager any more. They've promoted him for the first time in 20
years. He's not a "provider" any more; he's a senior production planner,
which effectively removes him from harm's way.

In many enterprises there needs to be basic questioning about whether the
current organization chart enables the essential processes to be carried out in the
most efficient way. *Overview modeling can therefore move out of the realm of
information systems and into the realm of business management thinking about
corporate reorganization.* In some cases *major* reorganization has resulted from
an information strategy planning study.

14 ENTITY-ACTIVITY ANALYSIS

In most cases, the techniques of Chapter 13 are all that are necessary to identify the business areas that become the subjects of business area analysis. Business area analysis then identifies the subject databases that are required by each business area. However, it is often useful to perform a more detailed analysis during information strategy planning to create a finer-resolution chart of where the enterprise uses data.

ACTIVITIES AND ENTITIES
Figure 8.6 showed how business functions can be decomposed into processes. We saw there that each of the processes constitutes an *activity* that must be performed in running the business. A typical enterprise might have 10 to 30 functional areas and 100 to 300 processes. In the coarse-resolution planning that we examined in Chapter 13, the business functions are mapped against broad data subjects. In the fine-resolution planning that we describe in this chapter, each business function is decomposed into activities and the activities are mapped against entities.

To carry out the fine-resolution planning of entity-activity analysis, the analyst makes an initial attempt at identifying individual business activities and then maps them against entities. This step is normally performed during business area analysis for a particular business area. However, it is sometimes appropriate to identify an initial set of activities during information strategy planning. These initial activities are then further analyzed during business area analysis.

An initial entity-activity analysis requires more work than the process described in Chapter 13, but in the experience observed, this does not seem to take much longer, *as long as computerized tools are used to support the process*. The clustering described in Chapter 13 could be done manually with pencil and paper, although the work would be tedious and error-prone. The more detailed analysis described in this chapter probably could not be accomplished without the help of CASE tools, unless a simple organization were the object of the information strategy planning study.

FUNCTIONAL
DECOMPOSITION

A function constitutes a task that must be accomplished in an enterprise. At the highest level a business can be regarded as one function. This may be broken into functional areas, and then to business functions, and so on. Figure 14.1 shows an example of a functional decomposition. We can call each of the blocks in Fig. 14.1 a *function*. Each function is broken into its component func-

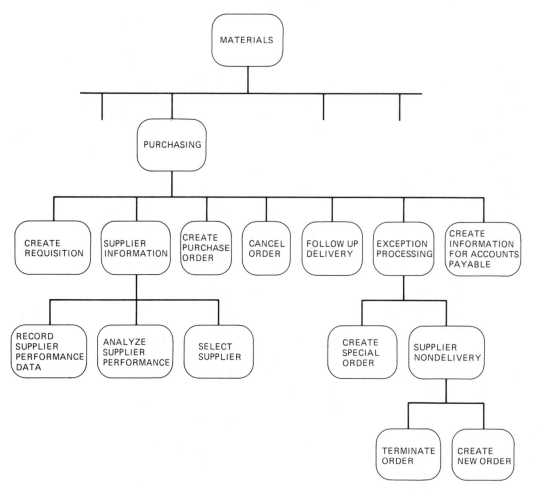

Figure 14.1   An example of functional decomposition.

tions until the lowest level is reached. The blocks at the lowest level of the tree are the *activities*. An activity is a function that can become a computer (or manual) procedure. Some activities become *prespecified* computer procedures (such as CREATE PURCHASE ORDERS); others are *nonprespecified* activities of a user at a terminal (such as ANALYZE SUPPLIER PERFORMANCE). The functions, including the lowest-level functions, are *logical*. They do not indicate *how* the task will be performed. Functional decomposition diagrams, like Fig. 14.1, are used for overall planning.

ON DRAWING HIERARCHIES

Most books and courses show hierarchical structures (tree structures) drawn vertically, as in Fig. 14.1, with the root at the top. In practice it is better to draw them horizontally with the root at the left, as in Fig. 14.2. The reason is that in

```
MATERIALS
.
.    PURCHASING
.    .
.    .    CREATE REQUISITION                              *
.    .
.    o    SUPPLIER INFORMATION
.    .    .
.    .    .    RECORD SUPPLIER PERFORMANCE DATA            *
.    .    .
.    .    .    ANALYZE SUPPLIER PERFORMANCE                *
.    .    .
.    .    .    SELECT SUPPLIER                             *
.    .    .
.    .    CREATE PURCHASE ORDER                           *
.    .
.    .    CANCEL PURCHASE ORDER                           *
.    .
.    .    FOLLOW UP DELIVERY                              *
.    .
.    .    EXCEPTION PROCESSING
.    .    .
.    .    .    CREATE SPECIAL ORDER                        *
.    .    .
.    .    .    SUPPLIER NONDELIVERY
.    .    .    .
.    .    .    .    TERMINATE ORDER                        *
.    .    .    .
.    .    .    .    CREATE NEW ORDER                       *
.    .    .
.    .    CREATE INFORMATION FOR ACCOUNTS PAYABLE    *
.    .
.    RECEIVING
```

Figure 14.2   The same diagram as in Figure 14.1, but with each layer listed vertically so that layers with many items fit on the page. This method of drawing is easy to handle and update. The asterisks mark the basic activities (the lowest nodes of the tree structure).

real situations (as opposed to textbook drawings), there can be many items at one level of the hierarchy—too many items to fit across one page. Drawing such a level horizontally becomes unwieldly, whereas listing it vertically as in Fig. 14.2 is no problem. Diagrams such as that in Fig. 14.2 are also more easily updated and redrawn with computers.

IDENTIFYING BASIC ACTIVITIES

How do we know when we have gone far enough in breaking down the functions into activities? Usually, one sentence can be used to describe the purpose of a basic activity. If more than one sentence is needed, the activity should probably be further decomposed. When you ask a member of the enterprise what he or she is doing, the answer will often identify a basic activity. For example, an order entry clerk might say "I'm preparing a purchase order" or "I'm paying a vendor." A similar sentence is needed to describe each basic activity. The clerk does not say "I am doing materials planning"; this is at too high a level. By the same token, the clerk will not say "I am entering the date on a purchase order"; this is too low a level.

A basic activity will typically be automated all at once as one procedure. If a function includes more than one procedure or would be automated in different stages, the analysis has not gone far enough.

When the characteristics just described are used to identify a basic activity, it is not worth having long arguments about what is a basic activity or what is the stopping point of the analysis. A sense of what is "natural" is more important than mechanical adherence to rules. If further subdividing a function promises interesting results, do it; if not, don't. The analysis should never be regarded as 100 percent complete and final. There will always be some activities not discovered or new activities added later. The model can be updated later.

When a function is broken down into lower-level functions, it is important to ensure that these are sufficient and that each of them is *necessary* to the overall purpose, no matter what reorganization or automation occurs. The analysts should feel confident that the entity-activity model that they are creating will survive organizational changes. Only if the activities are *necessary* and *sufficient* will this be true. Some activities currently practiced may be found to be extra or unnecessary. This is often the case, and entity-activity analysis sometimes leads to reorganizations of the procedures or to reorganizations of management structures.

PROPERTIES OF COHERENT ACTIVITIES

After working for some time on activity analysis, Ken Winter listed the following qualities to look for in well-formed activities [1].

1. A coherent activity produces some clearly identifiable result. Its purpose is to produce this result. The result may be a marketable product, a part of a product, an idea, a decision, a sale, a set of alternatives, a paycheck, a prospect, and so on. It should be possible to identify the purpose or result of the activity in a single simple sentence. By contrast, a poorly formed activity yields no identifiable result at all, or it produces a number of unrelated results.

2. A coherent activity has clear boundaries. At a given time, one can say unambiguously who is working on it and who is not. Over time, one can identify the moments when work on the activity starts and stops. Transitions between coherent activities are well marked. Incoherent activities overlap and blend into one another; one cannot localize when and where they are going on.

3. A coherent activity is carried out as a unit. It is done by a single person or by a well-defined group of people who work as a team to produce the result. Management responsibility for the activity is similarly well-defined and vested in a single person or group. An ill-defined activity may be carried out by an ill-defined group of people, that is, it may be unclear who does it. Or it may be done by a well-defined set of people whose jobs have something in common, but who do not work as a team: They do not interact, communicate, or cooperate to produce the activity's result, perhaps because they are dispersed throughout the enterprise in a way that never brings them into contact with one another.

4. Once initiated, a coherent activity is self-contained—it proceeds largely independently of other activities. If an alleged activity requires intense interaction along the way with another alleged activity, consider recasting them as a single activity. Another way of putting this is that the interactions within the team that carries out a coherent activity will be rich compared to the interactions between teams working on different activities

These points are heuristics, not absolute requirements when forming the activity model.

ENTITY-ACTIVITY MAPPING

Each activity relates to various data entities. A typical activity uses up to seven entities. It is recommended that if a function uses more than seven entities, the function should be broken down into more than one activity. An activity is intended to be performed by an employee in an efficient manner. Psychologists have demonstrated that most persons have great difficulty dealing with more than seven items or concepts at one time because the capacity of their short-term memory is about seven. A human activity should normally relate to no more than seven entities and preferably to less than seven.

REORGANIZING THE ENTERPRISE

Where management participates in the activity analysis, questions are often raised about what the activities *ought* to be. Some activities currently practiced may be found to be extra or unnecessary. Certain activities may be scattered in an ill-controlled manner throughout the enterprise. There may be alternative choices of activities in the model that represent policy decisions.

As with the techniques discussed in Chapter 13, entity-activity analysis often leads to a rethinking of procedures. It often leads to departmental reorganizations to a management review committee. An appropriate question for the entity-activity study team to ask is: "Which ways do you want the enterprise to be structured?" An ongoing search is necessary for ways to use databases and terminals to improve the enterprise procedures and structures. Often it is a surprise to senior management to see what data the different departments or divisions use. Often it reveals to them facts about the corporation that they had not known.

Entity Analysis Consultant:

It was an eye-opener to the DP steering committee to see where certain kinds of data were utilized. Senior management cannot be in touch with every area, and the data usage had simply never been mapped before. A project manager operates largely autonomously. He is responsible for most of what goes on in a multimillion-dollar program. He defines what he needs to achieve a product. They give him the budget and let him run. The study shows that many projects were doing the same thing as other projects, and nobody realized it. They were reporting to different managers in different areas.

Entity Analyst:

They had a total of eight autonomous divisions, all of which were competing furiously with one another, all of which were fighting tooth and nail to be top dog. The data analysis made it clear that most of them were essentially the same. Sixty percent of the operations of each division were common. But they all had different teams of programmers who never communicated. It became clear that they needed a thorough restructuring of the organization. Now this has happened. They are cutting the eight divisions to three.

AFFINITY ANALYSIS CLUSTERING

When the entities are mapped against activities, affinity analysis techniques are used to cluster them into subject databases. A matrix like the one in Fig. 14.3 can be computed showing the affinity that each entity has for each other entity. When numeric measures of affinities among objects can be calculated, a computer can group them into clusters of high affinity. The

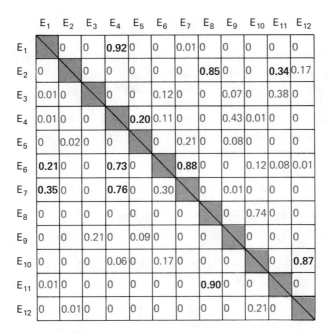

	E_1	E_2	E_3	E_4	E_5	E_6	E_7	E_8	E_9	E_{10}	E_{11}	E_{12}
E_1		0	0	0.92	0	0	0.01	0	0	0	0	0
E_2	0		0	0	0	0	0	0.85	0	0	0.34	0.17
E_3	0.01	0		0	0	0.12	0	0	0.07	0	0.38	0
E_4	0.01	0	0		0.20	0.11	0	0	0.43	0.01	0	0
E_5	0	0.02	0	0		0	0.21	0	0.08	0	0	0
E_6	0.21	0	0	0.73	0		0.88	0	0	0.12	0.08	0.01
E_7	0.35	0	0	0.76	0	0.30		0	0.01	0	0	0
E_8	0	0	0	0	0	0	0		0	0.74	0	0
E_9	0	0	0.21	0	0.09	0	0	0		0	0	0
E_{10}	0	0	0	0.06	0	0.17	0	0	0		0	0.87
E_{11}	0.01	0	0	0	0	0	0	0.90	0	0		0
E_{12}	0	0.01	0	0	0	0	0	0	0	0.21	0	

Figure 14.3 A matrix showing the computed affinity between different entities. This can be employed in the clustering of entities into subject databases.

planner can use the CASE workstation to control this clustering, adjusting parameters that affect the cluster sizes and applying manual overrides to take heuristic factors into account.

Let us suppose that we have two entities, E_1 and E_2. If the two entities are never used for the same activity, their affinity will be zero. If two entities are always used together for every activity, their affinity will be one. Many entities are used together for some activities only.

A computer can examine every activity and calculate

1. $a(E_1)$ = number of activities using entity E_1.
2. $a(E_1, E_2)$ = number of activities using both entities E_1 and E_2.

Using these figures, an affinity factor for the two entities can be calculated. One way of defining the affinity factor is

$$\text{affinity of } E_1 \text{ to } E_2 = \frac{a(E_1, E_2)}{a(E_1)}$$

The affinity factor can be printed in a matrix such as that in Fig. 14.3. If two entities have a high affinity, they should be in the same subject database. If they have an affinity of zero, they should definitely not be. Where is the dividing line?

A computer can group the entities into clusters based on their affinity factors. If it puts entities with affinity factor $= 0$ in the same cluster, there will be only one cluster. If it puts entities with affinity factor $= 1$ in the same cluster, there may be as many clusters as entities. A CASE planning tool can be instructed to set the affinity factor so as to produce 20 clusters, 30 clusters, or whatever the designer decides. These clusters are then used to determine the entities that are stored in subject databases.

The affinity factor does not take into account the volume of use of each activity. A different way of calculating affinity may take usage volumes into consideration. The method has given good results, in practice, when automatically clustering the entities into subject databases.

Suppose that we want to cluster the entities in Fig. 14.3 into databases. The entity pairs are sorted by affinity number, and we begin with the highest affinity numbers. Entity pairs with the highest affinity form the nuclei of the clusters; thus,

$$E_1, E_4 \qquad \text{(affinity} = 0.92)$$
$$E_{11}, E_8 \qquad \text{(affinity} = 0.90)$$
$$E_6, E_7 \qquad \text{(affinity} = 0.88)$$
$$E_{10}, E_{12} \qquad \text{(affinity} = 0.87)$$

Eventually, we arrive at an entity pair in which one of the entities is already in one of the clusters. The next entity pair we encounter is such:

$$E_2, E_8 \qquad \text{(affinity} = 0.85)$$

E_8 is already assigned to a cluster nucleus E_{11}, E_8. Should we now link E_2 to that cluster? To determine that, we need to calculate the weighted affinity of E_2 to cluster E_{11}, E_8.

$$\frac{[(\text{affinity to } E_2 \text{ to } E_{11}) \times a(E_{11})] + [(\text{affinity of } E_2 \text{ to } E_8) \times a(E_8)]}{a(E_{11}) + a(E_8)}$$

Suppose that entity E_{11} is used by 3 activities and entity E_8 is used by 48 activities. Then the composite affinity of E_2 to the cluster E_{11}, E_8 is

$$\frac{(0.34 \times 3) + (0.85 \times 48)}{3 + 48} = 0.82$$

This is higher than any remaining affinity number in Fig. 14.3, so the cluster E_2, E_{11}, E_8 is formed.

From now on, as we encounter new entities with an affinity to E_2, E_{11}, or E_8, we will compute their composite affinity to the cluster E_2, E_{11}, E_8. In this way the clusters of high-affinity entities grow steadily.

The next largest affinity number in Fig. 14.3 is the affinity of E_7 to E_4 (affinity = 0.76). However, both E_7 and E_4 are already allocated to a cluster. Should these clusters be combined? To determine that, we compute the composite weighted affinity of E_7 to the existing cluster E_1, E_4 and to a combined cluster E_1, E_4, E_6. Let us suppose that these affinity numbers were 0.55 and 0.37, respectively. These are lower than the next affinity number on the list, the affinity of E_8 to E_{10} (affinity = 0.74). This is therefore dealt with first. Each clustering decision is made in sequence by affinity number.

Some of the entities at the end of the affinity sequence may have little affinity with anything. These may be implemented as file systems or as simple isolated databases. The designer should review any remaining entities with low affinities to see whether they belong in any of the existing databases.

MANUAL ADJUSTMENT   When any entity clustering algorithm such as this is implemented, it is likely to require some intelligent human adjustment. The algorithm may group some entities that ought to be separate for other reasons, such as reliability, protecting one type of data when another type is involved with a failure, distributed system design, legal considerations, and so on. Sometimes the preservation of existing file or database systems may be the reason for a particular grouping. Sometimes the grouping may be adjusted so that one team can do the detailed modeling of a subject database. The analyst may run the algorithm several times, setting different affinity thresholds or forcing the data to be split in certain ways.

The clustering that results from affinity analysis can act as a cross-check on the clustering that results from the planning discussed in Chapter 13.

The overall results should be reviewed with the information strategy planning team and with senior management and adjusted if necessary. The subject databases that result from entity clustering can then be used to refine the choices of business areas that have been made.

REFERENCE

1. From a methodology working paper by Ken Winter and Rik Belew, KnowledgeWare, Inc., Atlanta, GA.

15 THE FOLLOW-ON PLAN

After the work of information strategy planning has been completed, the results of the study should be presented to top management. At this time, one or more business areas should be selected for further study. It is desirable that the information strategy planning study be immediately followed by vigorous action that leads to implementing better systems. Some strategic planning studies are not followed by action, and this makes them of little value. When the information strategy planning study results are presented to top management, a detailed action plan should accompany them saying what happens next.

If the enterprise has no experience with data modeling, the information strategy planning study may be followed by *one* business area analysis. The area selected should be one where the results will be especially valuable and the complexities are not too great. A function of this project should be to build a nucleus of experienced analysts who can move on quickly to analyze other areas of the business. If the enterprise has a well-established data administration function, it can act more quickly in business area analysis. It may be possible to move quickly into the system design and construction phases for areas that have already been modeled.

The information strategy planning project identifies certain critical and urgent needs for systems. These are often decision-support systems or executive information systems. Sometimes management wants these quickly, and they can indeed be built quickly with information center techniques, decision-support systems, spreadsheets, and so on. As we commented, these urgent needs can sometimes be met quickly so that senior management can see that important business needs can be addressed expediently.

CHOICE OF BUSINESS AREAS TO ANALYZE

When an enterprise has been split into areas for business area analysis, it is necessary to decide which area or areas to tackle first. It would be nice to have a simple return-on-investment computation for determining priorities, but in practice multiple considerations are likely to affect the choice.

Interviewer:

This is such a grand-scale plan, how do you split it up into what you do first? Obviously, it must take many years to implement.

Database Executive:

Well, quite frankly, at the beginning, it was kind of application driven and user driven. The need for corporate cash management systems became strong, for instance. However, we used that as an opportunity to put databases into place. Later it tended to change from being user driven because the databases were already in place. The data was available for us to implement those additional applications that users required.

Interviewer:

So you're saying that in the beginning it was driven by the demands of the users to get new applications, but then as you build up the set of subject databases you can design these in such a way that it becomes database driven?

Database Executive:

Yes, that's correct. The end result is that we get more and more requests and we're responding much faster. I've seen applications implemented in a matter of weeks in some cases because the database already exists.

It is recommended that the following criteria be used to help make the decision of what business area to be tackled first:

- Potential Benefit
    Return on investment (tangibles and intangibles)
    Achievement of critical success factors
    Achievement of goals
    Solution to serious problems

- Demand
  Pressure of demand from senior end users for new or improved systems
  Assessed need
  Political overtones

- Organizational Impact
  Number of organizations and people affected
  Whether the organizations are geographically dispersed
  Qualitative effect

- Existing Systems
  Adequacy or value of existing systems
  Relationship with existing systems
  Estimated future costs of maintenance

- Likely Success
  Complexity
  Degree of business acceptance
  Length of project
  Prerequisites
  Risks

- Resources Required
  Whether existing data or process models exist
  Whether a suitable tool kit is installed
  Quality of available analysts
  Funds required

- Concurrent Implementation
  Whether multiple business area analysis projects can proceed concurrently
  Whether one project will train people who can quickly move onto other projects
  Whether an existing data administration function has already done good data modeling

It is suggested that the areas for possible business area analysis be ranked on a scale of 1 to 7 for each of the foregoing categories. An informed decision can then be made about which area(s) to tackle first.

Since information should be treated as a business resource, information system projects should be evaluated by management in much the same way as business projects are evaluated. The return on investment, requisite resources, and possible risks should be evaluated like any new business venture. This can be done if the corporation as a whole is being examined with the involvement of suitably high executives.

ANALYSIS OF CURRENT SYSTEMS

An enterprise usually has many data processing systems that were established before strategic information planning came into use. They typically do not use stable data models. It is desirable to chart the existing systems and clarify how they currently support the business. Three matrices can be used for this, as shown in Fig. 15.1. Three of these matrices are shown in more detail in Figs. 15.2 through 15.4. They help to clarify system voids and redundancies. There are often major redundancies in systems developed using conventional techniques. There is often a major need to rebuild old systems. They have often been maintained by multiple programmers with different styles and are often lacking in integrated design. They become fragile and difficult to change. When they are rebuilt, this should be done with the data models and automated design techniques that we have been discussing.

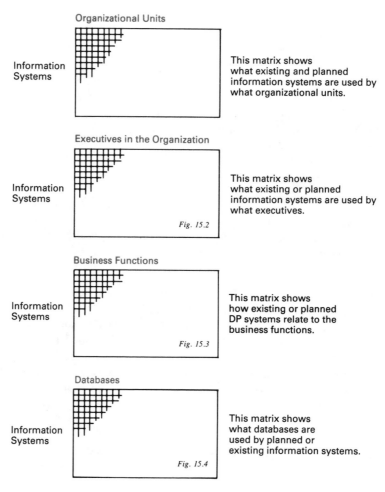

Figure 15.1 Matrices showing existing systems.

EXECUTIVE / INFORMATION SYSTEMS	President	Vice President of Finance	Controller	Personnel Director	Vice President of Sales	Order Control Manager	Electronic Sales Manager	Electrical Sales Manager	Vice President of Engineering	Vice President of Production	Plant Operations Director	Production Planning Director	Facilities Manager	Materials Control Manager	Purchasing Manager	Division Lawyer	Planning Director
Customer Order Entry	c/p				c/p	c/p	c/p	c/p		c/p	c/p	c/p					
Customer Order Control	C				C	C	C	C		C	C	C		C	C		
Invoicing		C	C														
Engineering Control									P								
Finished Goods Inventory	C	C	C		C		C	C		C		C	C				
Bills of Material									C	C	C	C	C				
Parts Inventory		C	C		C	C	C	C				C					
Purchase Order Control					c/p	c/p	c/p	c/p		c/p	c/p	c/p					
Routings									C	C	C	C					
Shop Floor Control										C	C	C	C				
Capacity Planning	P									P	P	P	P	P			P
General Ledger		P	P														
Expense			C		C												
Product Costing	c/p	c/p	c/p		c/p		c/p	c/p	c/p		c/p			c/p	c/p	c/p	
Operating Statements	C	C	C														
Accounts Receivable																C	
Accounts Payable	C	C	C														P
Asset Accounting	C	C	C													C	
Marketing Analysis	C				C		C	C									C
Payroll				C													

C = Current   P = Planned   c/p = Current and Planned

Figure 15.2 A matrix mapping existing (or planned) information systems against executives in the enterprise.

BUSINESS FUNCTION / INFORMATION SYSTEM	Marketing			Sales Operations				Engineering			Production				Materials Management				Facilities Management			Administration			Finance			Human Resources			Management			
	Planning	Research	Forecasting	Territory Management	Selling	Administration	Order Servicing	Design and Development	Product Specification Maintenance	Information Control	Scheduling	Capacity Planning	Material Requirements	Operations	Purchasing	Receiving	Inventory Control	Shipping	Work Flow Layout	Maintenance	Equipment Performance	General Accounting and Control	Cost Planning	Budget Accounting/Tax Accounting	Financial Planning	Capital Acquisition	Funds Management	Personnel Planning	Recruiting/Development	Compensation	Business Planning	Organization Analysis	Review and Control	Risk Management
Customer Order Entry				c/p			c/p				c/p	c/p	c/p																		c/p			
Customer Order Control							C			C	C		C		C																			
Invoicing																						C			C									
Engineering Control										P																								
Finished Goods Inventory															C	C	C					C	C											
Bills of Material									C	C	C				C								C											
Parts Inventory							C								C		C																	
Purchase Order Control											c/p	c/p	c/p		c/p																			
Routings										C		C		C																				
Shop Floor Control										C		C		C			C																	
Capacity Planning												P		P																				
General Ledger																						P					P							
Expense				C																		C												
Product Costing										c/p				c/p			c/p						c/p											
Operating Statements																						C									C	C		C
Accounts Receivable																						C												C
Accounts Payable																						C									C			C
Asset Accounting																								C		C								C
Marketing Analysis				C	C		C																											
Payroll																						C		C						C				

C = Current   *P* = Planned   *c/p* = Current and Planned

Figure 15.3 A matrix mapping business functions against current and existing information systems.

DATABASE / INFORMATION SYSTEM	Customer	Order	Vendor	Product	Routings	Bills of Material	Cost	Parts Master	Raw Material Inventory	Finished Goods Inventory	Employee	Sales Territory	Financial	Planning	Work in Process	Facilities	Open Requirements	Machine Load
Customer Order Entry	X	X	X	X			X			X			X					
Customer Order Control	X	X	X	X		X							X	X				
Invoicing	X	X	X				X						X					
Engineering Control				X	X	X		X									X	
Finished Goods Inventory		X		X						X				X	X			
Bills of Material				X	X	X		X						X			X	
Parts Inventory				X				X	X					X	X			
Purchase Order Control			X	X				X	X					X				
Routings				X	X	X		X							X			X
Shop Floor Control				X	X			X	X					X	X			X
Capacity Planning				X	X			X						X	X			X
General Ledger				X			X						X					
Expense												X	X					
Product Costing				X			X	X					X					X
Operating Statements												X	X					
Accounts Receivable	X	X	X										X					
Accounts Payable			X										X					
Asset Accounting													X			X		
Marketing Analysis	X	X		X								X	X					
Payroll											X							

Figure 15.4   A matrix mapping current information systems against databases.

STRATEGIC TECHNOLOGY PLANNING

Certain types of technology planning are of *strategic* importance. For example, it is desirable to have a data network that links all parts of the enterprise and goes to every knowledge worker's desk like a nervous system. Achieving full compatibility, so that any computer can be connected to this network, raises many complex issues and needs substantial planning and design. This planning can only be done at the top level in an enterprise because the network needs to serve all the divisions and locations. The network design relates to the permissible choice of computers and workstations.

Also complex is the choice of software in the enterprise. In the past, software was run in a largely stand-alone fashion on one computer. Increasingly today, integration of software is needed. Software on personal computers needs to link to software on departmental computers and then to corporate mainframes. Application software needs to link to database software, and data is increasingly distributed. Different knowledge workers with their own decision-support capabilities need to be able to discuss by telephone complex representations of information that they both have on their screens. Knowledge workers need to be able to exchange computerized business models or other computations.

Strategic technology planning involves a variety of issues that are beyond the scope of this book, such as production technology, network technology, standards for personal computers, and so on. In general, information engineering requires *open* networks, that is, networks that facilitate full interconnectability of facilities on machines of different vendors. Open networks require *standards*. The choice and implementation of standards for interconnectability is critical.

It is important that strategic plans and standards should not impede creativity. In practice, creativity in application building is enhanced if interconnectability is made easy. To achieve interconnectability we need networking standards and data standards. Machines must be easy to interconnect technically, and different locations must employ the same data model.

This book does not discuss technology planning such as network standards and design. The corporate network, and other technology, affects the implementation of business plans and offers opportunities for improving the functioning of the enterprise, for example, better connections with customers, agents, buyers, suppliers, and so on; better decision making; lower inventory; new types of business; and so on. Business strategy planning therefore needs to link to strategic technology planning as well as to strategic information planning:

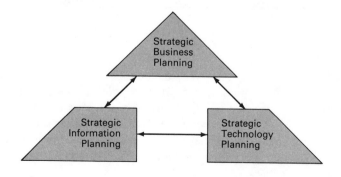

KEEPING THE PLANNING STUDY UP-TO-DATE

Some person should have an ongoing responsibility for keeping the information strategy planning information up-to-date. The technical information about entity types and business functions becomes more precise as business area analysis studies are completed. The charts of new technology and business opportunities should be kept up-to-date by a person who is enthusiastic about technology and who reads the current technical literature.

Goals and problems should be reviewed whenever management-by-objectives interviews are done for guiding executives and department heads.

Periodically, not less than once a year, strategic business planning meetings should take place. At these meetings the technology impact analysis and critical success factor analysis studies should be revisited and should help to guide the business planning. In some corporations critical success factors are part of the documentation for board meetings and modifications to them may be recommended by the board. This is useful and should be done for the board meetings of most corporations. Some corporations have a technical advisory board. This board should review the technology impact analysis and possibly also the critical success factor analysis. These aids to top management planning should be a live and vigorous part of the ongoing planning process.

16 BUSINESS AREA ANALYSIS

A business area analysis study establishes a detailed framework for building an information-based enterprise. It is not part of information strategy planning, but is done after the strategic information planning process has been completed. This chapter is intended only as an introduction to the business area analysis process; it is beyond the scope of this book to present all the techniques that are employed during a business area analysis study [1, 2].

Business area analysis takes one business area at a time and analyzes it in detail. It uses diagrams and matrices to record and analyze the data and activities in the enterprise and gives a clear understanding of the elaborate and subtle ways in which the information aspects of the enterprise interrelate. The diagrams and matrices are designed to be understood by management, end users, and information systems professionals and to greatly increase communication among these groups.

Business area analysis uses the information gathered during information strategy planning and expands it into more detail. The results are recorded and are used in subsequent system design. This detailed model of the enterprise must be kept up-to-date as the enterprise changes and as systems are built. It provides the architectural framework for the information-based enterprise.

Business area analysis is not an end in itself. Its purpose is to facilitate the design of systems and to ensure that they work together appropriately. There is often pressure to finish the analysis stage or avoid it completely and spend the effort on building much needed systems. However business area analysis is an essential stage in getting the right information to the right people at the right time. Box 16.1 gives the objectives of business area analysis. Box 16.2 lists some of the characteristics of a business area analysis study.

BOX 16.1   Objectives of business area analysis

- Provide a clear understanding of the business and how its activities interrelate.

- Provide an architectural framework for the building of systems in an information-based enterprise.

- Provide a framework such that separately built systems will work together. This framework consists of

  A fully normalized data model that becomes the foundation of application design and construction

  A model of the business activities and their interdependencies.

  A linkage of the preceding models to show what processes use what data.

- Trigger the rethinking of procedures in the enterprise so that they are as efficient as possible for the era of desktop computers, information networks, and flexible databases.

- Identify requirements of highest priority for information center activities and system design.

- Create an overview so that later design stages can proceed rapidly and coherently.

KEEP IT SIMPLE   Business area analysis should not be allowed to become too complex. In the author's view the steps described here represent the appropriate level of complexity. There is sometimes a tendency to make it more detailed or more bureaucratic. Finer detail than that described should be left for the system design stage. *The objective of business area analysis is not to design systems but to establish a framework that will ensure that separately designed systems will fit together.*

It establishes *what* data and *what* processes are required to operate the enterprise. It does not establish *how* procedures operate. Determining how procedures should operate is done in later design stages. Business area analysis should not be confused with requirements planning for a specific system. It will speed up subsequent system requirements planning, but the business area analysis itself is concerned with the fundamental data and processes, not with *how* a specific system should function.

SHORT PROJECT   The analysis of a business area should not take too long. The tools and procedures should be such that it

BOX 16.2　Characteristics of business area analysis

- Business area analysis is conducted for each business area independently. It takes from three to six months.

- It has strong end-user involvement.

- It studies *what* fundamental processes and data are used, not *how* procedures operate.

- It creates an architectural framework that will ensure the separately designed systems will fit together.

- The results are stored in the encyclopedia, and the encyclopedia tools are used to coordinate the results from different business areas.

- Over time the data and process models are kept up-to-date in the encyclopedia.

- The data half of business area analysis uses classical data administration and modeling techniques.

- It is independent of technology (because technology will change).

- It is independent of the current organization chart (because that will change).

- It is independent of the current systems and procedures (because often they need redesigning).

- It tends to cause a rethinking of the organization chart.

- It needs a high-level executive sponsor prepared to deal with political problems.

can be completed in three to six months. The enterprise should be subdivided into areas small enough to make this practical.

As with the methodologies of information strategy planning, automated CASE tools are needed for efficient business area analysis. The tools should be an extension of those used for information strategy planning. They should, in turn, become the tools used in later design stages. Computerized tools can provide analyses and coordination of the enterprise knowledge to an extent that far surpasses that of human analysts. An objective should be to avoid the burdensome paperwork and bureaucracy of earlier methodologies and replace it with diagrams and data designed for computerized analysis and coordination.

INDEPENDENT OF TECHNOLOGY AND ORGANIZATIONAL STRUCTURE

Business area analysis creates models of the fundamental data and processes that are necessary for the business. It does this in a manner that is *independent of technology*. This is important because technology is changing rapidly, but the fundamental processes such as factory scheduling, warehousing, and so on still have to be carried out.

The models are also *independent of the current systems*. The systems and procedures used are likely to change. Systems for an era of batch processing are different from online systems, and systems change fundamentally in an era of desktop computing, enterprisewide networks, and flexible databases. When the information needs of the enterprise are clearly understood, it is likely that different systems and procedures will be created.

The analysis should also be *independent of the current organizational structure*. It should not be tied to specific organizational units. The enterprise is likely to be reorganized periodically, but the fundamental data and processes remain. The model of its data and processes should be valid independently of how the organization is subdivided into departments. A specific organizational unit will frequently change its activities and composition to meet fluctuating business requirements.

ORGANIZATIONAL CHANGES

Some important questions to ask in business area analysis are: "What decisions must be made to run the business?" "What is the optimum place for each decision to be made?" and "What individual should be responsible for the decision?"

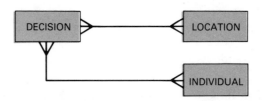

The answer to these questions often results in new systems, changed procedures, and organizational changes. An information-based enterprise needs to be organized differently from an older form of enterprise. Business area analysis studies, along with their parent information strategy planning study, make visible the need for organizational changes and have often, in practice, triggered major corporate reorganizations. One enterprise with 12 layers of management was restructured with only 5 layers as it became an information-based enterprise. The possibility of such upheavals can make the planning and business area analysis studies highly political. Because of this, the support of top management is essential. A suitably high executive needs to be the sponsor of a business area analysis, committed to making it happen efficiently and to acting upon the results. Top management commitment is needed to lessen the effects of middle management politics.

IDENTIFICATION OF THE BUSINESS AREA

The division of the enterprise into business areas is done as part of the information strategy planning study, with the aid of a tool for clustering the entity/ function matrix. There are no hard and fast boundaries to a business area, but experience shows that it is relatively easy to find pragmatic subdivisions of the enterprise.

For example, Fig. 16.1 shows a collection of business functions and entity types that are closely interconnected. Such a closely interconnected grouping may be defined as a business area. The clustering algorithms discussed in Chapters 13 and 14 help to find closely interwoven groupings in a large collection of entity types and business functions.

There may be multiple departments or organizational units involved with the cluster. For example the Purchasing, Warehouse and Goods Receipt departments are involved with the functions in Fig. 16.2, and there may be more than one factory and warehouse in different locations. Several organizational units employ the same data and interact in carrying out the business function.

A simple event such as a customer phoning and asking to place an order may trigger processing that involves multiple departments:

1. The order office receives the call.

2. The order office asks if the customer's credit is OK.

Business Functions

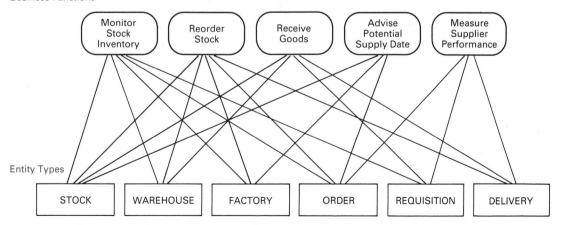

Figure 16.1 A business area is a collection of closely related business functions and entity types.

3. The credit office replies.

4. The order office asks when delivery can be scheduled.

5. The warehouse is low on stock and asks when it can have more stock.

6. Production scheduling asks when production will be available.

7. Plant maintenance replies.

8. Production scheduling determines that additional raw materials are needed and contacts a supplier.

9. The supplier replies.

10. . . . And so on.

An information system, as automated as possible, should enable the order clerk to respond to the customer quickly and accurately.

It is this complex interaction between separate business organizational units that makes providing good business information systems difficult. The traditional approach of building systems for business for each organizational unit fails to meet the underlying needs of business. Business area analysis needs to cross departmental boundaries to model how the business works and show what interdepartmental systems are needed. The departments may be reorganized, but

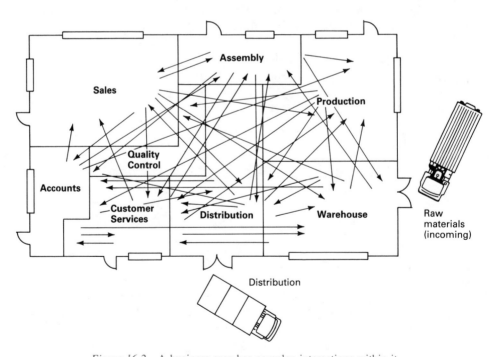

Figure 16.2   A business area has complex interactions within it.

the foregoing information processing still needs to be done to respond to a customer's request. Business area analysis charts the necessary processes and data.

SOLVING THE COMMUNICATION PROBLEM

The end user often has serious worries about computer systems:

- The current systems don't tackle my real problems.
- I'll have to wait years to get the new systems I need.
- Systems cost too much to develop and run.
- We have reorganized and my systems can't cope.
- I need to replace my existing procedures, but my current systems can't be changed for a year or more.

On the other hand, the business system developer has corresponding worries:

- What does the user want now?
- What will the user want? In six months' time? In six years' time?
- How can I respond quickly enough?
- How can I build a new application system when the users don't know what they want?
- Who will be the users?
- What happens if they change their minds?
- How can I avoid expensive long-term maintenance?

By creating a model of the data, processes, and their interactions, business area analysis addresses fundamental information needs. The diagrams used are easy to understand so as to facilitate communication between users and developers. The diagrams and their underlying details should be maintained in a computer, be readily available, and be updated as the business changes and its system needs are further clarified. The information gathered during business area analysis spans the business. It builds bridges between users who may be far apart and makes possible the creation of systems that interlink diverse parts of the business. Often this results in drastic simplification of business systems because complexity arises from inadequate communication and lack of understanding. Lack of communication in the past has resulted in massive redundancy and incompatibility of data files and programs. It has resulted in systems that do not work together and extensive human processing because of system inadequacies.

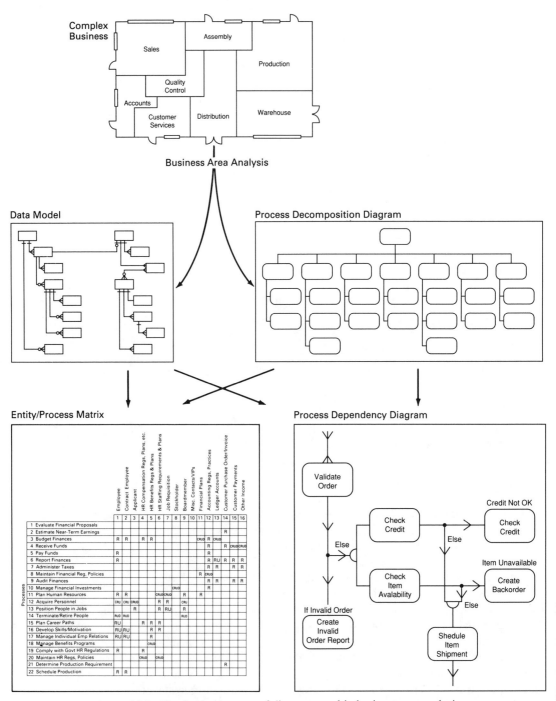

Figure 16.3　The four main types of diagrams used in business area analysis.

FOUR TYPES OF
DIAGRAMS

Four main types of diagrams are needed for business area analysis (Fig. 16.3).

- **Data Model Diagrams.** A fully normalized model is built of the data used in the business area. This is created by expanding the appropriate portion of the entity-relationship diagram that was created during information strategy planning.

- **Process Decomposition Diagrams.** The functions of the business area are decomposed into processes; high-level processes are decomposed into lower-level processes. A tree-structured decomposition is produced. If entity-activity analysis was conducted as part of information strategy planning, the results of that analysis can be used as the starting point for the more rigorous process decomposition done during business area analysis.

- **Process Dependency Diagram.** Some processes are dependent upon other processes; they can only be performed *after* the processes on which they are dependent. The dependency may be because data used by a dependent process are created by another process. A process dependency diagram maps the dependencies. Sometimes a process dependency diagram is called a *process flow diagram*. It shows the data flows from one process to another, but it does not show what this data is, as on a data flow diagram.

- **Process/Data Matrix.** A process/data matrix maps the processes against normalized data, showing which processes create, read, update, or delete the records. Creating this matrix helps to ensure that the process dependencies have been assessed correctly.

THE INITIAL
DIAGRAMS

The study proceeds by successive refinement of the four main diagram types. The initial versions of these will be extracted from the information gathered during information strategy planning. If time has elapsed since the information strategy planning was done, these models should be reviewed to determine whether they are an accurate description of the current business environment.

In some corporations data administration has existed for years before the business area analysis. The existing data models and descriptions may be subjected to further analysis. Sometimes a business area analysis is conducted when there has been no previous information strategy planning study. In this case the relevant planning information for the business area needs to be obtained.

LINKS WITH
OTHER BUSINESS
AREA ANALYSES

The different business areas in an enterprise are interlinked. Some data subjects are used in more than one business area. Some processes in one business area are dependent on processes in a different business area. The matrix developed during information strategy planning that maps

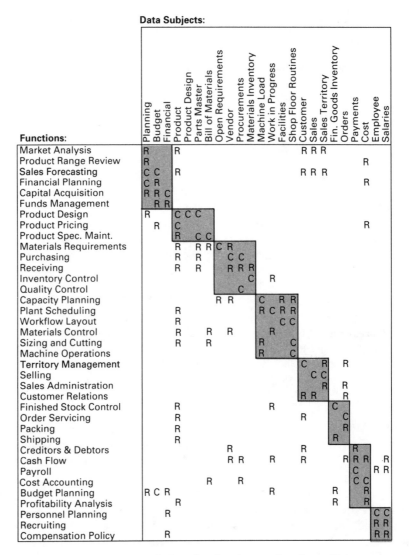

Figure 16.4   A matrix mapping functions against data subjects.

business functions against data subjects is shown again in Fig. 16.4. This matrix has been clustered into business areas. The information on this matrix can be condensed automatically into a smaller matrix that maps business areas against data subjects, as shown in Fig. 16.5. This matrix marks which business areas use data subjects exclusively, which have primary responsibility, and which have secondary responsibility. The following notation is used:

Data Subjects:

Business Areas:	Planning	Budget	Financial	Product	Product Design	Parts Master	Bill of Materials	Open Requirements	Vendor	Procurements	Materials Inventory	Machine Load	Work in Progress	Facilities	Shop Floor Routing	Customer	Sales	Sales Territory	Fin. Goods Inventory	Orders	Payments	Costs	Employee	Salaries
Planning	P	P	P	S												S	S	S			S			
Product Design	S	S		P	E	P	P														S			
Acquisition				S		S		P	P	P	E	S												
Manufacturing				S			S	S	S			E	P	E	E									
Sales																P	P	P	S					
Order Servicing				S								S				S			E	P				
Accounting	S	S	S	S		S			S	S		S				S	S		S		E	P		S
Personnel			S																				E	P

Figure 16.5 A matrix mapping business areas against data subject showing responsibility for data subject definition.

- **E — Exclusive.** The definition can proceed independently of any other business area.
- **P — Primary responsibility.** This business area defines the object in question and that others should use the definition (or negotiate to have it modified).
- **S — Secondary responsibility.** A different business area defines the object in question. In practice this business area may define it if it is done first, but the business area with primary responsibility is ultimately responsible.

Much data passes across the boundaries between different business areas. Where this interchange exists, coordination is necessary of the separate business area perspectives.

STAFFING A BUSINESS AREA ANALYSIS PROJECT

Business area analysis, like all information engineering, needs close cooperation between end users and information systems professionals. An enterprise is likely to conduct many business area analysis studies. It may conduct one initial study to gain experience and then conduct several studies in parallel until models of all or most of the enterprise are complete. Certain individuals develop a high level of skill at handling the subtleties of data modeling and process modeling. These professionals should move from one study to another. They become very valuable in enabling the study to be done quickly. A professional business area analysis team emerges from the training and experience. The most skilled members of this team have a promotion path that may lead them to become the *data administrator*.

The first study is often done with the aid of consultants who specialize in such work. The consultants should train internal staff to become skilled in the modeling processes and the coordination of information engineering. Often the team that performed the information strategy planning goes on to lead the business area analysis projects.

The business area analysis team members need skill in interviewing and human communication as well as in technical modeling. They need to have credibility and respect among operating management and end users.

End-user participation is essential in business area analysis studies. Sometimes one or two end users are allocated full time to the study. Such users should have thorough knowledge of the entire business area. Where full-time participation is not possible, users with an appropriate range of knowledge should be allocated on a part-time basis with, perhaps, a quarter of their time committed until the study of their area is complete. Other users will need to be interviewed but have less time committed.

A short seminar should be given to those users who will assist in the project and particularly those who will be asked to approve the decisions and plans. This should cover the motivation and objectives of the project, its scope, and the techniques used. The participants should be taught how to read the diagram types. Prior to this seminar, the relevant overview of the business area should be extracted from the encyclopedia. The relevant portion of the entity-relationship model and the function decomposition model should be explained to the participants. Relevant goals and problems, and critical success factors, relevant to the organizational units in question should be discussed.

Full-time team members should be given more complete education on information engineering as a whole. They should know how their analysis is likely to lead to the system design, joint application design sessions, prototyping, and information center operations. Some of these activities may follow on directly from the business area analysis.

An executive sponsor is needed for the study. This person should be committed to a successful completion of the study in the scheduled time.

Appendix II contains a complete action diagram for the business area analysis procedure. As with the other procedures of information engineering, it is useful to represent the procedure on an action diagram because the procedure can be quickly edited and adjusted to the circumstances in question. Business area analysis studies differ somewhat from one organization to another.

REFERENCES

1. Business area analysis is discussed in James Martin, *Information Engineering,* a report in four volumes, Savant Institute, 2 New Street, Carnsforth, Lancashire, England, 1986, 1987.

2. Business area analysis is also discussed in James Martin, *Database Analysis and Design* (Englewood Cliffs, NJ: Prentice Hall, 1989).

PART **III** EPILOGUE

17 INFORMATION SYSTEMS OF THE FUTURE

The corporation of the future will be highly dependent on its information systems, even more so than today. Its competitiveness and its survival will depend on how effectively it uses automation. Computers are changing fabrication techniques and changing products because products can have elaborate computation facilities built into them—a modern camera contains 150,000 transistors. Networks are changing the flows of information and the interactions between far-flung parts of the enterprise. Information can flow worldwide in seconds. Worldwide data can be made available on anyone's desk, with tools for processing the data. Computerized expertise will be available to decision makers.

The corporate data network, like the nervous system of an animal, will go to every part of the organism. Corporations will become highly interdependent as the electronic channel support systems discussed in Chapter 8 are used to link together cooperating enterprises. Networks will link suppliers directly to producers and producers to their customers. Computers in one organization will send information directly to computers in another organization. Knowledge workers with easy-to-use workstations will be able to interrogate databases anywhere. The vast infrastructure built for an obsolete world of paper shuffling will no longer be needed.

Innovative companies are perceiving how computers, networks, workstations, CD-ROMs, touch screens, and other technologies can enable them to launch preemptive marketplace attacks. It is clear that most corporations are still far from perceiving or capitalizing on the opportunities that information technology offers for maximizing their profits or market share. As technology increases the opportunities and competitive threats, so it becomes increasingly vital for top management to work with information systems executives to identify what are the new opportunities and how technology can best be put to work. The information systems executive who talks the language of top management and who can identify and categorize the opportunities is a valuable asset. The salaries of such executives have risen greatly as information technology has become perceived as a strategic weapon rather than merely a support tool.

WHERE SHOULD DECISIONS BE MADE

Given the ability to put a workstation on anyone's desk that can access databases anywhere, extract data, and do local computations with that data, the question arises: "Where should decisions best be made?" Information about any operations can be brought to the desk of any decision maker; the worldwide logistics can be made visible in the head office. Any decision maker can have access to great computer power and powerful decision-support software.

Certain types of decision ought to be made locally, as close to the problem as possible. Decisions about shop floor loading and routing should be made on the shop floor. Other types of decision should be made centrally where the worldwide operations can be viewed. Central decisions may be made about production planning, crew scheduling in an airline, inventory control with parts that can be flown around the world, currency control, and financial planning.

Many examples exist of decision making moving from distributed locations to a central location once the necessary information can be transmitted electronically. Many other examples exist of a skill that was developed centrally being moved to local operations. Examples exist of head office executives interfering in decisions that were best made locally. Many other examples exist of top management and their staff not having the information they need for effective control.

Information strategy planning showing the organization chart, geographical structure, goals, and hierarchy of critical success factors is essential in thinking about who needs what information and who should be making what types of decisions.

FLATTENING THE BUREAUCRATIC TREE

With networks able to deliver information to anyone who needs it, there is less need for organizational structures that are many layers deep. Decisions tend to be made either at the bottom of the tree close to the problem or else at the top of the tree where integrated planning is possible. The effect of powerful decision-support software is to enable an individual to have a greater span of control over events. Managers need fewer staff assistants. They can manage more with today's computers than they could without them.

New organizations built to take advantage of modern computing have wider, shallower, organization charts than do their paper-intensive predecessors. The vast office areas with stacked in baskets are replaced with electronics. Data flows directly from the bottom of the organization chart where staff interact with customers or production processes, to the top where planning and control is done. The Saturn plant in General Motors, for example, has a leaner, flatter, less bureaucratic management structure than do the older car plants in Detroit. Figure 17.1 illustrates the flattening of the bureaucratic tree as data networks facilitate new flows of information.

Many organizations have reshaped their managerial structure around the flow of information that computer networks make possible. In some this has been done on a worldwide basis. Some Japanese trading companies have adapted their management structure to take advantage of worldwide networks. Worldwide information can now be instantly available to decision makers in a

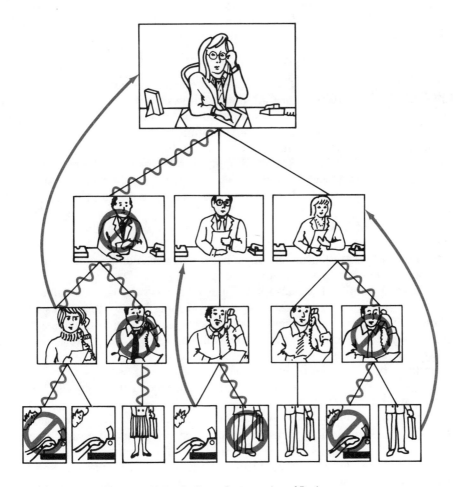

Computer Networks Cause Restructuring of Business

Figure 17.1 Executives can use new technologies to flatten the bureaucratic pyramid by cutting management layers and redefining work patterns.

head office location. Some organizations have reorganized the location at which they have inventories as central knowledge of all inventories was analyzed by computer and showed how the total world inventory could be reduced. Corporations implementing computer-integrated manufacturing have found it necessary to restructure and redesign their management as an information-based organization.

When a flatter organization chart is adopted, the executives who remain usually have more demanding, more responsible jobs. They control a higher volume of operations because they can handle more information with the computerized systems. They can span a wider area of operations because of networks. The supervisor in an automated plant controls a far higher volume of production. The financial decision maker can handle a far broader range of decisions and do more elaborate computations.

THE ORCHESTRA-LIKE STRUCTURE

The traditional organization has a hierarchical structure. Command flows down from the top. Information gathered at the bottom is successively summarized and passed to the top. The organization built around computer networks is often entirely different. Information passes horizontally from one operating unit to another. In principle all information can be made available to any person at one time. In practice this bulk of information is overwhelming, and careful design must be done of what information each operating unit needs. The corporate data resides in databases that any operating unit can access. Operating units extract information they need and restructure it for their own decision making.

Peter Drucker, the doyen of management consultants, compared the new corporate structures to a symphony orchestra [1].

The conventional organization of business was originally modeled after the military. The information-based organization more closely resembles the symphony orchestra. All instruments play the same score, but each plays a different part. They play together, but they rarely play in unison. There are more violins, but the first violin is not the "boss" of the horns; indeed the first violin is not even the "boss" of the other violins. Executives can use new technologies to flatten the bureaucratic pyramid by cutting management layers and redefining work patterns.

In the symphony orchestra type of enterprise some of the players are highly skilled. Some know how to use computerized tools and information access to make complex decisions or do complex design. The supervisor of the automated plant has a complex set of knowledge about how the plant works and how to control it. The information-based corporation tends to use far more "soloists"—bright individuals doing a highly skilled task on their own. They exist in a variety of different specializations—financial analysts, marketing experts, customer service personnel, production schedulers, decision makers with their own computerized models.

For example, Drucker describes how Citibank appointed a senior vice-president in its New York headquarters to take care of the bank's major Japanese customers and their worldwide financial needs. This man is not the "boss" of the bank's large branches in Japan. But he is not "service" staff either. He is very definitely "line." He is a soloist and is expected to function somewhat the way the pianist playing a Beethoven concerto is expected to function, and both he and the "orchestra" around him, that is, the rest of the bank, can function only because both "know the score." It is information rather than authority that enables them mutually to support each other [1].

The "score" of the well-orchestrated enterprise is the information in databases that anyone with authority can access. In the orchestra the score is given to both players and conductor. In business the score is being written as it is being played. To know what the score is, everyone in the information-based organization has to manage by objectives that are agreed on in advance and clearly understood. Management by objectives and self-control is, of necessity, the integrating principle of the information-based structure [1].

Without integrated planning and design of data, the orchestra model of an enterprise cannot work. Common language and common representation of data are essential; otherwise, the separate players create a cacophony.

It is sometimes thought that military-like hierarchical organizations have much more discipline than is possible with more horizontal organizations. To some people the horizontally structured organization conjures up an image of loose discipline and permissiveness. This is not the case in a successful information-based enterprise. A high level of self-control is necessary. Each organizational unit needs the other units to work well and follow the score. The semi-autonomous units cooperate tightly and have a common base of information, mutual understanding, and mutual respect. Digital Equipment Corporation (DEC) is a decentralized enterprise that places a high value on autonomous decision making, but it has achieved a product line much more unified than IBM, which has a military-like structure. DEC makes extensive use of computer networking. Autonomous organizational units with computer networks designed to get them the information they need can make fast decisions and give fast responses. The enterprise that consists of a network of autonomous units can be highly flexible, creative, and diverse.

The information-based organization with semiautonomous units needs a high level of discipline and an overall architecture. Each unit has to understand its objectives. Management by objectives is essential. A high value is placed on local initiative in meeting the objectives as excellently as possible. Each unit has to understand how it relates to other units, how other units can help it, and how other units depend upon it. This needs architectural planning and strong decisive leadership. The great corporation of the future will have highly disciplined overall leadership of many autonomous units, each doing the most excellent job it can within a framework architected by information strategy planning.

**COMPUTER-
INTEGRATED
MANUFACTURING**
Automation affects both physical work and information work. In some corporations robotized factories are leading to a new era of high-volume fabrication in which goods of great complexity will be mass-produced using startlingly few people. The robot-controlled production lines work 24 hours a day, 7 days a week. Most humans work only during the prime shift, preparing what the machines will need for the night shifts.

A factory in IBM was upgraded in 1984 from manufacturing Model 3278 terminals to Model 3178 terminals. A robot-operated production line was introduced. Before the change 700 terminals per day were produced by 130 people. After the change 2000 per day were produced by 5 people. Productivity in terms of numbers of products per person per day went from 5.4 to 400; a 7400 percent improvement in productivity. With the same reorganization the inventory turnover rose from 5 times per year to 80 times per year. In other words the cost of the inventory fell from ten weeks' supply to less than one week's supply. Before the change the mean time between failures of the product was one year; after the change it was eight years. This increase in reliability occurred partly because of the improvement in product design and partly because the product was made by robots, which do not make the types of mistakes that humans make.

The type of organization introduced in this factory is referred to as computer-integrated manufacturing (CIM). There are other equally dramatic examples of robot production lines. When an automated production line is introduced, many other changes are needed to maintain the flow of work that keeps the expensive machinery busy. The attempt is made to do this with ''just-in-time'' inventory control. In other words goods arrive shortly before they are needed so that inventory costs are kept low. This requires tight computerized control. Many different aspects of computerization need to be integrated.

The type of automated facility that enables IBM to produce 2000 machines per day with 5 people can be applied to the production of vacuum cleaners, hi-fi units, digital television sets, cameras, intelligent cookers, and all manner of other goods. The world is on the brink of a quantum leap in automated fabrication. All manner of goods, with highly elaborate built-in microelectronics, will be mass-produced in great quantity for low prices.

However, while IBM succeeded in achieving such a dramatic change in productivity with CIM, many factories are far from it. Some have as little chance of achieving it as a hang-glider pilot has of crossing the ocean. As the most efficient corporations automate, it is difficult to see how the least efficient ones can stay in business. As with most major advances in technology, CIM will cause a major shakeout.

The factor that makes CIM difficult is implied in its middle initial. Many different aspects of computerization have to be integrated to build today's factory automation. This aspect of complex integration applies not only to factories but to distribution channels, bank networks, insurance companies, military logistics, airline operations, and so on. We are moving into an era when many complex aspects of computing have to work together. The future of computing is a battle with complexity.

Online ordering and tracking of orders is necessary to minimize inventories or achieve just-in-time inventory control. Inland Steel provides services to customers enabling them to track orders of steel and estimates that the customers' saving in inventory costs from this are greater than the difference between American and Japanese steel prices.

AUTOMATED LINKS BETWEEN CORPORATIONS

When a computer generates a purchase order this should not be printed, mailed, and then key-entered into another computer. Rather, it should be transmitted electronically to the vendor computer. Key entering is tedious, error-prone work, and systems will be designed to avoid it where possible. To do this, the appropriate data formats need to be agreed among corporations, or, better, industry standard data formats should be used. The U.S. National Bureau of Standards has created standards for records exchanged among businesses, such as purchase orders and invoices. The Department of Defense has defined standard formats for the computer-aided design (CAD) representation of parts. Any such standards that facilitate electronic exchange among corporations should be well publicized. It would be valuable for the International Standards Organization (ISO) to agree upon and publicize such standards.

Corporations with many factories or worldwide operations should do all their intercorporate ordering and billing using their own standard data formats. These formats need to reside in the data models at each location.

The searching of catalogs and the placing of orders from a catalog should take place at workstation screens where possible. This helps the person doing the ordering and avoids the clumsy interim stages of writing, mailing, and key entering. Many corporations are providing customers or agents with terminals for placing orders, tracking the status of orders, searching catalogs, and so on. American Airlines gained great competitive advantage by placing such terminals in the offices of travel agents. Even though the terminals gave information about the flights of other airlines, they increased the probability that the agent would book American Airlines seats rather than those of competing airlines. Even if the agent books a seat on another airline, American collects a service fee. It is estimated that American increased its bookings by 15 to 20 percent with this system. The pretax profit from the system is estimated to exceed $150 million a year.

Workstations in one corporation, online to another corporation, sometimes provide complex services. Insurance companies provide agents with systems that enable them to make complex decisions about contracts and renewals. Some companies allow customers access to their database to track their orders and shipments. Sometimes customers can configure products online, examining and pricing many complex alternatives. In some cases financial or administration services are provided to small agencies. Some agencies worldwide are online to corporations whose products they market.

The new Saturn car plant of General Motors is designed so that many of the parts suppliers are in the same factory complex. The manufacturing schedules of the suppliers are then tightly linked to the assembly of the cars. The plant is online to car dealers. There are many options in configuring the car. The dealer works out with customers what options they desire, using a computer to assemble pictures of the car with different options and to price the resulting car. The order is transmitted to the computers at the Saturn plant and manufacturing of that car can begin quickly. The car being assembled travels on an automatically guided palette to only those assembly points that are needed for the order in question. The parts inventory and scheduling are adjusted accordingly. The customer can have the custom-configured car in a few days. This level of automation requires the integration of many different computer applications—a much higher level of integration than has been used in the past. The entire complex is designed to operate without paper to the maximum extent practical. Accounting is online. Expense accounts, for example, are handled by filling in details at a screen. This further complicates the integration of the separate systems.

We cannot design and maintain the complex integration of systems that is required unless we use computers themselves for this task. We need the automation of automation. There is today a vast difference between the design and maintenance of computer systems in the best and worst information systems organizations. The best are using disciplined techniques with automated CASE tools. The worst are using plastic templates and creating spaghetti code.

The sales representative of factory automation keeps away from the backward factories with vines covering the walls. The sales representative of design automation tools keeps away from the information systems departments that have not yet moved to structured programming and design. The best corporations upgrade to the most modern tools; the worst are left to fester in their disorganized mess.

RIGOROUS   Automation directly affects productivity. Information
ENGINEERING   systems directly affect decision making. Computers
                      and networks are growing rapidly in cost-effectiveness, and increasingly in the future, corporations with poor automation and information systems will not be able to compete.

As systems become more complex, they cannot sensibly be built without rigorous engineering. We cannot achieve rigorous engineering of software and information without automated tools. Tools for the design of systems must be linked to tools for code generation. Complex systems need tools that facilitate iterative or exploratory development. The tools must relate to the entire enterprise so that separately developed systems link together and strategic control of systems is practical. The tools should enforce full structuring of code and data, with automated editors so that systems are as easy to change as possible. The maintenance trap is extremely harmful; it prevents a corporation from changing its procedures to keep up with the dynamic evolution of the business. Well-engineered systems built with the most automated tools are designed so that they can be modified quickly. The tools should ensure this ease of modification.

INTEGRATION OF SYSTEMS

Separate systems are developed by separate teams. It is not practical for one team to build all the facilities of a complex corporation. To make the separately developed systems work together, the techniques of synthesis and coordination are needed. A top-down overview is needed of the processes and the data that are used. The data employed by the separately developed systems must be compatible—it should be derived from the same overall data model.

By developing the separate systems in conjunction with an overall information strategy plan, compatibility of data can be achieved. Synthesis using automated tools is essential because no one person has more than a fraction of the knowledge required. In addition to ensuring logical compatibility it is necessary that the systems are compatible from the networking point of view. Overall strategic planning of the corporate network is essential.

KNOWLEDGE BASES

Information systems of the future will increasingly use knowledge bases in conjunction with conventional databases. Expertise built into knowledge bases becomes steadily more refined as it has in Digital Equipment Corporation's pioneering use of expert systems. The existence of a maturing expert system affects everything that it touches. At DEC all sales representatives are expected to use an expert system for configuring, pricing, and controlling orders for computing systems. Designers of new computers must add to the knowledge base the knowledge needed for configuring the new systems. This computerized expert help must exist before the computer is announced. Details from the sales expert systems go to the factory expert systems, and delivery dates from the production planning expert system go to the sales representative. The production planning knowledge base in turn affects other factory expert systems. The knowledge in such systems steadily accumulates, building up a computerized base of expertise for running the corporation as efficiently as possible. These expert systems use data that is in the corporate databases.

NETWORKS AND STANDARDS

Data communication is vital to the running of corporations. Just as there is a telephone on everyone's desk today, so there will be a workstation on everyone's desk in the future. (This has already happened in many organizations.) The data network is the nervous system of the corporation; the workstations are its nerve endings. The workstations give access to information. The capability to process this information, display it graphically, do computations with it, and make decisions with it often resides locally even though the data may have been extracted from databases far away. Often the workstation is a personal computer; sometimes it will be a terminal of a departmental computer or system designed for a group of employees.

The workstation software and hardware will avoid the need to use coded commands and punctuation, which most people find difficult. It will replace any form of alien syntax with easy-to-learn forms of dialog employing techniques such as icons, graphics, a mouse, pull-down menus, windows, scrolling, a screen desktop analogy, and natural human language. All employees in efficient corporations of the future will be expected to be able to use the workstations. The databases to which these workstations have access will be designed to be flexible and to make it easy to extract information for local manipulation. The software connecting the workstation to the machines with databases will provide these machines with transparent windows.

To achieve the connectability that is desired, network standards are extremely important. The desktop workstation or departmental computer needs to access computers and databases anywhere in the organization in a transparent fashion. Network standards need to facilitate the transparent interconnection of machines from different vendors. Selecting and enforcing the network standards is a vital part of the strategic planning for networks in an organization. The standards apply to worldwide communication, communications satellites, local area networks, and other forms of transmission. Local area networks are important for obtaining fast response times, fast screen painting, and desk-to-desk communication within a building complex.

BUILDING HUMAN POTENTIAL

As computerized tools, robot machinery, and automated process control become more powerful, people tend to move into jobs of greater responsibility that require more skill. Often they are more interesting jobs, with higher pay. The annual revenue generated per person in highly automated corporations is often greater than $200,000 per person, whereas that in corporations with little automation is often less than $100,000 per person. The automated corporation demands greater skills for greater pay. In the Saturn plant of General Motors the mind-destroying job of the car production line worker has been replaced with a more intelligent job for workers who carry out a set of tasks as the car moves through automated assembly stations. Humans do not any more act like robots on a relentlessly moving production line; robot-like work is done by robots. A new union contract has been negotiated for the new-style car workers that gives them a salary and profit sharing. In a similar way moronic clerical work is tending to be replaced. Work with paper forms is disappearing. Bookkeepers are no longer adding up columns of figures. Financial staff, working with spreadsheets and decision support tools, is expected to make more intelligent decisions. Loan officers, maintenance personnel, diagnostic technicians, and production schedulers will have access to expert systems. Systems analysts and programmers use more sophisticated tools giving them more power to be creative.

As technological potential is built up, so human potential must be built up with it. Efficient technological corporations such as IBM and DEC pay much attention to building human skills to keep pace with the growing demands and opportunities of technology. If people are left to do moronic jobs for too long, the ability to upgrade their work skills becomes diminished. There has been a startling lack of success in attempts to retrain car production line workers to do more interesting work. If you are 40 and have spent 20 years of your life on a car production line, you probably have a level of mental fossilization that makes it almost impossible for you to learn more demanding jobs.

The corporation with its eye on the future attempts to develop the skills of its employees so that they can succeed well with the technology that is coming. Secretaries should use electronic mail and spreadsheets. Office workers should be made computer-literate. Blue-collar workers should be introduced to more automated machines or should operate multiple machine tools. Use of the most valuable types of personal computer software should be encouraged. Managers should be involved in information strategy planning and business area analysis studies. Experts of many types should take an interest in expert systems that might multiply their influence. All employees should be encouraged to think creatively about how the procedures they use can be improved.

THREE WAVES OF ENTRY IN TECHNOLOGY   Corporations tend to divide into three categories in their adoption of new technology. First, there are the pioneers (Fig. 17.2). These are a small fraction of all corporations. The cost of pioneering may be high. The pioneers face substantial startup costs in order to gain a major competitive advantage through being first. American Airlines, for example, gained a major competitive advantage from having the world's first online seat reservation sys-

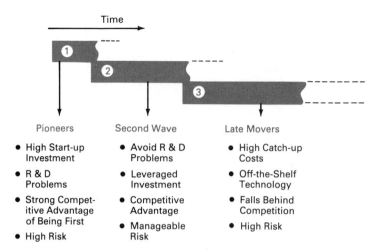

Figure 17.2   Three waves of technology application.

tem and, then, years later, gained a still larger advantage by placing terminals in the offices of travel agents, connected to an expanded version of its system. Both these pioneering systems were expensive, high-risk developments. But they both had large payoffs.

A second wave of corporations moves into a technology when the pioneers have demonstrated that it can be made to work. By this time there are lessons to be learned from the pioneers; there are seminars to attend; there are products on the market that have been tried, tested, and improved. There are far fewer research and development problems. The startup costs are lower. The risk is manageable. The first- and second-wave corporations are perhaps only 20 percent of all corporations, so there is still a strong competitive advantage to being second wave.

In the third wave are those corporations, production engineering departments, information systems departments, and so on that are set in their ways. They know how to manage their current technology and find many reasons for staying with it. Technicians, alarmed that they might become obsolete, find reasons for pouring scorn on the new ideas. The pioneers have already left to join another company. Many corporations and their technical departments avoid the need for upheaval until they are pushed into it. These late movers then have high catch-up costs. They often do not have the technical staff they need. By the time they implement the new technology, they have fallen severely behind their competition. Sometimes they never catch up with the early adaptors but instead buy services or move into less high-tech business areas. Being a late adaptor to advanced technologies constitutes a high business risk.

Late adaptors have the expense of conversion but do not gain competitive advantage from the conversion. They may have difficulty managing the conversion well, even though the technology is now off-the-shelf and stable. The last airlines to put in online reservation systems were not able to put terminals in travel agents' offices but had to buy services from their competition. The late adaptors to factory automation with robots and CIM may not be able to manufacture goods cheaply enough to sell them against their competition. With some technological changes the late adaptors will not stay in business.

GOVERNMENT

It is hoped that government departments of the future will be equally efficient in automation, but today, around the world, many public enterprises are not achieving the productivity through computers that is found in good private corporations. Government departments are usually immune from the intense competitive pressures that drive private corporations to automate. In industry there is a pressure to reduce headcount, to reduce costs, while in government, people-consuming bureaucracy tends to spread. In noncompetitive enterprises, tangible goals need to be established that replace the driving forces that stem from competition.

SUMMARY

It is difficult to see a revolution when one is in the middle of it. Today we are in the middle of a revolution concerning humankind's work. The social implications of this are great, and these have been discussed elsewhere [2]. When the revolution is complete, we will have highly automated factories, distribution channels, and services, with highly integrated networks of computers. The computer power in U.S. industry, measured in instructions per second, is increasing 1000-fold. Much of this increase is from the spread of personal computers and departmental computers. These widely distributed computers will become much more powerful and will need to be integrated with each other and with mainframes. The corporation of the future will be run with a vast mesh of interacting computers and database systems. It will be impossible to manage and build the procedures to take advantage of this technology with conventional unautomated tools.

Historians of the future will look back at the evolution of computing designed to change so much in society and will be amazed that the early attempts at data processing were done by hand. They will marvel that corporations survived the early incompatible spaghetti mess that computing was when manual methods were used.

REFERENCES

1. Peter F. Drucker, "Playing in the Information-Based 'Orchestra,' " *The Wall Street Journal,* June 4, 1985.

2. James Martin, *Technology's Crucible* (Englewood Cliffs, NJ: Prentice Hall, 1986).

PART **IV** APPENDICES

APPENDIX

I ENTITIES AND NORMALIZATION

An entity is something about which we store data. It can be a tangible object, such as an employee, a part, a customer, a machine tool, or an office. It can be intangible, such as a job title, a profit center, an association, a financial allowance, a purchase, an estimate, or an insurance claim. In analyzing information we study the entities of the enterprise in question. As discussed in Chapters 4 and 8, a typical corporation has several hundred entities. Its set of entities does not change much as time goes by unless the firm moves into a fundamentally different type of business.

An entity has various *attributes* that we wish to record, such as size, value, date, color, usage code, address, quality, performance code, and so on. Often in data processing we are concerned with a collection of similar entities, such as employees, and we wish to record information about the same attributes of each of them. A programmer commonly maintains a *record* about each entity, and a *data item* in each record relates to each attribute. Similar records are grouped into *files*. The result, shown in Fig. I.1 is a two-dimensional array.

Inside the box in Fig. I.1 is a set of data items. The value of each data item is shown. Each row of data items relates to a particular entity. Each column contains a particular type of data item, relating to a particular type of attribute. At the top of the diagram, outside the box, the names of the attributes are written. The leftmost column in the box contains the data items that *identify* the entity. The entity in this example is a person—an employee. The attribute referred to as the entity identifier in this case is *Employee-#*.

Such a two-dimensional array is sometimes referred to as a *flat file*. The use of flat files dates back to the earliest days of data processing when the file might have been on punched cards. Each card in a file or deck of cards such as that in Fig. I.2 might contain one record, relating to one entity. Certain card columns were allocated to each data-item type, or attribute, and were called a *field*. When magnetic tapes replaced decks of cards and disks replaced magnetic

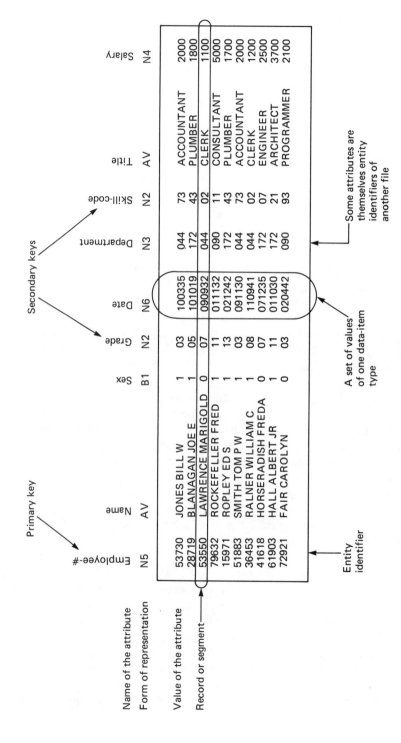

Figure I.1 Two-dimensional array.

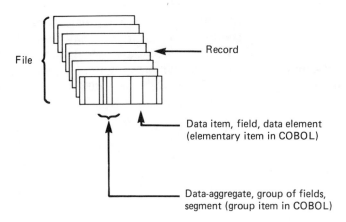

File

Record

Data item, field, data element
(elementary item in COBOL)

Data-aggregate, group of fields,
segment (group item in COBOL)

Figure I.2   A flat file, showing the wording commonly used to describe the application programmer's view of data.

tapes, many programmers retained their view of data as being organized into flat files. Today's database management systems store data in much more complex ways. However, the most sophisticated database management systems—those that use relational techniques—allow the user to retain the simplistic view of data as if it were organized as a series of flat files.

NORMALIZATION

A theory known as *normalization theory,* first described by E. F. Codd, has been used to aid in the design of all types of databases. Normalization theory can be described in rigorous mathematical terms. However, its underlying ideas are simple and have much to do with ordinary common sense. In this appendix, we will rely on simple explanations and examples to show how the normalization process can be used to help stabilize the design of databases.

The overall goals of the normalization process are to:

- Arrange data so that it can be represented in tabular form where each row-column position contains a single data item (no repeating groups).

- Ensure that data items are associated with the correct keys, and thereby minimize data redundancy.

Normalization involves a series of steps that change the column structure of the various records that make up a database by placing the data into a series of different forms called *first normal form, second normal form,* and so on. In this appendix, we will view data as if it were stored in the tables of a relational database. However, the same techniques can be employed to design the segment or record structures of other types of databases.

FIRST NORMAL FORM

The first step of the normalization process is to place the data into *first normal form*. This involves the removal of repeating groups. We remove repeating groups by simply creating a separate row, or record, for each of the elements in the repeating group. Suppose we begin with the following employee data:

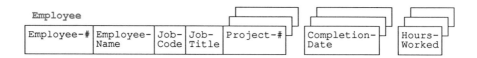

Here, a given record stores information about a number of different projects that a particular employee has worked on.

To represent this data in tabular form, we generate a separate record for each project an employee has worked on by repeating the employee information in each record. Here is how the data would look in tabular form; each row represents a separate record occurrence:

Employee

Employee-#	Employee-Name	Job-Code	Job-Title	Project-#	Completion-Date	Hours-Worked
120	Jones	1	Programmer	01	7/17	37
120	Jones	1	Programmer	08	1/12	12
121	Harpo	1	Programmer	01	7/17	45
121	Harpo	1	Programmer	08	1/12	21
121	Harpo	1	Programmer	12	3/21	107
270	Garfunkel	2	Analyst	08	1/12	10
270	Garfunkel	2	Analyst	12	3/21	78
273	Selsi	3	Designer	01	7/17	22
274	Abrahms	2	Analyst	12	3/21	41
279	Higgins	1	Programmer	01	7/17	27
279	Higgins	1	Programmer	08	1/12	20
279	Higgins	1	Programmer	12	3/21	51
301	Flannel	1	Programmer	01	7/17	16
301	Flannel	1	Programmer	12	3/21	85
306	McGraw	3	Designer	12	3/21	67

It is generally useful to define a unique key that identifies each row. (This is required with some database management systems.) In some cases, it is possible to identify a single data item that uniquely identifies each row; in other cases, two or more data items must be combined to form a *concatenated key*. In this case, we must use both the *Employee-#* and *Project-#* columns as a concatenated key that uniquely identifies each row, as shown:

Employee

Employee-#	Project-#	Employee-Name	Job-Code	Job-Title	Completion-Date	Hours-Worked
120	01	Jones	1	Programmer	7/17	37
120	08	Jones	1	Programmer	1/12	12
121	01	Harpo	1	Programmer	7/17	45
121	08	Harpo	1	Programmer	1/12	21
121	12	Harpo	1	Programmer	3/21	107
270	08	Garfunkel	2	Analyst	1/12	10
270	12	Garfunkel	2	Analyst	3/21	78
273	01	Selsi	3	Designer	7/17	22
274	12	Abrahms	2	Analyst	3/21	41
279	01	Higgins	1	Programmer	7/17	27
279	08	Higgins	1	Programmer	1/12	20
279	12	Higgins	1	Programmer	3/21	51
301	01	Flannel	1	Programmer	7/17	16
301	12	Flannel	1	Programmer	3/21	85
306	12	McGraw	3	Designer	3/21	67

One of the goals of the normalization process is to reduce data redundancy. At this point, it appears that we are actually increasing data redundancy by placing the data into first normal form; job code and job title data items are repeated many times, and the same completion dates are stored multiple times as well. This increase in data redundancy is an important argument for why further normalization steps are required to produce a stable design. A table that is only in first normal form may have many undesirable characteristics, of which data redundancy is only one. We will see how subsequent steps in the normalization process will reduce the redundancy that we have introduced and how additional normalization steps improve our data structure in other important ways as well.

SECOND NORMAL FORM

The second step in the normalization process places our data into *second normal form*. Second normal form involves the idea of *functional dependence*.

Functional Dependence

In general a given column, say, column *B,* is functionally dependent on some other column, say, column *A,* if for any given value of column *A* there is a single value of column *B* associated with it. Saying that column *B* is functionally dependent on column *A* is equivalent to saying that column *A* *identifies* column *B.* Notice in our table that there are three rows having an *Employee-#* value of *121,* but in each of those rows, the *Employee-Name* data item value is the same—*Harpo:*

Employee

Employee-#	Project-#	Employee-Name	Job-Code	Job-Title	Completion-Date	Hours-Worked
120	01	Jones	1	Programmer	7/17	37
120	08	Jones	1	Programmer	1/12	12
121	01	Harpo	1	Programmer	7/17	45
121	08	Harpo	1	Programmer	1/12	21
121	12	Harpo	1	Programmer	3/21	107
270	08	Garfunkel	2	Analyst	1/12	10
270	12	Garfunkel	2	Analyst	3/21	78
273	01	Selsi	3	Designer	7/17	22
274	12	Abrahms	2	Analyst	3/21	41
279	01	Higgins	1	Programmer	7/17	27
279	08	Higgins	1	Programmer	1/12	20
279	12	Higgins	1	Programmer	3/21	51
301	01	Flannel	1	Programmer	7/17	16
301	12	Flannel	1	Programmer	3/21	85
306	12	McGraw	3	Designer	3/21	67

A similar relationship exists between the *Employee-#* and *Employee-Name* columns in the other rows that have the same *Employee-#* value. Therefore, as long as we assume that no two employees can have the same employee number, *Employee-Name* is functionally dependent on *Employee-#*. We can use the same argument to show that *Job-Code* and *Job-Title* are also functionally dependent on *Employee-#*.

Full Functional Dependence

In some cases, a column will not be functionally dependent on a single column but will be functionally dependent on a *group* of columns. For example, *Hours-Worked* is functionally dependent on the combination of *Employee-#* and *Project-#*. This leads to the idea of *full functional dependence*. A column can be said to be fully functionally dependent on some collection of other columns when it is functionally dependent on the entire set but not on any subset of that collection. *Hours-Worked* is fully functionally dependent on *Employee-#* and *Project-#*. However, *Completion-Date* is not fully functionally dependent on *Employee-#* and *Project-#*, since *Completion-Date* is functionally dependent on *Project-#* alone.

To place into second normal form a group of columns that is in first normal form, we identify all the functional dependencies that exist and create a separate table, or record, for each set of these. We begin by identifying a likely key—in this case *Employee-#*—and determining which other columns are fully functionally dependent on that key. *Employee-Name, Job-Code,* and *Job-Title* are functionally dependent on *Employee-#*, so we move them to a separate *Employee* table that has *Employee-#* as its primary key:

Employee

Employee-#	Employee-Name	Job-Code	Job-Title
120	Jones	1	Programmer
121	Harpo	1	Programmer
270	Garfunkel	2	Analyst
273	Selsi	3	Designer
274	Abrahms	2	Analyst
279	Higgins	1	Programmer
301	Flannel	1	Programmer
306	McGraw	3	Designer

Of the remaining columns, *Completion-Date* is dependent on *Project-#*, so we move the *Project-#* and *Completion-Date* columns to a separate *Project* table that has *Project-#* as the primary key:

Project

Project-#	Completion-Date
01	7/17
08	1/12
12	3/21

This leaves the *Hours-Worked* column. *Hours-Worked* is fully functionally dependent on the concatenated key that consists of *Employee-#* and *Project-#*. So we create a third table called *Hours* that consists of *Employee-#*, *Project-#*, and *Hours-Worked*. The key of the *Hours* table consists of *Employee-#* and *Project-#*:

Hours

Employee-#	Project-#	Hours-Worked
120	01	37
120	08	12
121	01	45
121	08	21
121	12	107
270	08	10
270	12	78
273	01	22
274	12	41
279	01	27
279	08	20
279	12	51
301	01	16
301	12	85
306	12	67

We can now say that our set of columns is in second normal form because it is in first normal form and every nonkey column is fully functionally dependent on the primary key of its table.

Notice that we have repeated the *Employee-#* column in two of the tables and that we have repeated the *Project-#* column in two of the tables:

Employee

Employee-#	Employee-Name	Job-Code	Job-Title
120	Jones	1	Programmer
121	Harpo	1	Programmer
270	Garfunkel	2	Analyst
273	Selsi	3	Designer
274	Abrahms	2	Analyst
279	Higgins	1	Programmer
301	Flannel	1	Programmer
306	McGraw	3	Designer

Project

Project-#	Completion-Date
01	7/17
08	1/12
12	3/21

Hours

Employee-#	Project-#	Hours-Worked
120	01	37
120	08	12
121	01	45
121	08	21
121	12	107
270	08	10
270	12	78
273	01	22
274	12	41
279	01	27
279	08	20
279	12	51
301	01	16
301	12	85
306	12	67

Duplicating columns is perfectly valid and often occurs when converting a group of columns to second normal form. By duplicating columns in multiple tables, we are able to use relational operators to combine the tables in various ways to extract the data we need from them.

Notice that placing the data into second normal form has reduced much of the redundancy that existed in the original table. *Job-Code* and *Job-Title* data item values now appear only once per employee, and *Completion-Date* data item values appear only once per project.

Now that we have our data in second normal form, we can point out another undesirable characteristic of a table that is first normal form only. When our data was in first normal form only, we had a single table whose primary key consisted of *Employee-#* and *Project-#*. We need to have valid values for both *Employee-#* and *Project-#* in order to create a new row. This means that we would be unable to store a row for an employee that is currently not assigned to a project (null *Project-#* value). Similarly, we would be unable to store a row for a project that currently has no employees assigned to it (null *Employee-# value).

With our columns in second normal form, we can add a new employee by adding a row to the *Employee* table without having to change either of the other two tables. After the new employee has been assigned to a project and has logged some time on that project, we can add a row to the *Hours* table to describe the project assignment and the number of hours logged. In a similar manner, we can add a row to the *Project* table to describe a new project without changing either the *Employee* or *Hours* tables. Both these functions would be impossible if our tables were not in second normal form.

THIRD NORMAL FORM

The third step in the normalization process involves the idea of *transitive dependence*. Suppose we have a table with columns *A, B,* and *C:*

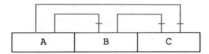

If column *C* is functionally dependent on column *B*, and column *B* is functionally dependent on column *A*, then column *C* is functionally dependent on column *A:*

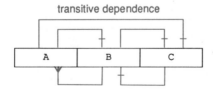

If similar dependencies are not true in the opposite direction (i.e., column *A* is not functionally dependent on column *B* or column *B* is not functionally dependent on column *C*), then column *C* is said to be transitively dependent on column *A:*

transitive dependence

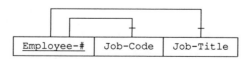

We said earlier that *Job-Code* and *Job-Title* were functionally dependent on *Employee-#:*

Assuming there is only one job title associated with a given job code, *Job-Title* is functionally dependent on *Job-Code:*

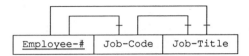

| Employee-# | Job-Code | Job-Title |

In the reverse direction *Job-Code* is functionally dependent on *Job-Title* as long as a given job title is associated with only one job code. However, many employees may have the same job code. So *Employee-#* is not functionally dependent on *Job-Code*. This means that *Job-Title* is transitively dependent on *Employee-#:*

transitive dependence

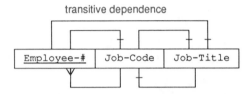

| Employee-# | Job-Code | Job-Title |

To place our data into third normal form, we must remove transitive dependencies. This is done by placing the *Job-Title* column in a separate table called *Jobs* with *Job-Code* as its primary key. The following tables show the data after it has been placed into third normal form:

Employee

Employee-#	Employee-Name	Job-Code
120	Jones	1
121	Harpo	1
270	Garfunkel	2
273	Selsi	3
274	Abrahms	2
279	Higgins	1
301	Flannel	1
306	McGraw	3

Jobs

Job-Code	Job-Title
1	Programmer
2	Analyst
3	Designer

Project

Project-#	Completion-Date
01	7/17
08	1/12
12	3/21

Hours

Employee-#	Project-#	Hours-Worked
120	01	37
120	08	12
121	01	45
121	08	21
121	12	107
270	08	10
270	12	78
273	01	22
274	12	41
279	01	27
279	08	20
279	12	51
301	01	16
301	12	85
306	12	67

A table is said to be in third normal form if it is in second normal form and every nonkey column is nontransitively dependent on the primary key. We can give a simpler definition of third normal form by saying that in third normal form, all the columns of a table are functionally dependent on the key, the whole key, and nothing but the key.

Placing data into third normal form eliminates more potentially undesirable characteristics of data that is in only first or second normal form. The preceding set of tables shows that a job title associated with a given job code now appears in only one place instead of appearing for each employee that has that job code. This makes it easier to change a job title, since the change has to be made in only one place. Also, we can now add a new job code with its associated job title even though no employee has yet been assigned that job code. And we will not lose the job title if we temporarily have no employees assigned a given job code.

FOURTH NORMAL FORM

In the great majority of cases, placing data into third normal form provides a sufficient level of normalization. Higher levels of normalization are possible, however, and it is occasionally beneficial to place data into *fourth normal form*.

Suppose that an employee can be assigned to several projects concurrently. Also suppose that an employee can possess a series of skills. If we record this information in a single table we need to use all three columns as the key, since no other column grouping produces unique row identification.

Employee-Project-Skill

Employee-#	Project-#	Skill
120	01	Design
120	01	Program
120	01	Document
120	08	Design
120	08	Program
120	08	Document

Using a single table like the foregoing one is not desirable because values have to be repeated, which could cause consistency problems when updating. However, since there are no columns in this table that are not part of the key, the table is in third normal form. We can represent the relationships in this table in a simpler manner if we split them into the following two separate all-key tables:

```
Employee-Project              Employee-Skill
```

Employee-#	Project-#
120	01
120	08

Employee-#	Skill
120	Design
120	Program
120	Document

These tables are in fourth normal form. Fourth normal form involves the idea of *multivalued dependencies,* in which a given value for a single column identifies multiple values of another column. A multivalued dependency is defined in terms of the set of values from one column that is associated with a given pair of values from two other columns. Look again at our original three-column table:

```
Employee-Project-Skill
```

Employee-#	Project-#	Skill
120	01	Design
120	01	Program
120	01	Document
120	08	Design
120	08	Program
120	08	Document

The relationship between *Employee-#* and *Project-#* is a multivalued dependency because for each pair of *Employee-#/Skill* values in the table, the associated set of *Project-#* values is determined only by *Employee-#* and is independent of *Skill*. Similarly, the relationship between *Employee-#* and *Skill* is a multivalued dependency, since the set of *Skill* values for an *Employee-#/Project-#* pair is independent of *Project-#*. Conversion to fourth normal form involves decomposing the original table into multiple tables so that the multivalued dependencies are eliminated.

Notice that the two individual tables better represent the true relationships between the columns because there is no real relationship between projects and skills. Also, there is less redundant data in the two separate tables, and the update behavior of the two separate tables is better as well. For example, if an employee acquires a new skill, we simply add a new row to the *Employee-Skill* table. With the single table, we would have to add multiple rows, one for each of the projects the employee is assigned to.

Another way of looking at fourth normal is that it gives us a good way of handling multiple repeating groups. We could view the original set of data in the following manner, where *Project-#* and *Skill* each takes the form of a repeating group:

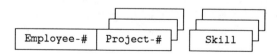

Placing the data into fourth normal form simply eliminates the repeating groups by placing each of them into a separate table. In actual practice, the earlier steps of normalization often identify such repeating groups and remove them, thus producing third normal form tables that are already also in fourth normal form.

FIFTH NORMAL FORM

Fifth normal form is of interest mainly to users of relational database management systems that will be performing relational operations on the tables that make up the database. The relational operations that are concerned with fifth normal form are quite simple, so this discussion of fifth normal form can be understood even if the reader currently has no background in the relational database architecture.

In all the normalization steps we have discussed thus far, we have split tables into their constituent parts by performing what is essentially a relational *project* operation. A *project* operation produces a new table that contains all the rows from the original table, but only a subset of the columns. Any rows that contain exactly the same values as another row are then eliminated from the result. For example, let us begin with the following table that we looked at previously:

Employee-Project-Skill

Employee-#	Project-#	Skill
120	01	Design
120	01	Program
120	01	Document
120	08	Design
120	08	Program
120	08	Document

One projection of this table would produce a new table with only *Employee-#* and *Project-#* columns:

Employee-Project-Skill

Employee-#	Project-#
120	01
120	01
120	01
120	08
120	08
120	08

Eliminating redundant rows, the final result would be

Employee-Project-Skill

Employee-#	Project-#
120	01
120	08

In all the previous examples, we were able to split a table into a set of its projections that together contain all the original columns while still retaining all the data contained in the original table. In other words, we were able to recombine the constituent tables to exactly re-create the original table.

There exist, however, some tables, in fourth normal form, that contain three columns but cannot be split into two projections and then recombined to form the original table. This phenomenon occurs because of the particular combination of data item values that occurs in the table and is the result of the inherent relationships in the data. Consider the following table:

Employee-Project-Skill

Employee-#	Project-#	Skill
120	01	Design
120	08	Program
120	01	Program
205	01	Program

Here an employee is assigned to one or more projects and uses one or more skills on each project. However, in this case the particular combinations of data item values that are stored in the table implies that there is a relationship not only between employees and skills (an employee has a particular skill) but also between projects and skills (certain skills are employed by each project). We can interpret these relationships to mean that an employee *uses* a skill that he or she possesses on a project only if that skill is *employed* by that project. This means that employees may *have* skills that are not *used* on projects to which they are assigned.

At first glance, the preceding table seems to have the same characteristics as the table in the example we looked at when examining fourth normal form. However, suppose we split the table into two of its projections as we did earlier:

Employee-Project   Employee-Skill

Employee-#	Project-#
120	01
120	08
205	01

Employee-#	Skill
120	Design
120	Program
205	Program

Since we have two tables that together contain all the columns from the original table, it appears as though these two tables are equivalent to the original table. Let us now perform a relational *join* operation in an attempt to re-create the original table. A relational *join* operation combines the rows from the two tables and results in a new table that combines all the rows from both tables. The *join* operation is based on data item values that are common between the two tables. In this case, the resulting table is formed by matching up the *Employee-#* values from both tables. By performing the *join* we get the following result:

Employee-Project-Skill

Employee-#	Project-#	Skill
120	01	Design
120	08	Design
120	01	Program
120	08	Program
205	01	Program

Notice that this table has an extra row that the original table did not have (the second row). *Project 08* now appears to use design skills when the original data shows no employee performing design tasks for that project. The reason this occurs is that the two tables that we created by performing *project* operations on the original table do not accurately represent all the associations inherent in the original table. In this case, the original combination of data item values implies that there *does* exist a relationship between projects and skills; each project only uses certain types of skills. This relationship is lost when we decompose the table into the two projections shown.

It is interesting to note that the original table does *not* contain multivalued dependencies and thus is already in fourth normal form. The set of *Project-#* values associated with each *Employee-Skill* pair *is* dependent on both *Employee-#* and *Skill* and not just on *Employee-#*. Similarly, sets of *Skill* values are dependent on both *Employee-#* and *Project-#*. Thus, it is not correct to separate the table into only *two* projections. One of the relationships is lost by doing so.

The table can, however, be further normalized by placing the data into *fifth normal form*. This involves decomposing the table into *three* projections, thus retaining all three relationships that exist between the various data items:

Employee-Project   Employee-Skill   Project-Skill

Employee-#	Project-#
120	01
120	08
205	01

Employee-#	Skill
120	Design
120	Program
205	Program

Project-#	Skill
01	Design
08	Program
01	Program

To join three tables, we first perform a relational *join* on the first two tables to form an intermediate result. We then join the intermediate table with the third table to form the final result of the three-way *join* operation. The result of the first *join* operation in this case corresponds to an intermediate result that shows all the skills that *might* be used on projects:

Employee-Project-Skill

Employee-#	Project-#	Skill
120	01	Design
120	08	Design
120	01	Program
120	08	Program
205	01	Program

The third table specifies the skills that each project *actually* uses. We then join the intermediate table with the third table:

Employee-Project-Skill

Employee-#	Project-#	Skill
120	01	Design
120	08	Design
120	01	Program
120	08	Program
205	01	Program

Project-Skill

Project-#	Skill
01	Design
08	Program
01	Program

In performing this *join*, we match up sets of both *Project-#* and *Skill* data item values. Because values for both project *08* and skill *Design* do not exist in both tables, the spurious row is eliminated, and we get a result that is identical to our original table:

Employee-Project-Skill

Employee-#	Project-#	Skill
120	01	Design
120	08	Program
120	01	Program
205	01	Program

The projections from the previous example, which *can* be rejoined to produce the original table, are in fifth normal form. This constraint on which projections can be validly rejoined is called a *join dependency*.

A table that is in fourth normal form but not in fifth normal form has strange update behavior. Consider the following table in which an employee uses design skills on one project and programming skills on some other project:

Employee-Project-Skill

Employee-#	Project-#	Skill
120	01	Design
120	08	Program

Suppose we added a new employee to the table, who uses programming skills on project *01:*

Employee-Project-Skill

Employee-#	Project-#	Skill
120	01	Design
120	08	Program
205	01	Program

The addition of that one row to the table on first glance seems to be valid. But let us now again decompose the table into its three fifth normal form projections:

Employee-Project

Employee-#	Project-#
120	01
120	08
205	01

Employee-Skill

Employee-#	Skill
120	Design
120	Program
205	Program

Project-Skill

Project-#	Skill
01	Design
08	Program
01	Program

We now rejoin the three preceding tables, producing the following result:

Employee-Project-Skill

Employee-#	Project-#	Skill
120	01	Design
120	08	Program
120	01	Program
205	01	Program

Notice that this table has one extra row than the table we began with. This result at first seems intuitively wrong. Does this mean that the three projections are not in fifth normal form? No, it means that it is not valid to add only that one row to the non–fifth normal form table. By adding the one new row to the non–fifth normal form table, we are actually stating three facts:

1. Employee *205* has been assigned to *Project 01*.

2. Employee *205* has *Programming* skills.

3. Project *01* now uses *Programming* skills.

By analyzing the contents of the original table together with the foregoing facts, we can see that when we add the new row for employee *205*, project *01*, and the *Programming* skill, then we must also add a new row for employee *120*, project *01*, and the *Programming* skill. This is because employee *120* already had the *Programming* skill and was already assigned to project *01*; thus, employee *120's Programming* skill is now available to project *01*, which, when we added the first row, we stated that project *01* is now using.

The join dependencies that exist in the single table that is not in fifth normal form create constraints on the updating of the table. If the table is left in fourth normal form, then we must sometimes add two rows to the table at a time instead of only one. There can be similar problems with deletions. It is often quite difficult to determine when these updating anomalies occur. Such arcane relationships are impossible for mere mortals to discern during normal update operations. But, by using the three individual tables (in fifth normal form) rather than the composite table, we can be sure that all three facts are reflected properly and completely in the table data. When the data is in fifth normal form, we can add the employee *205* data in a straightforward manner by simply adding a new row to each of the three individual tables. The two new rows will then automatically appear in the result if we rejoin the three fifth normal form individual tables.

Placing the data into fifth normal form also allows us to add data that couldn't be added to the composite table. For example, we can show an employee having a particular skill by adding a row only to the *Employee-Skill* table, even though no project currently uses that skill. This information cannot be added to the composite table, since it would require a null *Project-#* value.

Research is continuing on normalization, and even higher forms of normalization have been identified. However, it can be shown that fifth normal form is the highest form of normalization that is possible with respect to the relational operations of projection and join. Thus, fifth normal form is the highest form of normalization that is generally required in practice.

METHODOLOGY ACTION DIAGRAMS

This appendix contains action diagrams that describe the steps in the major methodologies that are discussed in this book. The action diagrams presented here include a high-level action diagram describing the information planning study as a whole and individual action diagrams describing the following methodologies:

- Technology impact analysis
- Critical success factor analysis
- Goal and problem analysis
- Business area analysis

The individual installation should tailor these action diagrams to the unique needs of the environment. An automated CASE tool that includes an action diagram editor is ideal for this purpose.

ACTION DIAGRAM FOR PERFORMING INFORMATION STRATEGY PLANNING

INFORMATION STRATEGY PLANNING

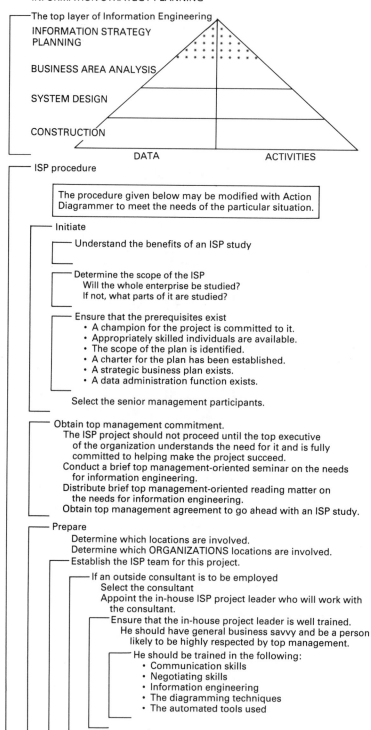

The top layer of Information Engineering

INFORMATION STRATEGY PLANNING

BUSINESS AREA ANALYSIS

SYSTEM DESIGN

CONSTRUCTION

DATA　　　　ACTIVITIES

ISP procedure

> The procedure given below may be modified with Action Diagrammer to meet the needs of the particular situation.

Initiate

Understand the benefits of an ISP study

Determine the scope of the ISP
Will the whole enterprise be studied?
If not, what parts of it are studied?

Ensure that the prerequisites exist
- A champion for the project is committed to it.
- Appropriately skilled individuals are available.
- The scope of the plan is identified.
- A charter for the plan has been established.
- A strategic business plan exists.
- A data administration function exists.

Select the senior management participants.

Obtain top management commitment.
The ISP project should not proceed until the top executive of the organization understands the need for it and is fully committed to helping make the project succeed.
Conduct a brief top management-oriented seminar on the needs for information engineering.
Distribute brief top management-oriented reading matter on the needs for information engineering.
Obtain top management agreement to go ahead with an ISP study.

Prepare
Determine which locations are involved.
Determine which ORGANIZATIONS locations are involved.
Establish the ISP team for this project.

If an outside consultant is to be employed
Select the consultant
Appoint the in-house ISP project leader who will work with the consultant.
Ensure that the in-house project leader is well trained.
He should have general business savvy and be a person likely to be highly respected by top management.

He should be trained in the following:
- Communication skills
- Negotiating skills
- Information engineering
- The diagramming techniques
- The automated tools used

Establish the in-house team who will work with the consultant.
A small team should be used. Two or three people are often
appropriate. There may be an end-user on the team.
Select future in-house BAA project leaders who will be trained
during this study.

Else

Appoint the in-house ISP project leader.
Ensure that the in-house project leader is well trained.
He should have general business savvy and be a person
likely to be highly respected by top management.
He should be trained in the following:
- Communication skills
- Negotiating skills
- Information engineering
- The diagramming techniques
- The automated tools used

Establish the in-house ISP team.
A small team should be used. Two or three people are often
appropriate. There may be an end-user on the team.
Select future in-house BAA project leaders who will be trained
during this study.

Ensure that the appropriate tools are installed and working
- An encyclopedia-based workbench appropriate for later
extension into the follow-on phases of information
engineering.

Ensure that the ISP team is adequately trained
They should be trained in the following:
- Communication skills
- Information engineering
- The diagramming techniques
- The automated tools used

Collect and evaluate existing strategic plans.
- The strategic business plan
- Existing ISP plans (if any)
- Strategic information technology plans (if any)
- Existing critical success factor studies (if any)
- Top management goals and objectives
- Existing data models (if any)
- Other relevant plans or system architecture documents.

Define a plan for successfully completing this ISP project
Modify this action diagram as required.

Determine the target date for completing the study.

Hold kickoff meeting
All the senior management participants should attend.
Have the chief executive of the enterprise make the opening speech.
Review with the participants the purpose and objectives.
Review the business assumptions that are to be made.
Review the agenda.
Give participants the preparatory material for them to study.

Conduct Linkage Analysis Planning Session

Create an overview of the enterprise

    Enter the following information into the encyclopedia:
        An organization chart showing all organizational units.
        The persons who manage the organizational units.
        Identify the major business functions.
        Decompose into lower-level functions with a function decomposition
          diagram.
        Identify the data subjects.
        Decompose into entity-types.
        Add detailed comments to the above diagrams where necessary.
        Create an initial entity-relationship diagram.

        Create a matrix mapping executives against business functions
        The involvement of the executive may be recorded with the
          following codes:
            R: Direct management RESPONSIBILITY
            A: Executive or policy-making AUTHORITY
            I: INVOLVED in the function
            E: Technical EXPERTISE
            W: Actual execution of the WORK

    Create a matrix mapping functions against organizational units.
    Create a matrix mapping functions against entity-types.
    Create a matrix mapping organizational units against entity-types.

Print relevant versions of the above diagrams from the
encyclopedia for the participants to review.

Conduct Technology Impact Analysis

> See TIA action diagram

Conduct Critical Success Factor Analysis

> See CSF action diagram

Conduct goal and problem analysis

    Obtain any existing documentation which relates to goals
    or objectives:
      • Business plans
      • Information system plans
      • Technology plans
      • Annual reports
      • Executive reports and memos
      • Reports on management-by-objectives interviews with
        executives.

    Comment
      • Goals should focus on results.
      • Goals should be as precise as possible.
      • Goals should be measureable.
      • Goals should be decomposable into work which has to be done.

    Create an initial inventory of goals
    Use an action diagram editor to represent the goal hierarchically.

> See GOALS action diagram

Determine which executives will be interviewed.
Establish the format of the interview.

For each executive

　　Conduct goal and problem interview
　　　　Review the portion of the business model which relates to
　　　　　　this executive.
　　　　Note any changes that are needed.
　　　　Establish the goals of the executive.
　　　　Identify the problems he perceives in achieving those goals.
　　　　Identify possible solutions to those problems.
　　　　Identify how information systems could help.
　　　　Rank the goals and problems.

　　Organize and record the interview information
　　　　Clean up the interview information and enter it into the
　　　　　　encyclopedia.
　　　　Refine the inventory of goals.
　　　　Rank the goals and problems.
　　　　Associate goals with organizational unit.
　　　　Associate problems with organizational unit.
　　　　Associate goals with problems.
　　　　Associate goals with information needs.
　　　　Associate problems with information needs.
　　　　Use the planning tool to analyze the goal and problem data.
　　　　Record any especially urgent information-system actions
　　　　　　that are needed.

　　Submit the record of the interview to the executive for validation.
　　Record any changes that are requested.

Refine the enterprise model
　　Make any improvements to the enterprise model as a result of
　　　　the executive interviews.
　　Complete an entity-relationship diagram.
　　Create a matrix of entity-types and business-functions.
　　Obtain approval of the enterprise model.

Group the enterprise model into natural clusters

　　Cluster the matrix to show natural systems.
　　　　Use the clustering algorithm of the strategic planning tool.
　　　　Cluster on the basis of what processes CREATE what entity-types.
　　　　Assign remaining processes and entity-types.
　　　　Refine the groupings manually.

　　Cluster the matrix to show natural business areas.
　　　　Use the clustering algorithm of the strategic planning tool.
　　　　Cluster on the basis of what processes CREATE what entity-types.
　　　　Assign remaining processes and entity-types.
　　　　Refine the groupings manually.

　　Refine BAA project boundaries
　　　　Consider:
　　　　　　• Time to implement BAA.
　　　　　　• Effort required to implement BAA.
　　　　　　• How the proposed BAA fits with the current organization.
　　　　　　• Risk assessment
　　　　　　　　User acceptance/participation
　　　　　　　　User sophistication/readiness
　　　　　　　　Technical complexity

Analyze current systems to determine what changes are needed
　　Build a matrix mapping I.S. systems against organizational units.
　　Build a matrix mapping I.S. systems against executives.
　　Build a matrix mapping I.S. systems against business functions.
　　Build a matrix mapping I.S. systems against entity-types.
　　Cluster the above matrices into business areas.
　　Identify which systems are in need of replacement or redesign.
　　Identify which systems are expensive in maintenance costs.

Prepare follow-on from Strategic Information Planning

Comment

When the ISP results are presented to top management a detailed action plan should accompany them saying what happens next. It is desirable that the ISP study is immediately followed by vigorous action which leads to implementing better systems.

Prioritize the business areas for Business Area Analysis
There are multiple factors which affect the prioritization of which business area to work on first.

Rank the factors below on a scale of 1 to 7

Potential benefits

Return on investment.
(This may be difficult to calculate and requires value judgements.)
- Tangibles.
- Intangibles.

- Achievement of critical success factors.
- Achievement of goals.
- Solution to serious problems.

Demand
- Pressure of demand from senior end-users for new or improved systems.
- Assessed need.
- Political overtones.

Organizational impact
- Number of organizations and people affected.
- Whether the organizations are geographically dispersed.
- Qualitative effect.

Existing systems
- Adequacy or value of existing systems.
- Relationship with existing systems.
- Estimated future costs of maintenance. (Systems which are fragile or have high maintenance costs should be replaced.)

Likely success
- Complexity. (Relatively simple areas should be the first to be tackled until experience is gained.)
- Degree of business acceptance.
- Length of project.
- Prerequisites.
- Risks.

Resources required
- Whether existing data or process models exist.
- Whether a suitable toolkit is installed.
- Quality of available analysts.
- Funds required.

Concurrent implementation
- Whether multiple Business Area Analysis projects can proceed concurrently.
- Whether one project will train people who can quickly move to other projects.
- Whether an existing data administration function has already done good data modeling.

312

Initiate Business Area Analysis

| See BAA action diagram |

Determine what systems should be built immediately
    The ISP generates certain urgent needs for systems for senior
    management. These should be satisfied as quickly as possible
    with relatively simple techniques such as spreadsheet tools,
    decision-support software, or executive-information-system
    software.

| See EIS action diagram |

Initiate actions to keep the ISP up-to-date
    Appoint technology-minded person to keep the Technology
    Impact Analysis up-to-date.
    Plan that Critical Success Factors should be reviewed periodically
    at business strategy planning meetings.
    Plan that Critical Success Factors should be presented at Board
    meetings for review.
    Plan that the goal and problem analysis shall be updated when
    management appraisal interviews are conducted as part of the
    management-by-objective procedure.
    Ensure that the business-function decomposition diagrams and
    entity-relationship diagrams are updated in the encyclopedia
    when Business Area Analysis is done.
    Ensure that the ISP is re-examined when major changes
    occur in the enterprise (such as a takeover).

Make top management presentation
    Obtain agreement to follow-on actions.

ACTION DIAGRAM FOR PERFORMING TECHNOLOGY IMPACT ANALYSIS

Technology Impact Analysis can be done by a team of two people in two months. It often results in changes in an organization which strongly affect profits. It therefore has an exceptionally high return on investment. Every enterprise should conduct a TIA.

Procedure for TECHNOLOGY IMPACT ANALYSIS

> The procedure given below may be modified with Action Diagrammer to meet the needs of the particular situation.

Establish the TIA team
  The team may consist of two highly experienced people, one external consultant who specializes in conducting TIAs, and one technology-minded staff person whom top management will respect.
  The consultant should have a broad knowledge of the industry.
  The in-house person should have a broad knowledge of the enterprise, and technology.

Preparation by the TIA team
  Become fully familiar with the TIA methodology.
  Become fully familiar with current trends in technology.
  Be fully familiar with the industry
  Study the corporation (Annual reports, History, Organization chart, Policies, Products, Competitive products, Literature)
  Spend time with the company management and people who have views on its competitive position, problems and opportunities.
  List the mission of the enterprise, along with its perceived goals and problems

Conduct an introductory workshop with a small key top management group
  Explain the TIA procedure
  Give them literature on the TIA procedure.
    Chapter 19 of "Information Engineering" by James Martin
  Determine which managers should participate.
  Solicit the active involvement of a key member of top management
  Set a date of the focusing workshop in which the results will be examined and discussed

Establish an action diagram showing a taxonomy of new technology
  Start with an existing action diagram.

  > See Technology Action Diagram

  Brainstorm what other technology changes might be relevant.
  ... Description

Establish an action diagram showing potential business opportunities.
  Start with an existing action diagram.

  > See Opportunities Action Diagram

  Brainstorm what other opportunities might be relevant.
  ... Description

Establish a matrix mapping technology against business opportunities.

  Mark the matrix with time scale codes
      0: Immediate.
      1: 1 year away.
      2: 2 years away.
      3: 3 years away.
      Etc.

  Mark the matrix with priority codes
      A: Very Critical. Immediate implementation is needed.
      B: Critical. Should be implemented with some urgency.
      C: Should be implemented with medium priority.
      D: Required, but with no urgency.
      E: Desirable, but not absolutely required.

  Eliminate unimportant items.
  Print the matrix.

Redefine and redistribute the matrix.
Determine any needs for immediate action.
  Determine any business actions which should be taken immediately.
  Determine any needs for immediate action in creating information systems.

ACTION DIAGRAM
FOR PERFORMING
CRITICAL SUCCESS
FACTOR ANALYSIS

Initial Determination of Critical Success Factors

Establish the CSF team

(This may contain one external CSF consultant and at least one internal analyst)

Preparation by the CSF team

Study CSF methodology

Study CSF interviewing techniques

Be fully familiar with the industry

Study the corporation (annual reports, history, organization chart, policies, products, competitive products, literature)

Spend time with the company management and people who have views on its competitive position, problems and opportunities

Probe and try to understand the internal company politics

List the mission of the enterprise, along with its perceived goals and problems

List possible CSFs and measure for the enterprise (this is done as preparation for the introductory workshop and should not be allowed to bias the collecting of goals, problems and CSFs from top management)

Conduct an introductory workshop with a small key top management group

Explain the CSF procedure

Establish the goals of the enterprise

Establish the major problems

Determine which managers should be interviewed

Solicit the active involvement of a key member of top management

Set a date of the focusing workshop in which the results will be examined and discussed

Set up the interviews

Send letters to the interviewees

Explain the purpose of the interview

Show top management support

Send them a copy of this chapter, or book

Send them an outline of the interview

Arrange dates and times, interviewing the lowest level managers first

For each manager interviewed (with the lowest level managers first)

Prepare for the interview

Assume the role of the interviewee

List his probable goals, problems

List possible CSFs and CSF measures

List possible critical decisions, critical assumptions and critical information (this is done as an aid to preparation and should not be allowed to bias the interviewee's statements of CSFs, etc.)

Conduct the interview

Discuss the interviewee's views of the enterprise (possibly gathering information that will help in subsequent interviews)

Clarify the interveiwee's understanding about the CSF procedure

Obtain the interviewee's description of his mission and role

Discuss the interviewee's goals (the goals for his organizational unit

Determine the problems the interviewee perceives in meeting his goals

Develop critical success factors

Establish priorities for the CSFs

Discuss ways to measure the CSFs

Record all of the above with a computerized planning tool

Aggregate the results

Produce a coordinated listing of critical success factors

Establish a critical information set

Establish a critical assumption set

Establish a critical decision set

Review results

Distribute the statements of goals and CSFs to the top management team

Conduct a top management focusing workshop

Discuss the goals and CSFs with top management team (this is a key meeting which usually provokes much argument about the enterprise, its goals, problems and CSFs)

Modify the goals and CSFs as appropriate

Achieve consensus

Revise critical information

Revise critical assumptions

Revise critical decisions

Refine and distribute the goals and CSFs

ACTION DIAGRAM FOR PERFORMING GOAL AND PROBLEM ANALYSIS

Conduct goal and problem analysis

Obtain any existing documentation which relates to goals
or objectives:
- Business plans
- Information system plans
- Technology plans
- Annual reports
- Executive reports and memos
- Reports on management-by-objectives interviews and
  executives.

Comment
- Goals should focus on results
- Should be as precise as possible
- Goals should be measurable
- Goals should be decomposable into work which has to be done

Create an initial inventory of goals
Use an action diagram editor to represent the goal hierarchically

> See GOALS action diagram

Determine which executives will be interviewed
Establish the format of the interview
For each executive

Conduct goal-and-problem interview
Review the portion of the business model which relates to
    this executive
Note any changes that are needed
Establish the goals of the executive
Identify the problems he perceives in achieving those goals
Identify possible solutions to those problems
Identify how information systems could help
Rank the goals and problems

Organize and record the interview information
Clean up the interview information and enter it into the
    encyclopedia
Refine the inventory of goals
Rank the goals and problems
Associate goals with organizational unit
Associate problems with organizational unit
Associate goals with problems
Associate goals with information needs
Associate problems with information needs
Use the planning tool to analyze the goal and problem data
Record any especially urgent information-system actions
    that are needed

Submit the record of the interview to the executive for validation
Record any changes that are requested

ACTION DIAGRAM FOR PERFORMING BUSINESS AREA ANALYSIS

┌─ BUSINESS AREA ANALYSIS.

   ┌─ The second layer of Information Engineering

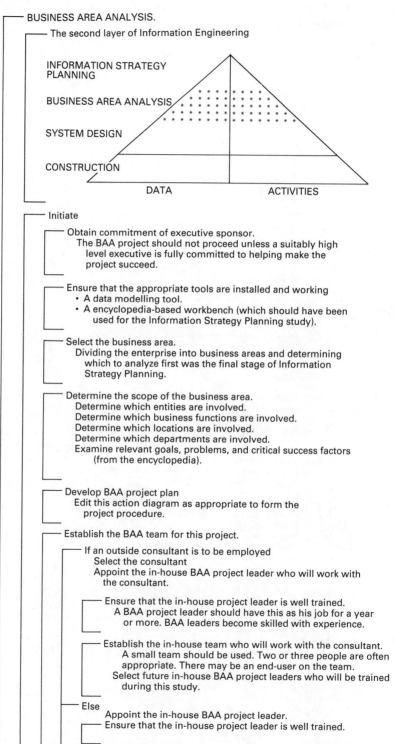

INFORMATION STRATEGY PLANNING

BUSINESS AREA ANALYSIS

SYSTEM DESIGN

CONSTRUCTION

DATA   ACTIVITIES

┌─ Initiate

   ┌─ Obtain commitment of executive sponsor.
   │   The BAA project should not proceed unless a suitably high
   │   level executive is fully committed to helping make the
   │   project succeed.

   ┌─ Ensure that the appropriate tools are installed and working
   │   • A data modelling tool.
   │   • A encyclopedia-based workbench (which should have been
   │   used for the Information Strategy Planning study).

   ┌─ Select the business area.
   │   Dividing the enterprise into business areas and determining
   │   which to analyze first was the final stage of Information
   │   Strategy Planning.

   ┌─ Determine the scope of the business area.
   │   Determine which entities are involved.
   │   Determine which business functions are involved.
   │   Determine which locations are involved.
   │   Determine which departments are involved.
   │   Examine relevant goals, problems, and critical success factors
   │   (from the encyclopedia).

   ┌─ Develop BAA project plan
   │   Edit this action diagram as appropriate to form the
   │   project procedure.

   ┌─ Establish the BAA team for this project.

      ┌─ If an outside consultant is to be employed
      │   Select the consultant
      │   Appoint the in-house BAA project leader who will work with
      │   the consultant.

         ┌─ Ensure that the in-house project leader is well trained.
         │   A BAA project leader should have this as his job for a year
         │   or more. BAA leaders become skilled with experience.

         ┌─ Establish the in-house team who will work with the consultant.
         │   A small team should be used. Two or three people are often
         │   appropriate. There may be an end-user on the team.
         │   Select future in-house BAA project leaders who will be trained
         │   during this study.

      └─ Else
          Appoint the in-house BAA project leader.
        ┌─ Ensure that the in-house project leader is well trained.

Establish the in-house BAA team.
  A small team should be used. Two or three people are often
  appropriate. There may be an end-user on the team.
  Select future in-house BAA project leaders who will be trained
  during this study.

Ensure that the BAA team is adequately trained
  They should be trained in the following:
  • Information engineering
  • Analysis and design
  • Data modeling
  • The diagramming techniques
  • The automated tools used
  • Communication skills

Prepare

Create initial documentation.
  Extract the relevant functional decomposition diagram from
    the encyclopedia.
  Extract the relevant entity-relationship diagram from
    the encyclopedia.
  Add detailed comments to the above diagrams where necessary.
  Print relevant versions of the above diagrams from the
    encyclopedia for the participants to review.

Select the user participants.

Prepare the user participants.
  Give user participants literature on the BAA procedure.
  Give them the initial printouts from the encyclopedia.

Conduct training class for the user participants.
  Introduce user participants to the BAA technique.
  Train user participants in the diagramming techniques.
  Review the initial printouts from the encyclopedia.

Determine the target date for completing the study.

Hold kickoff meeting
  Have the executive sponsor make the opening speech.
  Review with participants the purpose and objectives.
  Review the agenda.
  Give participants the preparatory material for them to study.
   Inform them that they must understand it well before the first
   workshop
  Review the initial data models and process models with the
    participants.
  Review relevant goals, problems, and critical success factors.
  Review the business assumptions that are to be made.

Create a preliminary data model
  Extract the entity-relationship model for this business area
    from the encyclopedia.
  Determine what events occur in this business area.
  Associate the events with entity-types (A behavior model)
  Draw the life-cycle of each entity.
  Enter initial attributes of each entity.

Create a preliminary process model
  Extract the business-function decomposition model for this
    business area from the encyclopedia.
  Decompose the functions into processes.

Successively refine the information
in the following stages until a complete representation of the
data and processes is achieved.

Create a detailed data model
Perform economical synthesis

Create a process decomposition diagram
Decompose processes eventually into elementary processes.
An elementary process is one which cannot be decomposed
further without stating HOW a procedure is carried out.

Create a process dependency diagram
Correlate this with the process decomposition diagram.
Consider what information flows from one process to another.

Create a process data-flow diagram
Correlate this with the data model.

Build matrices

Generate an entity-type/process matrix.
Indicate what process CREATES each entity record.
Indicate what processes UPDATE, READ or DELETE each entity record

Associate entity-types, processes and events with organizational
units and locations.
Associate entity-types, processes and events with goals and
problems.

Analyse and correlate (automatically) the above information.
Use a workbench tool which analyses and correlates the above
information with a knowledge coordinator.
Use the knowledge coordinator of the design tool to ensure
that the BAA is internally consistent, and consistent with
other knowledge in the encyclopedia.

Prepare for system design

Review the analysis of current systems created during the ISP study.
Identify system design projects.
Refine system design project boundaries.
Prioritize the system-building projects

There are multiple factors which affect the prioritization
of system building.

Rank the factors below on a scale of 1 to 7
□ Return on investment.
□ Achievement of critical success factor.
□ Achievement of goal.
□ Solution to serious problem.
□ Adequacy of current system.
□ Maintenance cost of current system.
□ Speed of implementation.
□ Manpower or resource availability.
□ Risk

Other business areas are likely to be competing for the
same development resources, so the decision of what to build
first may be taken at a higher level than the business area.

Schedule the system-building projects.
Obtain approval for system projects.

Present the results to the executive sponsor.

INDEX

A

Action diagrams, 30, 32, 44, 52, 114
  automatic navigation in, 59
  brackets in, 52–53
  of business and management
    opportunities, 177–80
  for business area analysis, 268,
    318–20
  CASE structures in, 54–55
  compound database actions, 58–60
  for critical success factor analysis,
    315–16
  escapes in, 56
  for goal and problem analysis, 317
  GO TO instruction in, 57
  hierarchy of goals represented as,
    210, 215
  for information strategy planning,
    308–13
  input and output data, 63
  for management procedures, 64, 67
  next-iteration construct in, 57
  organization chart represented as,
    140, 142
  repetition in, 53–54
  sets of data in, 55
  simple database actions, 57–60
  steps involved in information strategy
    planning in an, 66
  subprocedures in, 55–56
  of technological changes, 172–77
  for technology impact analysis, 314
  ultimate decomposition in, 60–64
Activities, 237–39
  diagrams for, 28–36
  identifying basic, 240
  properties of coherent, 240–41
Affinity analysis clustering, 106,
    227–28, 242–45
Allen, Brandt, 124
American Airlines, 279, 283
Analysis, 26–27, 106–107
Application databases, 83, 85–86
Arrows in diagrams, 45–46, 51
Attributes, 80–81, 289
Automatic navigation, 59

B

Batch systems, 126–27
Boxes in diagrams, 44–45
Brackets in action diagrams, 52–53